ASIA-PACIFIC COUNTRIES WITH SPECIAL NEEDS DEVELOPMENT REPORT 2016

Adapting the 2030 Agenda
for Sustainable Development
at the National Level

UNITED NATIONS
ESCAP
Economic and Social Commission for Asia and the Pacific

ASIA-PACIFIC COUNTRIES WITH SPECIAL NEEDS DEVELOPMENT REPORT 2016

Adapting the 2030 Agenda for Sustainable Development at the National Level

Shamshad Akhtar

Executive Secretary

Hongjoo Hahm

Deputy Executive Secretary

Aynul Hasan

Director, Macroeconomic Policy and Financing for Development Division

United Nations publication

Sales No. E.16.II.F.11

Copyright © United Nations 2016

All rights reserved

Printed in Bangkok

ISBN: 978-92-1-120717-0

e-ISBN: 978-92-1-057 950-6

ISSN: 0252-5704

ST/ESCAP/2752

Cover photo credit: Shutterstock (Lightspring)

FOREWORD

National circumstances and priorities will shape the approach of every member State to implementation of the 2030 Agenda for Sustainable Development. Although the Sustainable Development Goals are universal, integrated and indivisible, specific national contexts define the most pressing needs and the resources available for governments to incorporate the Goals and targets into their planning processes, policies and strategies.

The translation of the global 2030 Agenda into national action is particularly important to Asia-Pacific countries with special needs: the least developed countries, landlocked developing countries and small island developing States, which constitute the majority of ESCAP members. These countries face a range of structural challenges, related to lower levels of development, smaller productive capacities and increased vulnerability to external shocks, such as those arising from volatile commodity prices, climate change and natural disasters.

These structural challenges are, in most cases, associated with remoteness, geographic features, availability of resources, demography, weather or, most commonly, a combination of these factors. The result has been limited progress in structural transformation and slower development of productive capacities. Successful national implementation of the 2030 Agenda will, therefore, require careful adaptation to these specific developmental challenges.

ESCAP is committed to support member States, especially our countries with special needs, in adapting the global Goals to national circumstances and in the subsequent follow-up and review of implementation.

Although different for each country, many of the challenges have similar elements. Regional cooperation can facilitate exchanges of experiences, mutual learning and identification of best practices.

To address these issues, the five United Nations regional commissions have jointly developed an action framework to prioritize support to member States in the following areas:

    (a) Analytical work to promote policy integration, coherence, and linkages among the different Goals.

    (b) Regional coordination of national statistical development and indicators.

    (c) Support to follow-up and review processes.

    (d) Mobilizing the necessary means of implementation.

    (e) Translating regional policy models into global public policy goods.

    (f) Regional integration to enhance productivity and address cross-cutting issues such as regional inclusiveness and inequality.

    (g) Coordinating the United Nations system at the regional level.

This 2016 edition of the *Asia-Pacific Countries with Special Needs Development Report* contributes to the first of these areas, by focusing on how countries with special needs can best adapt the 2030 Agenda to their national contexts.

A significant obstacle to implementation of the Goals is the lack of clear road map or strategy for implementation. The 169 targets provide a comprehensive framework for tracking progress, but do not provide guidance about how to achieve the Goals or about prioritization or sequencing.

This report therefore presents an analytical framework, based on a set of 82 indicators, representing all 17 Goals and the 174 countries for which data are available. This includes details about the interlinkages, synergies and trade-offs across different indicators, from the viewpoint of each individual country. It also allows the calculation of a summary measure of the attainment of the Goals for individual countries. Taken together, this information can be used to inform optimal, country-specific pathways on progress towards the Goals.

Building on the analytical work started in this edition of the *Report*, and other modelling approaches to be developed, ESCAP aims to provide guidance to policymakers, contribute to policy dialogues and build national capacities for the design of plans and strategies for the national adaptation of the global 2030 Agenda in each of our region's countries with special needs.

Shamshad Akhtar
Under-Secretary-General of the United Nations and
Executive Secretary, United Nations Economic and
Social Commission for Asia and the Pacific

EXECUTIVE SUMMARY

Although the 17 Sustainable Development Goals and 169 targets of the 2030 Agenda for Sustainable Development are integrated, indivisible, global in nature and universally applicable, their implementation should take into account different national realities, capacities and levels of development, while respecting national policies and priorities. As such, the 2030 Agenda suggests that Governments set their own national targets and decide how to incorporate them in national development planning processes, policies and strategies. In other words, the 2030 Agenda gives countries policy space to adapt the Goals in the way they deem most suitable. The present report contributes to regional discussions on how countries with special needs (CSN), such as least developed countries, landlocked developing countries and small island developing States, can best adapt the 2030 Agenda to their unique national contexts.

Tracking the progress of the global programmes of action

Of the region's 12 least developed countries, 7 met the criteria for graduation as of 2015

At its latest triennial review in March 2015, the Committee for Development Policy found that Bhutan, Nepal, Solomon Islands and Timor-Leste had met the graduation criteria for the first time. Three other countries, Kiribati, Vanuatu and Tuvalu, had already met the criteria for graduation at two or more consecutive triennial reviews, and the Committee had already recommended two of them for graduation. As such, the Asia-Pacific region has already met an important goal of the Programme of Action for the Least Developed Countries for the Decade 2011-2020 (Istanbul Programme of Action), namely that half of the least developed countries meet the graduation criteria by 2020. However, the high level of economic vulnerability, especially for the small island developing States, leaves doubts on the ability of these countries to sustain their development gains in the long term.

Linking the Asian landlocked developing countries with the rest of the world

Two successful experiences of landlocked developing countries enhancing their connectivity with the rest of the world are the Lao People's Democratic Republic and Azerbaijan. The former cut the average transit time between the capital and the closest seaport from 60 days in 2007 to about 20 days in 2015. This improvement was due to a number of policy initiatives and institutional reforms, leading to improvements in road infrastructure and border clearance procedures. The latter increased access to broadband Internet from about 1 subscriber per 100 people in 2009 to about 20 in 2014, exceeding the average for Asia-Pacific developing countries that are not CSN. This achievement is largely due to the country's leading efforts to build the Trans-Eurasian Information Superhighway, which is expected to supply Central Asian countries with Internet and telecommunications systems. In spite of these success stories, the majority of the Asia-Pacific landlocked developing countries continue to experience serious challenges in these areas, as well as in diversifying their production.

Renewable energy in small island developing States

Because small island developing States remain highly dependent on expensive fuel imports to meet their energy requirements, increasing renewable energy investments has been seen as a means to mitigate the financial risks associated with oil price fluctuations. Among Pacific island developing States, Fiji, Papua New Guinea and Samoa are the ones that rely the most on renewable sources of energy, especially hydroelectricity, for generating electricity. Challenges to a further expansion of renewable energy in small island developing States include: the need to develop adequate storage capacity for electricity; generating data to guide policy formulation on the potential of hydropower, geothermal, wind and other renewable sources of energy; and lack of local technical capacity for installing, operating and maintaining renewable systems.

From the global programmes of action to the 2030 Agenda

Mapping the contribution of the global programmes of action to the 2030 Agenda

The Istanbul Programme of Action covers the 17 Goals of the Agenda, with an emphasis on Goal 2 (zero hunger), Goal 8 (decent work and economic growth), Goal 10 (reduced inequalities), Goal 16 (peace, justice and strong institutions) and Goal 17 (partnerships for the Goals). In contrast, the actions of the Vienna Programme of Action address exclusively Goal 7 (affordable and clean energy), Goal 8, Goal 9 (industry, innovation and infrastructure) and Goals 10 and 17. Finally, the actions of the Samoa Pathway cover most of the Goals, with an emphasis on Goal 5 (gender equality), Goal 13 (climate action), Goal 14 (life below water), Goal 15 (life on land) and Goal 17. By identifying overlaps between actions in the global programmes of action and targets and Goals of the 2030 Agenda, the mapping exercise suggests that the region's least developed countries, landlocked developing countries and small island developing States could make progress towards the achievement of the latter by pursuing actions in their respective programmes of action.

Prioritization, sequencing and implementation challenges of the 2030 Agenda

A survey of experts and practitioners from across the Asia-Pacific region conducted by ESCAP gathered views on a number of issues related to adapting the 2030 Agenda at the national level, including prioritization and sequencing of the Goals, unfinished Millennium Development Goals, institutional arrangements, sources of finance, roles of different stakeholders and more. A total of 160 respondents from 38 Asia-Pacific countries completed the survey, including 95 respondents from 25 CSN.

With regard to implementation priorities, the survey found that while experts from least developed countries expressed a strong preference for prioritizing the social pillar of sustainable development, experts from landlocked developing countries focused on the economic pillar and those from small island developing States expressed a preference for a balanced prioritization of the social, economic and environmental pillars. Survey respondents from CSN also noted that horizontal and vertical coordination among different government agencies, the availability of technical and administrative capacities and the availability of statistical data are key implementation challenges.

Remarkably, the opinion of experts and practitioners on the prioritization and sequencing of the Goals in CSN coincides with the focus areas set forth in the programmes of action of their respective country groups. This suggests that specific actions agreed in such programmes can provide guidance to Governments for the implementation of the 2030 Agenda.

Pathways to enhance capacities for sustainable development

A unique analytical framework

This report proposes a unique analytical framework for the implementation of the 2030 Agenda based on cutting-edge methods from complexity science coupled with economic analyses. The Sustainable Development Goals system is conceptualized as a network consisting of (a) a set of 82 indicators representative of the 17 Goals, (b) 174 countries for which there are adequate data available for the indicators, and (c) the linkages among and between countries and indicators. The framework also provides the computation of a country-specific measure — termed "SDG capacity" — which quantifies the capacity of each country to implement the Goals. The analytical framework allows for the identification of optimal strategies of implementation of the Goals, including specific recommendations for their prioritization and sequencing.

Identifying priorities in selected CSN

The report illustrates the functioning of the framework in three CSN: Bangladesh, Kazakhstan and Fiji. The results suggest that, in Bangladesh, the initial priority should be on education, reduction of inequalities and infrastructure. The first two elements could be related to the importance of human capital for a country to increase the diversification and sophistication of its production and the potential for a more even distribution of income to boost aggregate demand. In Kazakhstan and Fiji, the results show that the initial priority should be directed towards infrastructure. However, the composition of this initial high investment in infrastructure is different for both countries, with Fiji assigning a significantly larger role to telecommunications. This may be due to the greater distance of Fiji from international markets, which may make the cost of international trade in services lower compared with merchandise trade.

Identifying bottlenecks and trade-offs

The exercise allows not only the identification of optimal strategies but also of country specific bottlenecks and trade-offs in attaining different Goals. An important regularity found in the three countries was the absence of progress in the environmental Goals of the 2030 Agenda. As discussed in chapter 3, this result seems to be due to the isolation of the environmental indicators in the countries' networks from the core socioeconomic indicators. This finding suggests that the integration of the three pillars envisioned in the 2030 Agenda is not going to be easy to achieve.

Both the lack of progress of the environmental pillar and the identification of bottlenecks that can potentially impede progress in the attainment of the Goals require careful consideration by national policymakers and development partners. With respect to the latter, they could contribute to focusing the support of the international community on sectors that require the most attention and for which additional financial resources could be most effectively allocated.

The need to exploit synergies in devising optimal policies for sustainable development

A comparison of different scenarios of prioritization and sequencing strongly suggests the importance of a thorough understanding of linkages, synergies and trade-offs across the 17 Goals, as well as the relative benefits of different implementation plans for each country. Devising an implementation plan based on a narrow selection of sectors could result in a substantially lower attainment of the Goals. The main areas of focus of the Istanbul Programme of Action provide good guidance for the implementation of the 2030 Agenda in least developed countries. However, those of the Vienna Programme of Action and the Samoa Pathway may be limited to boost sustainable development in, respectively, landlocked developing countries and small island developing States.

ACKNOWLEDGEMENTS

This report was prepared under the overall direction and guidance of Shamshad Akhtar, Under-Secretary-General of the United Nations and Executive Secretary of the Economic and Social Commission for Asia and the Pacific. Hongjoo Hahm, Deputy Executive Secretary, provided valuable advice and comments. The report was coordinated by a core team under the direction of Aynul Hasan, Director of the Macroeconomic Policy and Financing for Development Division. The core team, led by Alberto Isgut, included Naylin Oo, Gabriela Spaizmann, Yusuke Tateno, Heather Taylor and Marin Yari. Debapriya Bhattacharya, Jaebeum Cho and Ran Kim were part of the core team as external experts.

ESCAP staff who contributed substantively include: Daniel Jeongdae Lee, Hamza Ali Malik and Oliver Paddison of the Macroeconomic Policy and Financing for Development Division; Katinka Weinberger of the Environment and Development Division; Yanhong Zhang of the Statistics Division; Iosefa Maiava and Sanjesh Naidu of the ESCAP Pacific Office; Tiziana Bonapace and Hong Pum Chung of the ESCAP Subregional Office for North and Central Asia; and Matthew Hammill and Nagesh Kumar of the ESCAP Subregional Office for South and South-West Asia. Valuable advice was also received from Clovis Freire of the Department of Economic and Social Affairs.

The report benefited from the discussions of the Expert Group Meeting held from 1 to 3 December 2015 at ESCAP, during the Committee on Macroeconomic Policy, Poverty Reduction and Inclusive Development.

The graphic design was created by QUO Bangkok, Ltd. with the support and facilitation of Chavalit Boonthanom, Martin Dessart, Katie Elles and Patricia de la Torre Rodriguez of the ESCAP Strategic Publications, Communications and Advocacy Section. The layout and printing were provided by Clung Wicha Press.

Pannipa Jangvithaya, Achara Jantarasaengaram, Kiatkanid Pongpanich and Nucharat Tuntiwigit of the Macroeconomic Policy and Financing for Development Division proofread the manuscript. Sutinee Yeamkitpibul, supported by Sukanitt Jarunveshsuti, Sirinart Suanyam and Woranooch Thiusathien of the Macroeconomic Policy and Financing for Development Division undertook all administrative processing necessary for the issuance and dissemination of the publication.

CONTENTS

CONTENTS *(continued)*

BOXES

FIGURES

FIGURES *(continued)*

TABLES

EXPLANATORY NOTES

Analyses in the *Asia-Pacific Countries with Special Needs Development Report 2016* are based on data and information available up to the end of March 2016.

Groupings of countries and territories/areas referred to in the present issue of the *Report* are defined as follows:

- Countries with special needs: least developed countries, landlocked developing countries and small island developing States.

- ESCAP region: Afghanistan; American Samoa; Armenia; Australia; Azerbaijan; Bangladesh; Bhutan; Brunei Darussalam; Cambodia; China; Cook Islands; Democratic People's Republic of Korea; Fiji; French Polynesia; Georgia; Guam; Hong Kong, China; India; Indonesia; Iran (Islamic Republic of); Japan; Kazakhstan; Kiribati; Kyrgyzstan; Lao People's Democratic Republic; Macao, China; Malaysia; Maldives; Marshall Islands; Micronesia (Federated States of); Mongolia; Myanmar; Nauru; Nepal; New Caledonia; New Zealand; Niue; Northern Mariana Islands; Pakistan; Palau; Papua New Guinea; Philippines; Republic of Korea; Russian Federation; Samoa; Singapore; Solomon Islands; Sri Lanka; Tajikistan; Thailand; Timor-Leste; Tonga; Turkey; Turkmenistan; Tuvalu; Uzbekistan; Vanuatu; and Viet Nam.

- Developing ESCAP region: ESCAP region excluding Australia, Japan and New Zealand.

- Developed ESCAP region: Australia, Japan and New Zealand.

- Least developed countries: Afghanistan, Bangladesh, Bhutan, Cambodia, Kiribati, Lao People's Democratic Republic, Myanmar, Nepal, Solomon Islands, Timor-Leste, Tuvalu and Vanuatu.

- Landlocked developing countries: Afghanistan, Armenia, Azerbaijan, Bhutan, Kazakhstan, Kyrgyzstan, Lao People's Democratic Republic, Mongolia, Nepal, Tajikistan, Turkmenistan and Uzbekistan.

- Small island developing States: Cook Islands, Fiji, Kiribati, Maldives, Marshall Islands, Micronesia (Federated States of), Nauru, Niue, Palau, Papua New Guinea, Samoa, Solomon Islands, Timor-Leste, Tonga, Tuvalu and Vanuatu.

- Pacific: American Samoa, Australia, Cook Islands, Fiji, French Polynesia, Guam, Kiribati, Marshall Islands, Micronesia (Federated States of), Nauru, New Caledonia, New Zealand, Niue, Northern Marina Islands, Palau, Papua New Guinea, Samoa, Solomon Islands, Tonga, Tuvalu and Vanuatu

Bibliographical and other references have not been verified. The United Nations bears no responsibility for the availability or functioning of URLs.

The designations employed and the presentation of the material in this publication do not imply the expression of any opinion whatsoever on the part of the Secretariat of the United Nations concerning the legal status of any country, territory, city or area, or of its authorities, or concerning the delimitation of its frontiers or boundaries.

Mention of firm names and commercial products does not imply the endorsement of the United Nations.

Growth rates are on an annual basis, except where indicated otherwise.

Reference to "tons" indicates metric tons.

References to dollars ($) are to United States dollars, unless otherwise stated.

The term "billion" signifies a thousand million. The term "trillion" signifies a million million.

In dates, a hyphen (-) is used to signify the full period involved, including the beginning and end years, and a stroke (/) indicates a crop year, fiscal year or plan year.

Country or area in the ESCAP region	ISO Alpha-3 code	Country or area in the ESCAP region	ISO Alpha-3 code	Country or area in the ESCAP region	ISO Alpha-3 code
Afghanistan	AFG	Japan	JPN	Papua New Guinea	PNG
American Samoa	ASM	Kazakhstan	KAZ	Philippines	PHL
Armenia	ARM	Kiribati	KIR	Republic of Korea	KOR
Australia	AUS	Kyrgyzstan	KGZ	Russian Federation	RUS
Azerbaijan	AZE	Lao People's Democratic Republic	LAO	Samoa	WSM
Bangladesh	BGD	Macao, China	MAC	Singapore	SGP
Bhutan	BTN	Malaysia	MYS	Solomon Islands	SLB
Brunei Darussalam	BRN	Maldives	MDV	Sri Lanka	LKA
Cambodia	KHM	Marshall Islands	MHL	Tajikistan	TJK
China	CHN	Micronesia (Federated States of)	FSM	Thailand	THA
Cook Islands	COK	Mongolia	MNG	Timor-Leste	TLS
Democratic People's Republic of Korea	PRK	Myanmar	MMR	Tonga	TON
Fiji	FJI	Nauru	NRU	Turkey	TUR
French Polynesia	PYF	Nepal	NPL	Turkmenistan	TKM
Georgia	GEO	New Caledonia	NCL	Tuvalu	TUV
Guam	GUM	New Zealand	NZL	Uzbekistan	UZB
Hong Kong, China	HKG	Niue	NIU	Vanuatu	VUT
India	IND	Northern Mariana Islands	MNP	Viet Nam	VNM
Indonesia	IDN	Pakistan	PAK		
Iran (Islamic Republic of)	IRN	Palau	PLW		

ACRONYMS

ADB	Asian Development Bank
CSN	countries with special needs
DESA	United Nations Department of Economic and Social Affairs
ESCAP	Economic and Social Commission for Asia and the Pacific
FAO	Food and Agriculture Organization of the United Nations
FDI	foreign direct investment
GDP	gross domestic product
GNI	gross national income
ICSU	International Council for Science
ICT	information and communications technology
IEA	International Energy Agency
ILO	International Labour Organization
IMF	International Monetary Fund
IRENA	International Renewable Energy Agency
ISSC	International Social Science Council
MW	megawatt
NGO	non-governmental organization
ODA	official development assistance
SDG	Sustainable Development Goal
SMEs	small and medium-sized enterprises
SPREP	Secretariat of the Pacific Regional Environment Programme
UNCTAD	United Nations Conference on Trade and Development
UNDP	United Nations Development Programme
UNESCO	United Nations Education, Scientific and Cultural Organization
UNHCR	United Nations High Commissioner for Refugees
UNICEF	United Nations Children's Fund
UNODC	United Nations Office on Drugs and Crime
UN-OHRLLS	United Nations Office of the High Representative for the Least Developed Countries, Landlocked Developing Countries and Small Island Developing States
UNSD	United Nations Statistics Division
WHO	World Health Organization

INTRODUCTION

This report focuses on the implementation of the 2030 Agenda for Sustainable Development in the Asia-Pacific countries with special needs (CSN). These 36 countries include least developed countries, landlocked developing countries and small island developing States (figure A). These countries face a number of structural challenges related to their low levels of development of productive capacities and vulnerability to external shocks arising from volatile commodity prices, climate change and natural disasters. Their structural challenges are generally highly idiosyncratic and, in most cases, associated with remoteness, geographic features, availability of resources, demography and weather. Over the years, international programmes of action specifically tuned to the needs of CSN have come into being. The most recent of them are the Istanbul Programme of Action, the Vienna Programme of Action and the Samoa Pathway.

The 2030 Agenda, adopted by more than 150 world leaders on 25 September 2015, is an ambitious agenda of unprecedented scope and significance. Its 17 Goals and 169 associated targets aim at ending poverty and hunger, protecting the planet from degradation, ensuring that all human beings can enjoy prosperous and fulfilling lives and fostering peaceful, just and inclusive societies. The 2030 Agenda recognizes that CSN deserve special attention and states that their relevant strategies and programmes of action are an integral part of it.

In light of its high level of ambition and comprehensiveness, the 2030 Agenda recognizes that differences across countries in capacities and levels of development must be taken into account in its implementation. To that end, it states that "each Government will ...decide how these aspirational and global targets should be incorporated in [their] national planning processes, policies and strategies..." (see A/RES/70/1, para. 55). The freedom accorded to Governments on how to achieve the universal and indivisible Goals leads to the question of what is the best way for countries to adapt the 2030 Agenda to their unique circumstances. The difficulties in adapting the 2030 Agenda are amplified in the Asia-Pacific CSN because of their limited capacities.

This report explores ways to address the challenges for achieving the Sustainable Development Goals in the Asia-Pacific CSN and proposes a set of policy actions to adapt the 2030 Agenda to their unique capacities and levels of development. It aims to provide useful insights to policymakers on how to prioritize and sequence the Goals, as well as how to overcome structural impediments to sustainable development.

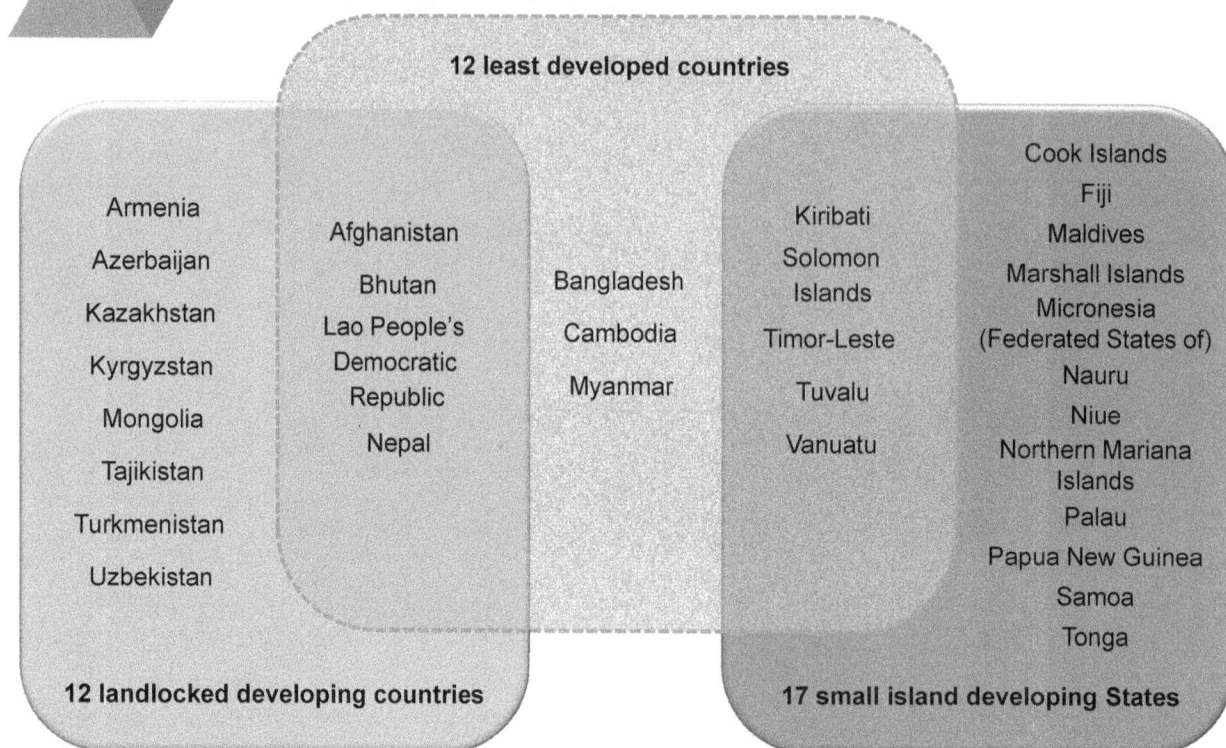

Figure A — Countries with special needs in Asia and the Pacific

12 least developed countries

12 landlocked developing countries			17 small island developing States
Armenia	Afghanistan	Bangladesh	Kiribati	Cook Islands

Armenia
Azerbaijan
Kazakhstan
Kyrgyzstan
Mongolia
Tajikistan
Turkmenistan
Uzbekistan

Afghanistan
Bhutan
Lao People's Democratic Republic
Nepal

Bangladesh
Cambodia
Myanmar

Kiribati
Solomon Islands
Timor-Leste
Tuvalu
Vanuatu

Cook Islands
Fiji
Maldives
Marshall Islands
Micronesia (Federated States of)
Nauru
Niue
Northern Mariana Islands
Palau
Papua New Guinea
Samoa
Tonga

12 landlocked developing countries   **17 small island developing States**

Source: ESCAP.

For that purpose, the report aims to provide answers to the following questions:

(a) What are the progress and challenges of CSN towards meeting the objectives of their respective global programmes of action?

(b) How can CSN benefit from the global programmes of action to advance towards the implementation of the 2030 Agenda?

(c) What are the views of experts and practitioners from the Asia-Pacific CSN on the prioritization, sequencing, and implementation challenges of the 2030 Agenda?

(d) How can policymakers from CSN identify synergies, trade-offs and bottlenecks across Goals and effectively sequence their attainment?

(e) Can the three dimensions of the 2030 Agenda be achieved at the same time?

The report finds that, although the Asia-Pacific CSN are advancing towards meeting the targets of their programmes of action, they continue to face structural impediments to their sustainable development. The report also finds that there are complementarities between the global programmes of action and the 2030 Agenda, and that the opinions of experts and practitioners tend to coincide with the focus areas of the programmes of action of their respective countries. The analytical framework proposed in the report allows the identification of synergies, trade-offs and bottlenecks across indicators in each country, as well as the derivation of optimal, country-specific pathways for the prioritization and sequencing of the Goals.

The report is organized as follows. Chapter 1 takes stock of the progress of CSN in the implementation of their respective programmes of action and identifies their challenges and vulnerabilities. Chapter 2 considers two elements for the discussion of the adaptation of the 2030 Agenda at the national level. It first analyses the relationship between the programmes of action and the 2030 Agenda, and second it examines current perceptions of experts and practitioners from 25 CSN on how their countries should prioritize and sequence the achievement of the Goals. Chapter 3 presents a unique analytical framework for the implementation of the 2030 Agenda based on conceptualizing the Sustainable Development Goals as a network of 82 indicators, representative of the 17 Goals, and 174 countries.

TRACKING THE GLOBAL PROGRAMMES OF ACTION

Despite recent technological advances and the commitments of international communities to provide help, the Asia-Pacific countries with special needs (CSN) continue to face structural challenges in their development processes. Such challenges are highly idiosyncratic and, in most cases, associated with disadvantages in their initial endowments and geographic features, including remoteness, costly access to international markets, insufficient human, natural and financial resources and vulnerability to disasters.

In recognition of their unique development challenges and vulnerabilities, the international community has adopted specific programmes of action to support them at various United Nations conferences, starting with the First United Nations Conference on the Least Developed Countries in Paris in 1981. Other important conferences include the Global Conference on the Sustainable Development of Small Island Developing States of 1994 and the International Ministerial Conference of Landlocked and Transit Developing Countries and Donor Countries and International Financial and Development Institutions on Transit Transport Cooperation of 2003. The current global programmes of action for least developed countries, landlocked developing countries and small island developing States are the following:

(a) The Programme of Action for the Least Developed Countries for the Decade 2011-2020, informally called the Istanbul Programme of Action;
(b) The Vienna Programme of Action for Landlocked Developing Countries for the Decade 2014-2024;
(c) The SIDS Accelerated Modalities of Action (SAMOA) Pathway of 2014, referred to as the Samoa Pathway.

The present chapter, following on from last year's report, tracks the progress of Asia-Pacific least developed countries, landlocked developing countries and small island developing States in meeting the goals of their respective programmes of action. The first section updates the indicators for graduation of least developed countries and assesses their progress towards graduation. It also discusses their difficulties in reducing economic vulnerabilities. The second and third sections of the chapter track selected indicators that are relevant to implementation of the Vienna Programme of Action and the Samoa Pathway. They contain short case studies of landlocked developing countries that exhibited an exceptional performance in selected aspects of the Vienna Programme of Action and an in-depth discussion of renewable energy in the Pacific, which is a particularly important element of the Samoa Pathway.

1. GRADUATION FROM THE STATUS OF LEAST DEVELOPED COUNTRY

The category of least developed countries was established in 1971 to articulate international support measures for low-income developing countries that face severe structural impediments to growth. Since then, the Committee for Development Policy has been mandated to identify and make recommendations on which countries should be added or removed from this category.

Since 1991, the Committee has been conducting triennial reviews of least developed countries to assess which countries should be added to or dropped from the list through three criteria: (a) the income criterion; (b) the human assets criterion; and (c) the economic vulnerability criterion. During such reviews,

the three indicators for each least developed country are measured against specific graduation thresholds. If a country satisfies at least two of the three criteria for graduation in two consecutive triennial reviews, the Committee recommends to the Economic and Social Council that the country should be considered for graduation.

More specifically, the income criterion requires that the three-year moving average of the gross national income (GNI) per capita exceed the threshold, defined as 20% above the three-year moving average of the level of GNI per capita that the World Bank uses to identify low-income countries. The human assets criterion and the economic vulnerability criterion require that the respective indices satisfy the corresponding threshold levels set by the Committee. As an alternative, the "income-only" option allows countries to graduate if their income per capita is at least twice as high as the regular income graduation threshold.[1]

The graduation of least developed countries has been a slow process. Globally, only four countries graduated, including two from Asia and the Pacific: Maldives in 2011 and Samoa in 2014. The Istanbul Programme of Action, however, aims at expediting the graduation process by including the goal that half of the least developed countries (as at 2010) meet the criteria for graduation by 2020. After the graduation of Samoa, there remain 12 least developed countries in the Asia-Pacific region. Although the graduation goal is global in nature, it is useful to track the graduation status of the region's least developed countries.

For that purpose, it is encouraging to note that at its latest triennial review in March 2015, the Committee found that Bhutan, Nepal, Solomon Islands and Timor-Leste had met the criteria for graduation for the first time and that two other countries, Tuvalu and Vanuatu, had met the criteria for graduation at more than two consecutive triennial reviews. This means that the region has already met the goal established by the Istanbul Programme of Action. The Committee had already recommended Tuvalu and Vanuatu for graduation.

A seventh Asia-Pacific least developed country, Kiribati, met the criteria for graduation for the second consecutive triennial review. However, Kiribati was not recommended for graduation at the 2015 review because of concerns about the sustainability of the country's income level in view of its acute vulnerability. According to the report, Kiribati is the world's most structurally vulnerable country (Ocampo, 2015).

The status of the graduation process at the March 2015 review is summarized in table 1.1. With 7 out of the 12 Asia-Pacific least developed countries having met the criteria for graduation, the Asia-Pacific region has already reached the ambitious goal established in the Istanbul Programme of Action.

1.1. Tracking the graduation indicators

In order to track the progress of the least developed countries towards graduation, this subsection provides annual updates of the three indicators used for identification of least developed countries, based on the latest data available. Although these updates are estimates and do not reflect the review process of the Committee, they provide a detailed assessment of the progress towards graduation of the region's least developed countries, which is otherwise only available every three years at its triennial reviews.

To simplify the review of progress towards graduation, in what follows the 12 Asia-Pacific least developed countries are divided into three groups: (a) least developed countries that are neither landlocked developing countries nor small island developing States (Bangladesh, Cambodia and Myanmar); (b) least developed countries that are also landlocked developing countries (Afghanistan, Bhutan, the Lao People's Democratic Republic and Nepal); and (c) least developed countries that are also small island developing States (Kiribati, Solomon Islands, Timor-Leste, Tuvalu and Vanuatu).

Figures 1.1-1.3 show the evolution of the three indicators for graduation from the status of least developed country for the three types of countries noted above. The first figure for each country illustrates the evolution of the three-year moving average of GNI per capita and its corresponding graduation threshold. During the 2015 review, the value of this threshold, based on the average for the period from 2011 to 2013, was $1,242. The updated value based on the average for the period from 2012 to 2014 is $1,250. The figures also show the "income-only" graduation threshold.

The second figure for each country shows the evolution of the human assets index and its graduation threshold, while the third figure shows the evolution of the economic vulnerability index and its graduation threshold. The graduation threshold for the human assets index has been fixed at 66 since the 2009 review, while the graduation threshold of the economic vulnerability index has stood at 32 since the 2012 review. For simplicity, the figures show these fixed thresholds throughout the period under analysis. The three indicators for graduation have been computed

---

Table 1.1   **Status of the graduation process at the March 2015 triennial review**

Country	GNI per capita	Human assets index	Economic vulnerability index	Have the criteria been met?	Recommended for graduation? (year)
Afghanistan	$ 672	43	35	-	
Bangladesh	$ 926	64	**25**	-	
Bhutan	**$ 2 277**	**68**	40	✓	
Cambodia	$ 852	**67**	38	-	
Kiribati	**$ 2 489**	**86**	72	✓	
Lao People's Democratic Republic	$ 1 232	61	36	-	
Myanmar	$ 1 063	**73**	34	-	
Nepal	$ 659	**69**	**27**	✓	
Solomon Islands	**$ 1 402**	**72**	51	✓	
Timor-Leste	**$ 3 767**	57	55	✓[a]	
Tuvalu	**$ 5 788**	**89**	54	✓	2012[b]
Vanuatu	**$ 2 997**	**81**	48	✓	2015
Graduation thresholds	≥ $ 1 242	≥ 66	≤ 32		

Sources: Based on data from the Development Policy and Analysis Division (www.un.org/en/development/desa/policy/cdp/ldc/ldc_data.shtml); and the "Report on the seventeenth session (23-27 March 2015)" of the Committee for Development Policy, E/2015/33.

Notes: The table shows the values of the indicators for graduation and the corresponding thresholds at the March 2015 triennial review of the Committee for Development Policy. The numbers in bold represent the values that satisfy the graduation thresholds.

[a] Timor-Leste has met the "income-only" criterion for graduation.
[b] Tuvalu was recommended for graduation by the Committee in 2012, but the Economic and Social Council of the United Nations has deferred its decision on this matter until 2018. See ECOSOC Resolutions 2012/32 and 2013/20.

annually for the period between 2000 and 2014 using the same methodology and data sources as the Committee in its 2015 review. See annex I for details.[2]

Among the first group of least developed countries, Bangladesh, Cambodia and Myanmar, GNI per capita has been converging towards the graduation threshold (figure 1.1). Myanmar experienced the fastest growth in its GNI per capita over this period.

These three countries have also continued to improve their human assets index, with Cambodia and Myanmar having already met the threshold and Bangladesh being very close to meeting it in 2014, which is the latest year for which data are available. With regard to the economic vulnerability index, Bangladesh has already met the threshold and Cambodia has shown remarkable progress over the past decade. Further analysis shows that the progress of Cambodia in reducing its economic vulnerability index was due to

Figure 1.1	Evolution of indicators for graduation from the status of least developed country for those countries that are neither landlocked developing countries nor small island developing States

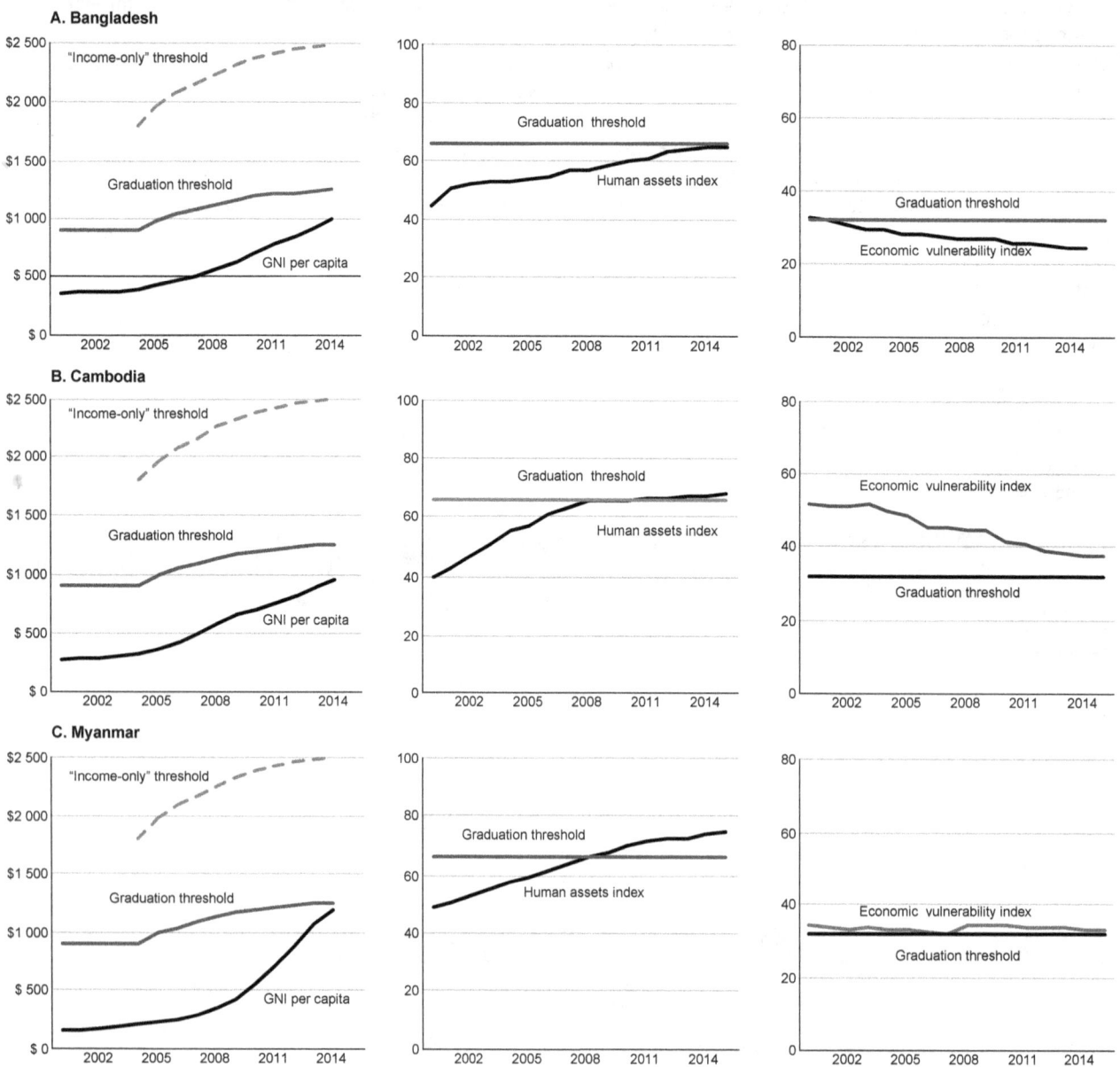

A. Bangladesh

B. Cambodia

C. Myanmar

Source: ESCAP calculations based on data from various sources.
Note: See annex I.

Figure 1.2 Evolution of indicators for graduation from the status of least developed country for those countries that are also landlocked developing countries

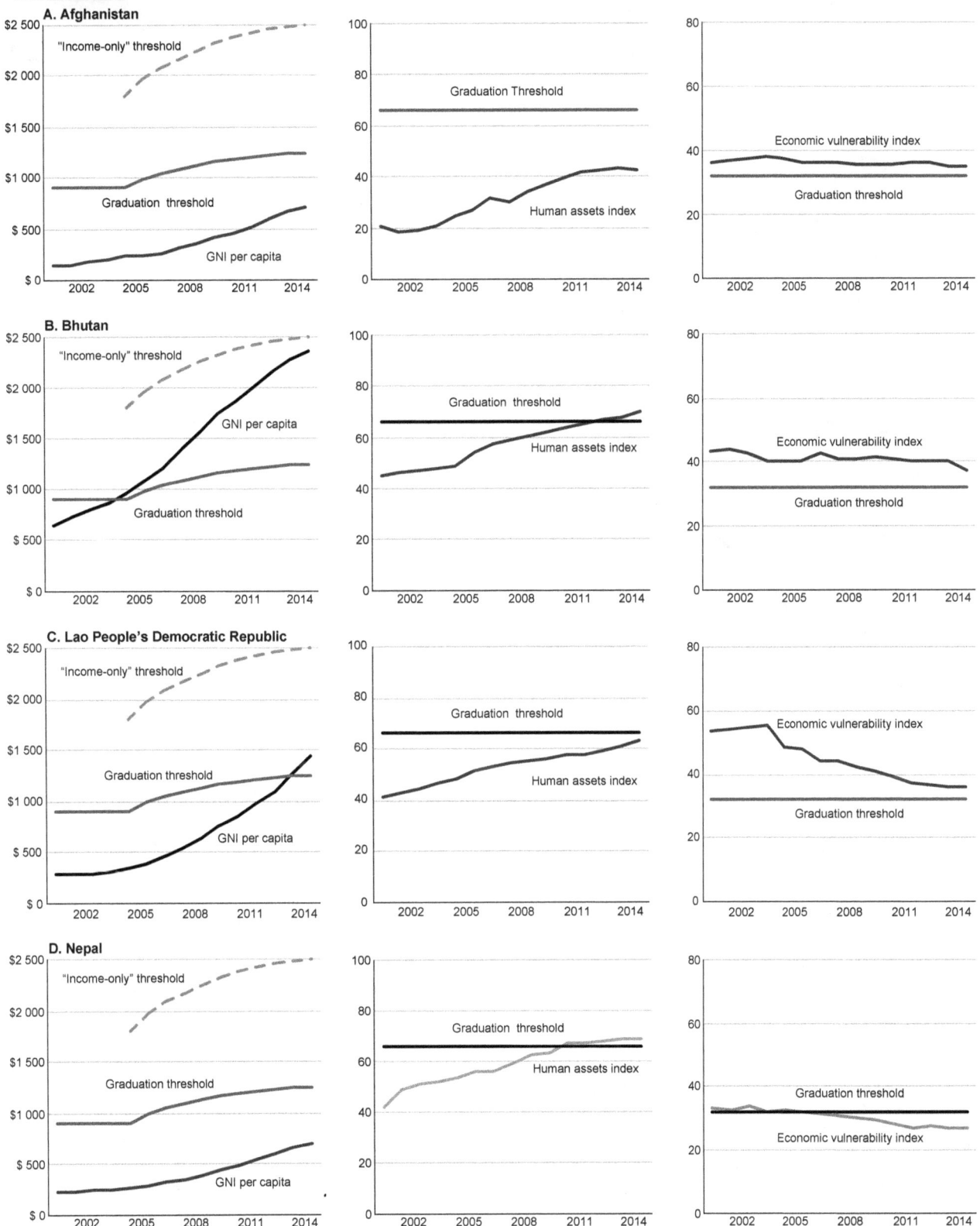

A. Afghanistan

B. Bhutan

C. Lao People's Democratic Republic

D. Nepal

Source: ESCAP calculations based on data from various sources.

Note: See annex I.

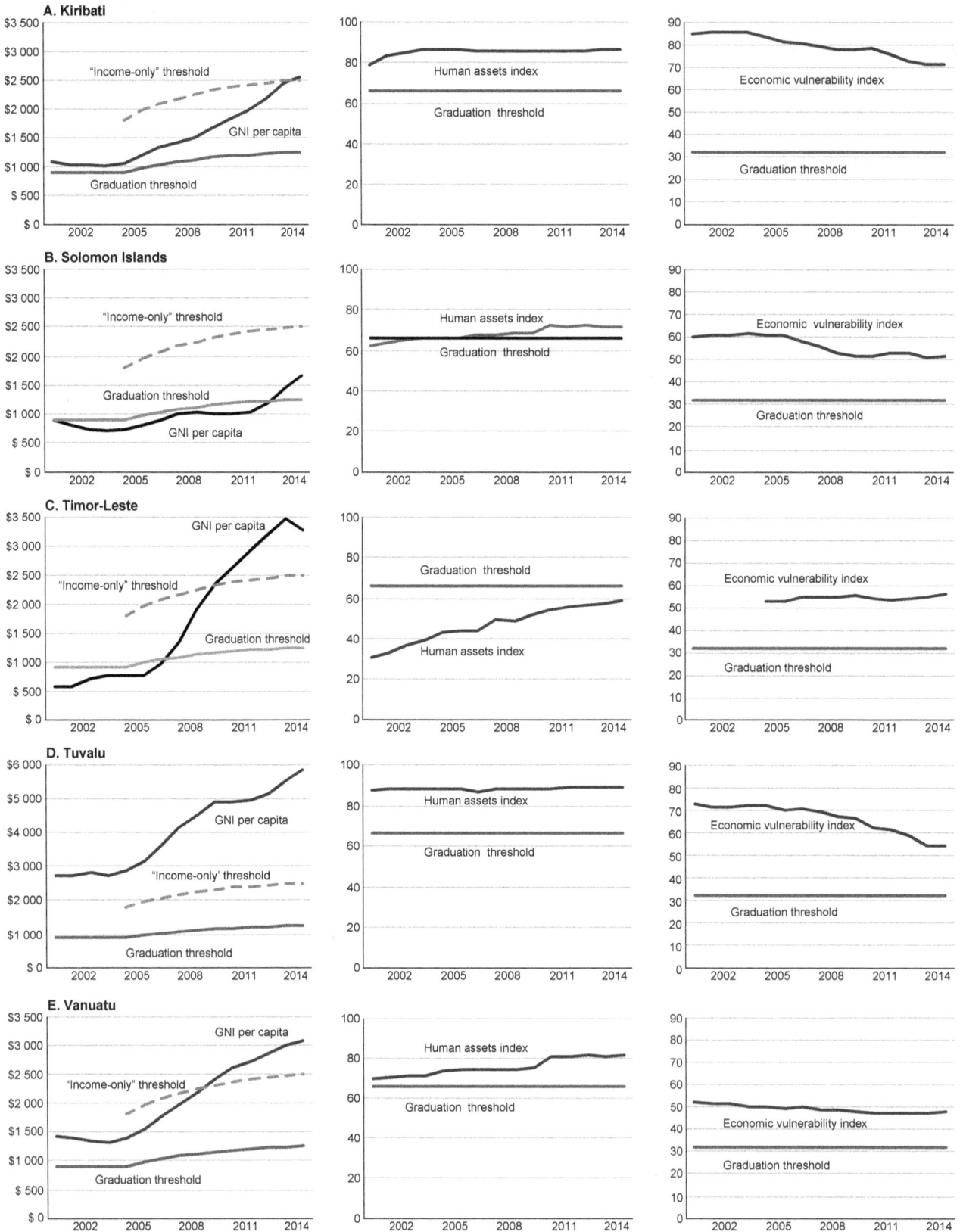

Figure 1.3 Evolution of indicators for graduation from the status of least developed country for those countries that are also small island developing States

A. Kiribati

B. Solomon Islands

C. Timor-Leste

D. Tuvalu

E. Vanuatu

Source: ESCAP calculations based on data from various sources.

Note: See annex I.

its success in reducing the instability of its exports of goods and services.

Among the four countries in the second group of least developed countries, those that are also landlocked developing countries, Bhutan and the Lao People's Democratic Republic have already met the GNI per capita graduation criterion (figure 1.2). According to the latest data for 2012-2014, the GNI per capita of Bhutan is comfortably above the regular income graduation threshold and only a short distance away from the "income-only" threshold. The Lao People's Democratic Republic, which has been consistently improving on the three graduation indicators over the past decade, cleared the income threshold in 2013, in time for the 2015 review. In contrast, progress towards meeting the GNI per capita criterion has been slower in Afghanistan and Nepal.

In terms of the human assets index criterion, these four countries have made remarkable progress. Bhutan and Nepal have already cleared the graduation threshold, while the Lao People's Democratic Republic has been constantly narrowing the gap with the threshold. In Afghanistan, the human assets index remains relatively low, although it has made some progress over the past decade.

With regard to the economic vulnerability index criterion, Nepal is the only country in this group that has cleared it. In Afghanistan, the economic vulnerability index has hardly changed in recent years. The economic vulnerability index of Bhutan, which had stalled for a decade, showed some progress in 2014 due to the reduced numbers of victims of natural disasters in recent years. In contrast, the Lao People's Democratic Republic had lowered the economic vulnerability index significantly between 2003 and 2012, although its progress slowed between 2013 and 2014.

As regards the third group, the least developed countries that are also small island developing States (Kiribati, Solomon Islands, Timor-Leste, Tuvalu and Vanuatu), they all meet the "income-only" criterion for graduation, with the exception of Solomon Islands (figure 1.3). Although the GNI per capita of Timor-Leste dropped in 2014, its level is still considerably above the "income-only" threshold of $2,500 for the period between 2012 and 2014. Solomon Islands met the regular income threshold for the first time during the 2015 review.

With regard to the human assets index criterion, although Timor-Leste is the only country in this group that has not cleared it as of 2014, the country has made steady progress in recent years. Reducing the economic vulnerability index remains a major challenge for each of the least developed countries that are also small island developing States. Given the significance of economic vulnerability for these countries, this issue is further explored in the following subsection.

Table 1.2 summarizes the latest status of the progress towards meeting the graduation criteria based on the annual updates of the indicators. The progress is reported in terms of "gaps", defined as the difference between the graduation threshold and the value of the indicator divided by the graduation threshold. In the case of GNI per capita or the human assets index, which need to exceed the value of their respective graduation thresholds, the gap is measured as the value of the threshold minus the value of the indicator. In the case of the economic vulnerability index, which needs to attain a value lower than the graduation threshold, the gap is defined as the value of the indicator minus the value of the threshold.

Table 1.2 reveals that, apart from the seven countries that have already fulfilled the graduation requirements at the March 2015 review, three countries have cleared one of the three criteria and missed a second threshold by a margin of 5% or less. The observations on the three groups of least developed countries in the region can be summarized as follow:

(a) **Least developed countries that are neither landlocked developing countries nor small island developing States:** Although none of them has met the criteria for graduation yet, they have made considerable progress since the 2012 review. The three countries in this group have all met one of the three graduation criteria and two of them were very close to meeting a second criterion according to the latest data available. Bangladesh met the economic vulnerability index criterion but missed the human assets index criterion by 2%, and Myanmar met the human assets index criterion but missed both the income and economic vulnerability indices criteria by 4%. Although Cambodia has met the human assets index criterion, as of 2014 it had a 17% gap in meeting the economic vulnerability index criterion and a 24% gap in meeting the GNI per capita criterion. These observations suggest that both Bangladesh and Myanmar have good chances of meeting the graduation criteria at the 2018 review if they continue progressing at the same pace;

(b) **Least developed countries that are also landlocked developing countries:** The four countries in this group follow diverse paths towards

Country	GNI per capita	Human assets index	Economic vulnerability index	Income only	Have the criteria been met?
Least developed countries that are neither landlocked developing countries nor small island developing States					
Bangladesh	20%	2%	✓	-	-
Cambodia	24%	✓	17%	-	-
Myanmar	4%	✓	4%	-	-
Least developed countries that are also landlocked developing countries					
Afghanistan	43%	35%	9%	-	-
Bhutan	✓	✓	17%	5%	✓
Lao People's Democratic Republic	✓	5%	13%	42%	-
Nepal	45%	✓	✓	-	✓
Least developed countries that are also small island developing States					
Kiribati	✓	✓	122%	✓	✓
Solomon Islands	✓	✓	62%	34%	✓
Timor-Leste	✓	11%	75%	✓	✓
Tuvalu	✓	✓	69%	✓	✓
Vanuatu	✓	✓	49%	✓	✓

Source: ESCAP calculations based on data from various sources.

Note: See annex I.

graduation from least developed country category. Both Bhutan and Nepal met the criteria for graduation for the first time at the 2015 review. As such, they will be considered for possible graduation at the Committee's next review. Bhutan has met the graduation threshold for income and the human assets index, while falling short in the economic vulnerability index criterion. On the other hand, Nepal met the human assets index and economic vulnerability index criteria but failed to meet the income criterion by a large margin. The Lao People's Democratic Republic, which has met the income criterion, may be able to meet the human assets index criterion in time for the 2018 review if its pace of progress in this indicator continues over the next two years;

(c) **Least developed countries that are also small island developing States:** All five countries in this group have already met the graduation criteria by clearing either the "income-only" threshold or a combination of the income and human assets index criteria. However, there remains a significant margin for meeting the economic vulnerability index criterion. As of 2014, Kiribati had the highest economic vulnerability index, 122% above the graduation threshold, followed by Timor-Leste (75%), Tuvalu (69%), Solomon Islands (62%) and Vanuatu (49%), leaving serious concerns about their economic and environmental vulnerabilities.

1.2. Deconstructing the economic vulnerability index

As mentioned above, the Asia-Pacific least developed countries have had great difficulty in lowering their economic vulnerability indices. Out of the 12 Asia-Pacific least developed countries, only Bangladesh and Nepal met the economic vulnerability index criterion for graduation at the 2015 review. Kiribati, Solomon Islands, Timor-Leste, Tuvalu and Vanuatu remain particularly vulnerable. As of 2014, the average gap of the economic vulnerability index for these countries was 75%, compared with 12% for the other five least developed countries that did not meet the economic vulnerability index criterion as of 2014 (Afghanistan, Bhutan, Cambodia, the Lao People's Democratic Republic and Myanmar).

Concerns over such a high degree of vulnerability have been reflected in the decision of the Committee for Development Policy at its 2015 review. It did not recommend Kiribati for graduation, even though the country had met the income and human assets index criteria for the second time, due to the country's high economic vulnerability index. In addition, Cyclone Pam, which hit the South Pacific two weeks before the Committee met in New York to undertake its review, was one of the worst natural disasters in the history of Vanuatu; it also caused significant damage in Tuvalu and Kiribati. The Committee will revisit the possibility of recommending Kiribati for graduation at its 2018 review.

Solomon Islands met the graduation criteria for the first time at the 2015 review, clearing the income and human assets index criteria. However, though decreasing during recent years, the country's vulnerability remains high: its economic vulnerability index was 62% above the threshold in 2014. The country will be considered for graduation at the next review. Timor-Leste also met the eligibility criteria for graduation in the "income-only" category, but it lags behind in the human assets index, with a gap of 11% and has a persistently high economic vulnerability index, with a gap of 75%.

Tuvalu has one of the highest income levels and the highest human assets indices among the world's least developed countries, and it has met both thresholds by large margins. The Committee had already recommended Tuvalu for graduation in its 2012 review. However, as is the case for other Asia-Pacific small island developing States, the country's high level of vulnerability, 69% above the threshold level in 2014, is of great concern to the Economic and Social Council,[3] which postponed its recommendation for graduation for the second time in 2015.

Finally, Vanuatu was initially scheduled to graduate in 2017 as it had met and continued to advance in the GNI per capita and human assets index

criteria. However, its vulnerability remains high with an economic vulnerability index of 49% above the threshold. It should be added that the devastation caused by Cyclone Pam had not been fully assessed at the time of the March 2015 review. In December 2015, taking into account the serious disruption caused by this natural disaster to the economic and social progress that Vanuatu had been demonstrating for several years, the General Assembly decided to postpone graduation until December 2020.[4]

To understand the sources of economic vulnerability of the Asia-Pacific least developed countries, figure 1.4 shows the composition of the economic vulnerability index for three groups of least developed countries: the five least developed countries that are also small island developing States; the other five least developed countries that did not meet the economic vulnerability index criterion for graduation; and the two Least Developed Countries that met the economic vulnerability index criterion. For the purposes of comparison, the composition of the index is also shown for a reference group of non-CSN developing countries in Asia.[5] Each bar in the figure is based on the average values of the eight components of the economic vulnerability index for each group of countries. Data for the least developed countries are for 2014.

As mentioned above, the least developed countries that are also small island developing States have significantly higher vulnerability scores than other

Figure 1.4 **Composition of the economic vulnerability index, 2014**

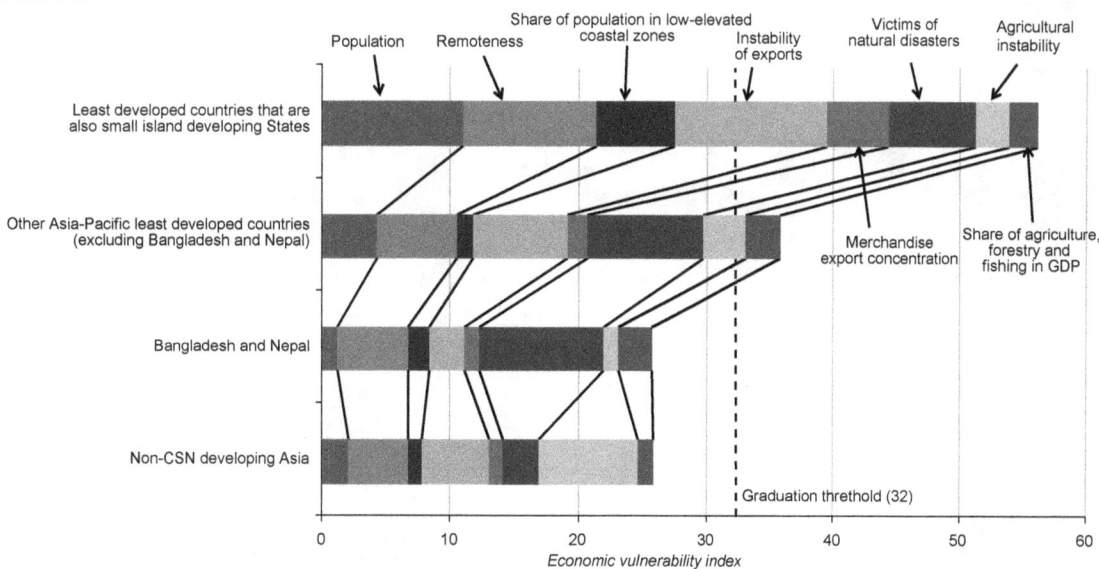

Source: ESCAP calculations based on data from various sources.
Note: See annex I.

least developed countries in the region. Although the composition of the economic vulnerability index varies across these countries, the instability of exports of goods and services is on average its single largest component, accounting for 21% of the total.[6] Export concentration is another important component of the economic vulnerability index for the least developed countries that are also small island developing States, accounting for 9% of the total. Thus, the contribution of export instability and concentration to the economic vulnerability index is 30%. However, the largest source of economic vulnerability for these countries comes from the small sizes of their populations and geographic characteristics, such as remoteness and the share of the population living in low-elevated coastal zones.[7] On average, these three components explain 49% of the economic vulnerability index.

For the other five least developed countries that did not meet the economic vulnerability index criterion in 2014, the demographic and geographic characteristics are less significant, representing on average 33% of the economic vulnerability index, followed by instability and concentration of exports, which account for a further 25%. For these countries, however, the share of victims of natural disasters in their economic vulnerability index is 25%, twice as high as for the least developed countries that are also small island developing States. The share of agriculture, forestry and fishing in the GDP together with agricultural instability is also more important for these countries than for the least developed countries that are also small island developing States.

For the two least developed countries (Bangladesh and Nepal) that have already met the economic vulnerability index criterion, the main component of this index is victims of natural disasters, which accounts for 38% of the total. The average economic vulnerability index for these two countries is almost the same as for the reference group of non-CSN developing countries. The most important components of the economic vulnerability index for the reference group are export and agricultural instability.

Table 1.3 illustrates how the economic vulnerability index and its components changed between 2004 and 2014. In order to make this comparison, economic vulnerability indices for the year 2004 have been re-estimated based on the weighting and calculation schemes used for the 2014 figures. The results are reported by component, separately for the three groups of least developed countries described above.

The table shows that the three groups of least developed countries reduced their economic vulnerability indices between 2004 and 2014. However, the reduction was most significant for Bangladesh and Nepal, some 17%. The second fastest reduction in the economic vulnerability index was for the five countries that were not small island developing States. For these countries, the reduction of the economic vulnerability index was 14%. Since, on average, these countries have a gap of 10% to reach the graduation threshold of 32, it seems feasible that they will do so over the next 10 years, if their pace of progress during the previous decade continues. However, for

| Table 1.3 | Changes in the composition of the economic vulnerability index between 2004 and 2014 |

	Least developed countries that are also small island developing States		Other Asia-Pacific least developed countries (excluding Bangladesh and Nepal)		Bangladesh and Nepal	
	2004	2014	2004	2014	2004	2014
Population	11.0	11.0	4.6	4.3	1.3	1.2
Remoteness	11.0	10.4	7.7	6.2	7.0	5.6
Merchandise export concentration	3.6	4.8	1.6	1.6	1.3	1.1
Share of agriculture, forestry and fishing in GDP	2.7	2.2	3.9	2.7	2.9	2.6
Instability of exports of goods and services	13.7	12.0	10.4	7.3	5.4	2.7
Share of population in low-elevated coastal zones	3.7	6.1	1.3	1.3	1.6	1.6
Victims of natural disasters	9.6	7.0	8.9	8.9	10.3	9.7
Agricultural instability	3.9	2.6	3.3	3.4	1.3	1.2
Economic vulnerability index	59.1	56.1	41.8	35.8	31.0	25.7

Source: ESCAP calculations based on data from various sources.
Note: See annex I.

Box 1.1

Estimating the impact of natural disasters in 2015 on the progress towards graduation of selected Asia-Pacific least developed countries

Although data to calculate the value of the economic vulnerability indices for 2015 will not be available until late 2016, it is possible to estimate their future values by taking advantage of the timely updates of the Emergency Disasters Database of the World Health Organization and the population forecasts of the United Nations Statistics Division. Using these data, ESCAP has estimated the economic vulnerability indices for 2015 by updating two of their eight components, population and victims of natural disasters, keeping the other six components unchanged from 2014. This procedure can be justified in that the additional six components vary relatively little from year to year. See annex I for more details. "Victims of natural disasters" measures the share of a country's population that is killed, injured, left homeless or requiring basic necessities such as food, water, shelter, sanitation and immediate medical assistance after a natural disaster. In order to account for fluctuations of disasters over time, this indicator is calculated as a 20-year moving average. Thus, a major disaster will affect the value of this component of the economic vulnerability index, and the economic vulnerability index itself, for many years.

The estimates show that the impact of natural disasters in 2015 was sizable in terms of both the indicator for victims of natural disasters and the total economic vulnerability index (figure A). In Nepal, the share of the population that are victims of natural disasters more than doubled from the average of 0.7% between 1995 and 2014 to 1.7% for the period between 1996 and 2015, which corresponds to an increase from 65 to 77 in the indicator for victims of natural disasters. This change is large enough to reverse the downward trend of the economic vulnerability index that Nepal had been following over the previous decade. According to this estimation, Nepal's economic vulnerability index is expected to rise from 26.9 in 2014 to 28.3 in 2015. Although this is still below the graduation threshold of 32, it is possible that Nepal's economic vulnerability index could worsen even more once the impact of the earthquake on other components of the economic vulnerability index, such as the instability of exports of goods and services and agricultural instability, is accounted for in the 2015 data. Similarly, in Vanuatu, the average share of the population that are victims of natural disasters jumped from 3.4% (over the 20 years leading up to 2014) to 6.6% (over the 20 years leading up to 2015). As a consequence, the indicator for victims of natural disasters increased from 86 to 94, and the total economic vulnerability index from 47.7 to 48.7. Although Vanuatu has already met all the other criteria and this deterioration in the economic vulnerability index will not directly affect the review by the Committee for Development Policy, such a high level of economic vulnerability could affect the country's post-graduation transition process, as was the case for Maldives and Samoa (see the next section).

Figure A. Evolution of the economic vulnerability index and the score for victims of natural disasters, Nepal and Vanuatu

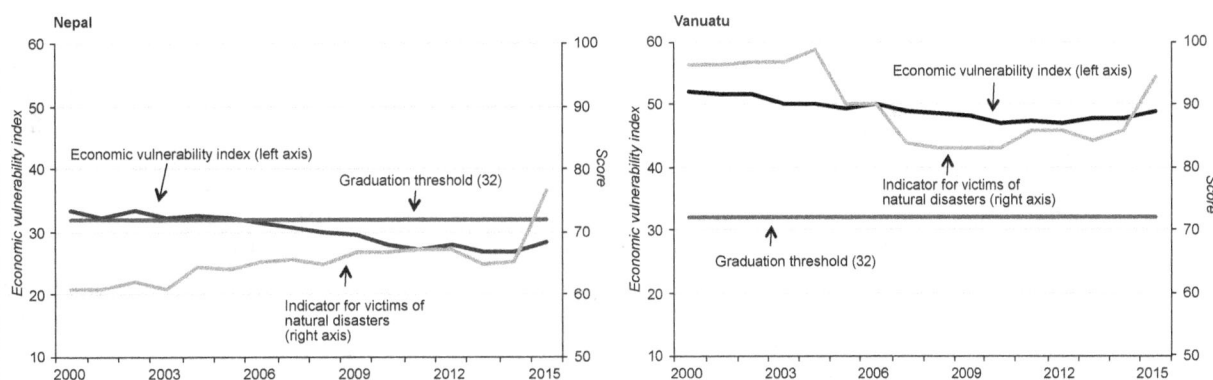

Source: ESCAP calculations based on data from various sources.

Notes: The figures for 2015 are estimates. See annex I for more details.

the least developed countries that are also small island developing States, the average reduction in their economic vulnerability index was only 5%. With a remaining average gap of 43% over the threshold of 32, it is highly unlikely that these countries will meet the graduation criterion in the near future.

Looking at the pace of progress in individual components of the economic vulnerability index provides further information. For both Bangladesh and Nepal and for the aforementioned group of non-small island developing States, more than half of the reduction in the economic vulnerability index is due to a marked improvement in export stability. The second most important factor is an improvement in the remoteness indicator. As noted in annex I, the remoteness indicator depends not only on the distance of a country to world markets but also on the share of world trade accounted for by neighbouring countries. Because of the economic buoyancy of Asia, Asian least developed countries have experienced a decrease in their remoteness indicator, contributing to a reduction in their economic vulnerability indices. Although this factor has also been favourable to the Pacific least developed countries, their remoteness is almost twice as great as for the Asian least developed countries due to the long distances to world markets.

For the least developed countries that are also small island developing States, a decrease in export instability was also an important factor in the reduction in the economic vulnerability index. Encouragingly, the most important factor was a decrease in the victims of natural disasters. However, these favourable factors were almost completely offset by increases in export concentration and in the share of the population living in low-lying coastal areas. Furthermore, the combined value of the demographic and geographic factors for these countries (population, remoteness and share of the population living in low-lying coastal areas) increased from 25.7 in 2004 to 27.5 in 2014. Because these factors are largely exogenous, and in 2014 represented 86% of the graduation threshold (32), the obstacles for these countries to meet such a criterion are enormous.

As encouraging as the reduction in the victims of natural disasters is for the least developed countries that are also small island developing States, the increase in the share of the population living in low-lying coastal areas is increasing future risks associated with natural disasters and climate change. Such risks should be taken into account when assessing possible future trajectories for the economic vulnerability index. Two major natural disasters that hit the Asia-Pacific least developed countries in 2015 exposed the great

vulnerability of these countries. In addition to Cyclone Pan mentioned above, which killed 11 people and affected over 60% of the population of Vanuatu, in April 2015 an earthquake with a magnitude of 7.8 killed over 8,000 people and affected more than 20% of the population of Nepal. Box 1.1 contains estimates of the impact of these natural disasters on the 2015 values of the economic vulnerability index for these countries.

1.3. Smooth transition and sustainable graduation

The losses and damages caused by natural disasters, to which least developed countries are highly vulnerable, make the implementation of the so-called smooth transition from the status of least developed country particularly important. This concept was articulated in General Assembly resolutions 59/209 and 67/221. These resolutions emphasize that graduation should not disrupt the development progress of the graduating countries and that specific measures to support least developed countries, including preferential market access, should be phased out in a gradual and predictable manner.

Resolution 59/209 was endorsed on the same day, 20 December 2004, on which Maldives was officially removed from the list of least developed countries; namely, six days before the Indian Ocean earthquake and tsunami, one of the deadliest natural disasters on record. Although Maldives was 2,500 km away from the epicentre of the earthquake, the country suffered significant damage and loss of lives. As a consequence of the tsunami, in 2005 the General Assembly granted Maldives a three-year moratorium to allow the country more time for post-disaster recovery and reconstruction. After the end of the moratorium, in 2007, Maldives entered a three-year transition period to negotiate a gradual phasing out of the benefits derived from being a least developed country, as recommended in resolution 59/209; Maldives eventually graduated in January 2011. The experience of Samoa is similar. The country was scheduled to graduate in 2010, but the General Assembly extended the transition period by three years until January 2014, due to the disruption caused by the Pacific Ocean tsunami of 2009.

The experiences of Maldives and Samoa made it clear that graduates from the status of least developed country category still remain vulnerable to major natural disasters, as well as to global economic shocks emanating from financial or commodity markets, which can wipe out their development progress. There is also a suggestion that a three-year transition towards graduation may still be insufficient to enhance the graduates' resilience to natural disasters and the impact of climate change. It is important to note that the five least developed countries that are also small island developing States have already met the conditions for graduation but still have very large economic vulnerability indices.

This fact further suggests the need for an alternative framework to deal with the graduation of such countries and ultimately to rebalance international support towards vulnerable countries. While such a framework can be established either within or outside the least developed country category, it should address the specific vulnerabilities of countries that reflect their economic, environmental and climate-related challenges. One possible framework could be based on the use of vulnerability data to determine the allocation of climate finance for adaptation. Recent research by Patrick Guillaumont (2015) offers promising new ideas for the design of such a framework. This area deserves more research and will be discussed further in next year's *Asia-Pacific Countries with Special Needs Development Report*.[8]

2. LINKING THE ASIAN LANDLOCKED DEVELOPING COUNTRIES WITH THE REST OF THE WORLD

Landlocked developing countries face special challenges associated with their lack of direct territorial access to the sea, remoteness and isolation from world markets. High transport costs due to long distances to the nearest seaport, cumbersome transit procedures and inadequate infrastructure negatively affect their competitiveness and economic growth potential. As a result, the Vienna Programme of Action emphasizes measures aimed at linking the landlocked developing countries with the rest of the world.

2.1. Tracking selected indicators of landlocked developing countries

This section aims to capture the progress of the Asian landlocked developing countries in some aspects of the Vienna Programme of Action by tracking selected indicators: the time for delivery of goods between the main commercial centre and a ship at the nearest seaport; the export product concentration index; and the number of fixed broadband Internet subscribers per 100 people.[9] The first indicator measures progress in the first goal of the Vienna Programme of Action, "to promote unfettered, efficient and cost-effective access to and from the sea by all means of transport …". The second indicator captures progress towards the fifth goal of the Vienna Programme of Action, "to promote growth and increased participation in global trade, through structural transformation related to enhanced productive capacity development, value addition, diversification and reduction of dependency on commodities". The third indicator focuses on an important element of the second priority of the Vienna Programme of Action, "infrastructure development and maintenance". See annex I for details about the construction and data sources of the three indicators.

To simplify the analysis, the 12 Asian landlocked developing countries are divided into two groups: (a) landlocked developing countries that are also least developed countries (Afghanistan, Bhutan, the Lao People's Democratic Republic and Nepal); and (b) landlocked developing countries that are not least developed countries (Armenia, Azerbaijan, Kazakhstan, Kyrgyzstan, Mongolia, Tajikistan, Turkmenistan and Uzbekistan). The performance of each of these countries is compared with a benchmark based on the performance of a reference group of Asian developing countries that are not CSN.[10] Figures 1.5 and 1.6 show the evolution of the three selected indicators for the two types of landlocked developing countries.

With respect to the number of days to/from ship, the data show a widening gap in the performances of Afghanistan, Bhutan and Nepal compared with the benchmark. In the case of Bhutan and Nepal, this is mostly due to the downward trend in the value of this indicator for the benchmark countries. In Afghanistan, the number of days to/from ship increased over time. As noted in the *Asia-Pacific Countries with Special Needs Development Report 2015*, the most successful landlocked developing country in reducing the time to reach the closest seaport is the Lao People's Democratic Republic. Its experience is discussed in box 1.2.

High values of the export product concentration index represent a lack of economic diversification. With the exception of Nepal, the landlocked developing countries that are also least developed countries have high levels of export concentration compared with the benchmark. It is important to note that this indicator is sensitive to fluctuations in relative prices and increases in commodity prices make commodity exporters look more concentrated.

In the case of Nepal, the export product concentration index is not only the lowest among all landlocked developing countries of the region but even lower than the benchmark. This is also one of the elements that explain the country's low economic vulnerability index among least developed countries.

Figure
1.5

Selected structural indicators of landlocked developing countries that are also least developed countries

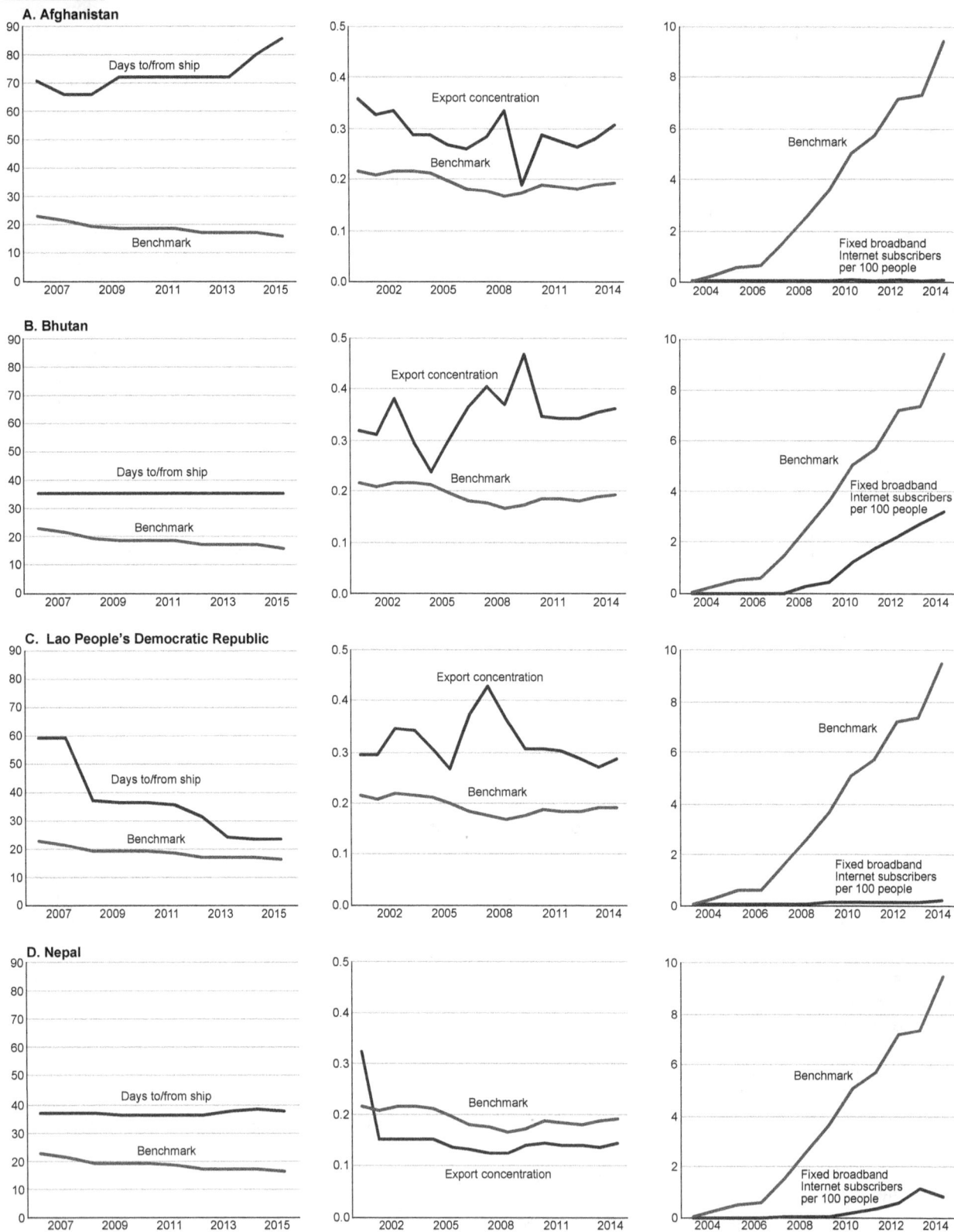

A. Afghanistan

B. Bhutan

C. Lao People's Democratic Republic

D. Nepal

Source: ESCAP calculations based on data from various sources.

Note: See annex I.

Figure 1.6 Selected structural indicators of landlocked developing countries that are not least developed countries

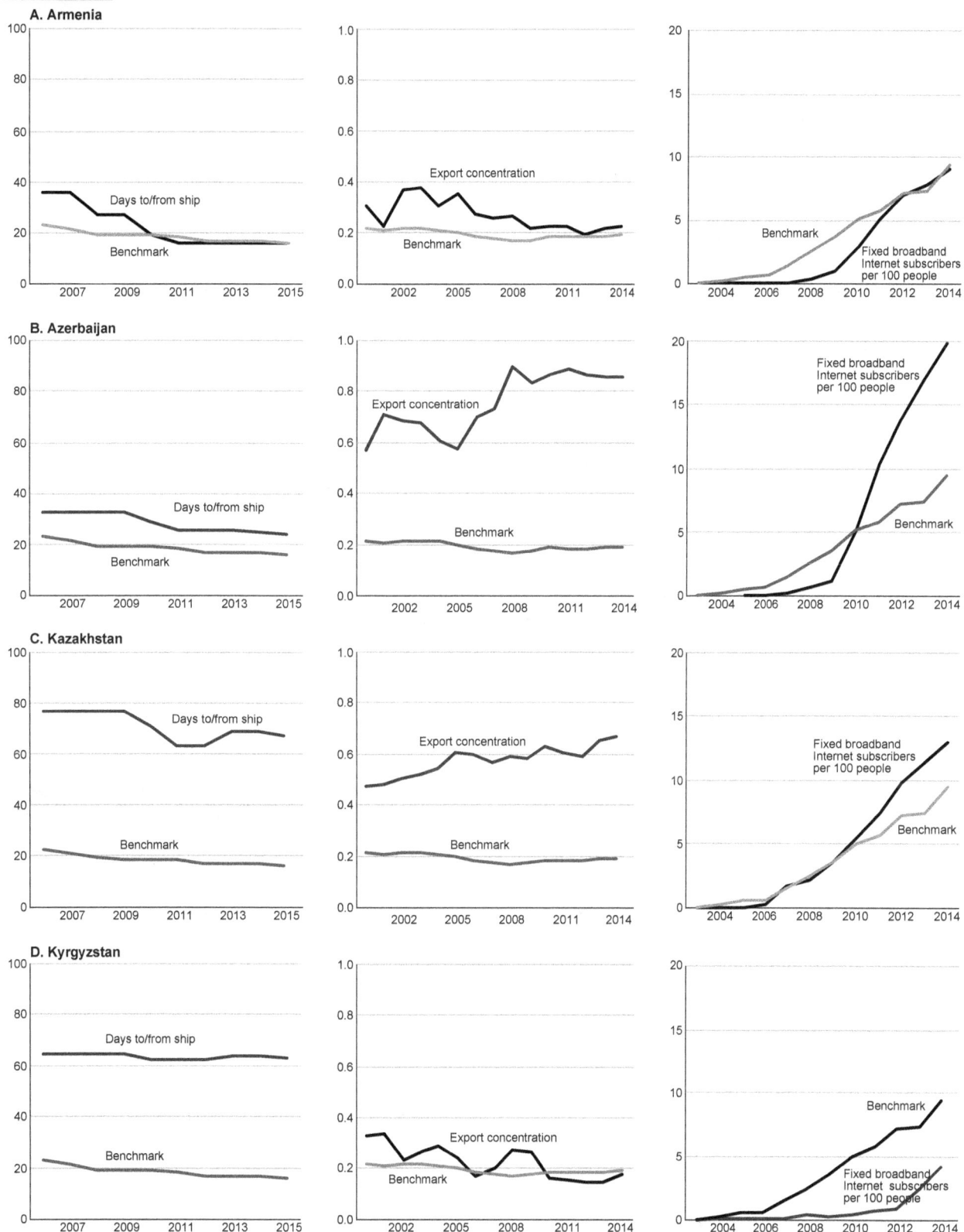

A. Armenia

B. Azerbaijan

C. Kazakhstan

D. Kyrgyzstan

Figure 1.6 *(continued)*

E. Mongolia

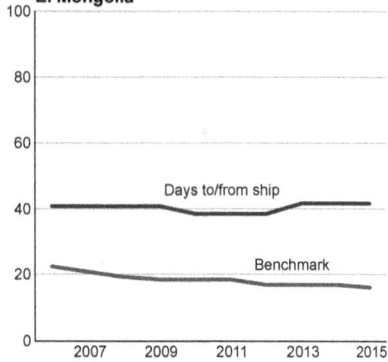
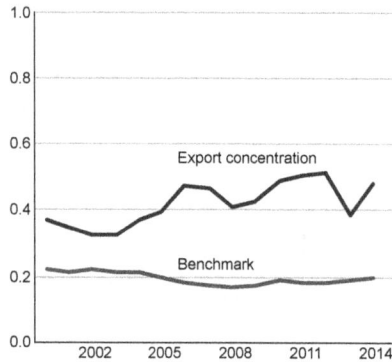
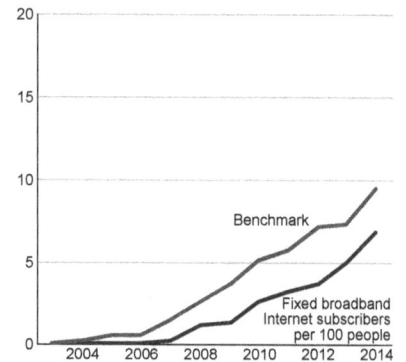

F. Tajikistan

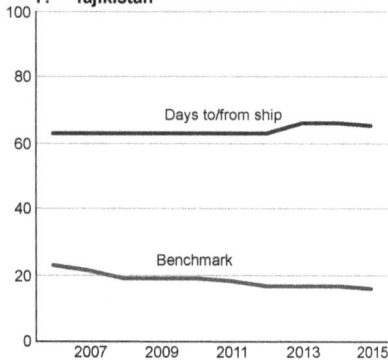
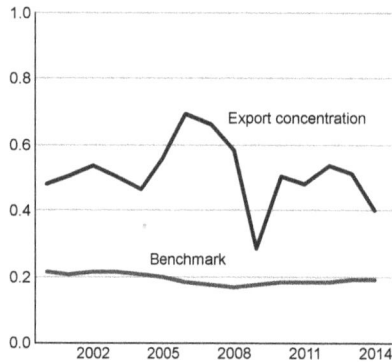
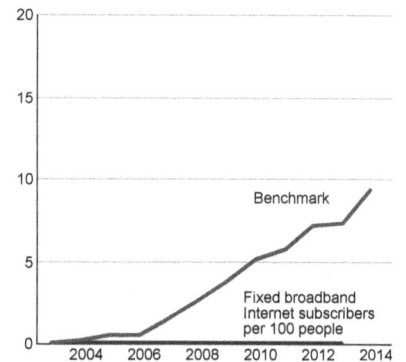

G. Turkmenistan

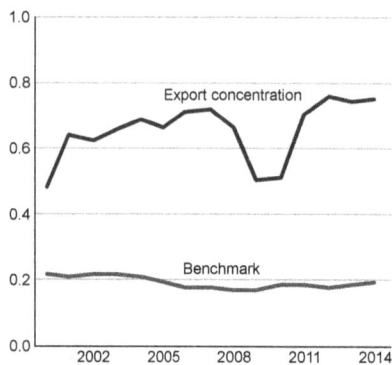
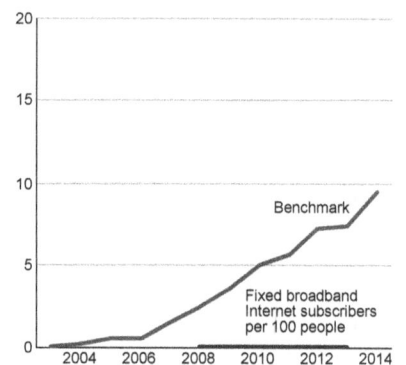

H. Uzbekistan

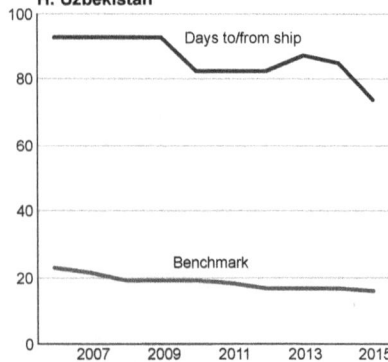
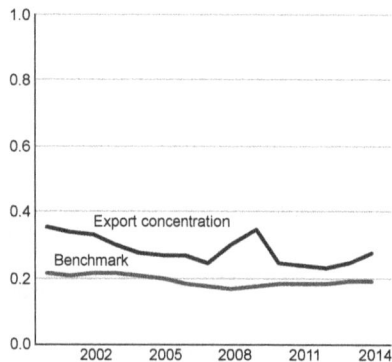
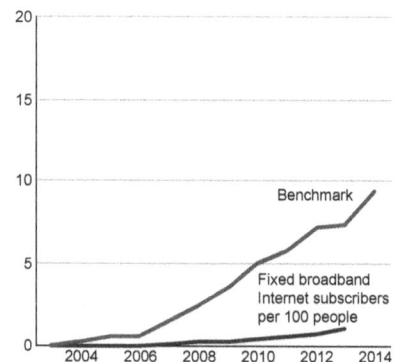

Source: ESCAP calculations based on data from various sources.

Note: See annex I.

Box 1.2   Decreasing trade time and costs in the Lao People's Democratic Republic

Driven by investments and exports of hydropower, gold, copper and wood products, the economy of the Lao People's Democratic Republic has grown at an average annual rate of 7% over the past two decades. The country's buoyant growth has been supported by public investment, increased private consumption and robust inflows of foreign direct investment. In February 2013, the Lao People's Democratic Republic became a member of the World Trade Organization, which resulted in a number of trade policy reforms, simplified investment procedures and an overall improvement in the business environment.

In addition, the Government established the Trade Facilitation Secretariat in October 2010, and it approved a Trade Facilitation Strategy and Action Plan in July 2011. The latter identified an agenda for improving trade facilitation and cooperation among border agencies with a proposed implementation structure, clear responsibilities for lead agencies and predefined performance indicators. The Trade Facilitation Strategy and Action Plan also aims at increasing trade competitiveness through the simplification and standardization of trade procedures (Lao People's Democratic Republic, 2014).

Although the country's rural infrastructure remains weak, the Government has made much progress in improving road infrastructure and streamlining border clearance procedures. In particular, it has rehabilitated and improved road connections with Viet Nam, China, and Cambodia. Furthermore, rationalized and simplified border clearance procedures have resulted in substantially decreased transport costs. For instance, a Single Stop-Single Window Inspection procedure established at the border between the Lao People's Democratic Republic and Viet Nam on the East-West Economic Corridor has been estimated to reduce the time spent at that border checkpoint by half.

In addition, the costs for transporting cargo have declined significantly due to greater competition from Thai transporters. The improvements in both transport infrastructure and facilitation resulted in reduced delivery times to and from the country's nearest seaport and its principal trading partners: Thailand, Viet Nam and China. Remaining delays occur when shipments require approvals from multiple government agencies (World Bank, 2014a). Therefore, the attainment of effective cross-sectoral coordination among various government agencies remains an important challenge.

Regarding fixed broadband Internet subscribers per 100 people, only Bhutan shows some progress, having reached a value of 3 in 2014, compared with 9 for the benchmark. Notice that the benchmark increased significantly between 2013 and 2014, widening the gap for this group of countries.

Among the second group of landlocked developing countries, the days to/from ship have decreased significantly in the period under consideration in only two countries: Armenia and Azerbaijan. The value of this indicator for Armenia has been comparable to that of the benchmark since 2010. The gap for this indicator vis-à-vis the benchmark has been relatively low and constant for Azerbaijan, with a noticeable reduction between 2009 and 2011. The number of days to/from ship has been significantly higher for the other landlocked developing countries in this group, and this indicator has remained roughly constant for Mongolia, Kyrgyzstan and Tajikistan over the period under consideration. Some progress has been made by Kazakhstan and, especially, Uzbekistan in 2014 and 2015.

The values of the export concentration index of Azerbaijan, Kazakhstan and Turkmenistan are not only high but have also increased over time. Export concentration is also high, but less so, in Mongolia and Tajikistan, with an upward trend in the former and a volatile pattern in the latter. The most diversified economies in this group are Armenia, Kyrgyzstan and Uzbekistan. Armenia has reduced its export concentration over time, reaching values close to the benchmark since 2012. The export product concentration index has also decreased over time in Kyrgyzstan, reaching values lower than the benchmark since 2010.

As regards the number of fixed broadband Internet subscribers per 100 people, the performance varies significantly within this group of countries. Armenia, Kazakhstan and Mongolia have, respectively, caught up with, exceeded and approached the benchmark, while very little progress has been made in Tajikistan, Turkmenistan and Uzbekistan. Kyrgyzstan made significant progress between 2012 and 2014.

The performance of Azerbaijan in Internet connectivity is remarkable, reflecting its leading efforts to build the Trans-Eurasian Information Superhighway, which is expected to supply Central Asian countries with Internet and telecommunications systems and to serve as a major element of the East-West Transport Corridor (box 1.3).

Table 1.4 presents the latest readings of the three selected indicators for landlocked developing countries. It also provides a comparison across the two types of landlocked developing countries and with the benchmark of the reference group. The observations and implications drawn therefrom for the two groups of Asian landlocked developing countries can be summarized as follows:

(a) **Landlocked developing countries that are also least developed countries:** The time it takes for the delivery of goods between the main commercial centres and the nearest seaport is still lengthy for countries in this group. Compared with the benchmark, it takes, on average, 2.7 times as long for goods to be delivered to/from these countries. Although the Lao People's Democratic Republic has managed to reduce this time considerably, more efforts should be made to reduce procedural delays, including at border-crossing points, as well as operational inefficiencies at the seaport. In addition, improvements on access to broadband Internet have been rather limited in this group of countries, with the exception of Bhutan. In the light of their physical distance to shipping networks,

---

Box 1.3   **Improving information and communications technology connectivity in Azerbaijan**

The information and communications technology (ICT) sector of Azerbaijan has been expanding at an average annual rate of between 25% and 30% since 2005. The gradual extension of fixed broadband networks, which is taking place mostly in urban areas, and a significant reduction in the wholesale and retail prices of broadband access are the main drivers behind this boom. At the end of 2013, the number of fixed broadband subscribers was 605,233, which represented 30.26% household penetration (World Bank, 2014b).[a]

Two important recent initiatives are likely to reinforce the boom in fixed broadband Internet: one at the national level and the other at the regional level. At the national level, the Government has developed a National Broadband Development Plan with the objective of deploying broadband networks over fibre-optic cables in the country's unserved and underserved rural areas at a cost of over $550 million for the period between 2014 and 2016. In addition, the State Programme on Poverty Reduction and Sustainable Development for 2008-2015 contained ambitious targets, including the complete access of all school children to computers and the Internet by 2015 (Azerbaijan, 2008).

At the regional level, the fifth and sixth sessions of the Special Programme for the Economies of Central Asia Project Working Group on Knowledge-based Development in 2013 welcomed a decision by the Government of Azerbaijan to establish a specialist centre on public-private partnerships in the ICT sector in Baku. Also, at the end of 2013, the leading telecommunications operators of Azerbaijan, China, Kazakhstan, the Russian Federation and Turkey signed a memorandum of understanding to establish a consortium for the implementation of the Trans-Eurasian Information Superhighway project, which aims at creating a transnational fibre-optic backbone between Europe and Asia.

The project was launched at the ministerial summit held within the framework of the 14th Azerbaijan International Telecommunications and Information Technologies Exhibition and Conference in November 2008. The project was subsequently supported by a resolution co-sponsored by 30 countries and adopted by consensus at the sixty-fourth session of the General Assembly in 2009.[b] The project is expected to boost the development of the Internet, telecommunications systems and related electronic services in Eurasia.

A major challenge for the expansion of access to broadband Internet is the difficulty in connecting rural areas. Greater promotion of mobile broadband could be an alternative to fixed broadband in connecting rural areas in the short term. The price of Internet services plays an important role in promoting broadband diffusion. In addition, the long-term sustainability of the sector's growth will greatly depend on the design and adoption of a proper regulatory framework aimed at the promotion of competition.

[a] The data of the International Telecommunication Union used in figures 1.6 and 1.7 are based on the percentages of individuals subscribed to broadband Internet. The two figures would be compatible if the average household size of Internet subscribers is smaller than the average household size for the population at large. This is likely to be the case, as Internet access is more common initially among younger, urban and more affluent individuals.

[b] General Assembly resolution 64/186.

---

investing in Internet infrastructure could be an important element in linking the Asian landlocked developing countries that are also least developed countries to the rest of the world;

(b) **Landlocked developing countries that are not least developed countries:** For this group of countries, the delivery of goods between the main commercial centres and the nearest seaport requires an average of 3.3 times the benchmark of the reference group, which is even longer than the first group of Asian landlocked developing countries. As such, time delays and inefficiencies should be addressed through the concerted efforts of these countries with the cooperation of neighbouring transit countries. Finally, export diversification is uncommon among these countries. An excessive dependence on exports of a small set of goods, especially primary commodities, exposes their economies to external shocks, such as volatility in the global commodity markets. Progress is required to diversify their economies through, for instance, strong enforcement of market competition laws and relevant investment in infrastructure, which could potentially improve the business environment and contribute to the development of new high value-added sectors (ESCAP, 2012; 2015).

3. RENEWABLE ENERGY IN THE SMALL ISLAND DEVELOPING STATES

The small island developing States of the Pacific face unique development challenges because of their small size, remoteness from major markets, limited export base and exposure to global environmental challenges. Energy security is another important area of concern for these countries, with an estimated 70% of their population lacking modern electricity services. There is also very high dependence on imported petroleum fuels for electricity generation and, in particular, for the transport sector (Johnston, 2012).

For that reason, in 2004, 18 Pacific island countries and territories, together with regional and international development agencies, developed the Pacific Islands Energy Policy, which was followed by the Framework for Action on Energy Security in the Pacific 2010-2020. The Framework, among other things, calls for increasing investment in proven renewable energy technologies, including biomass, to supplement and replace expensive petroleum fuels as the predominant source of energy. More recently, the Samoa Pathway, signed by 20 Pacific island countries in 2014, includes renewable energy as one of its priority areas.

Table 1.4 Indicators of landlocked developing countries, latest data available

Group/country	Days to/from ship (2015)	Export concentration index (2014)	Fixed broadband Internet subscribers per 100 people (2014)
Landlocked developing countries that are also least developed countries			
Group average	46	0.27	1.1
Afghanistan	86	0.31	0.0
Bhutan	36	0.36	3.3
Lao People's Democratic Republic	24	0.28	0.2
Nepal	38	0.15	0.8
Landlocked developing countries that are not least developed countries			
Group average	56	0.48	6.8
Armenia	16	0.22	9.1
Azerbaijan	24	0.86	19.8
Kazakhstan	67	0.67	12.9
Kyrgyzstan	63	0.17	4.2
Mongolia	42	0.48	6.9
Tajikistan	66	0.41	0.1
Turkmenistan	98	0.76	0.0
Uzbekistan	74	0.28	1.1
Benchmark	17	0.19	9.5

Source: ESCAP calculations based on data from various sources.
Note: See annex I.

3.1. Tracking selected indicators of small island developing States

Given the importance of renewable energy for the small island developing States, the share of renewables in total electricity generation is one of the selected indicators used in this section to track the progress of these countries towards the goals of their global programme of action, the Samoa Pathway. To capture progress towards meeting some of the social and economic pillars contained in the Samoa Pathway, two other indicators were chosen: access to improved sanitation facilities and access to mobile phones. The former is one of its priority areas and the latter is included in the access to technology section as an important means of implementation. See annex I for details about the construction and data sources of the three indicators.

To facilitate the present analysis, in what follows the 11 Asia-Pacific small island developing States, for which data for at least two of the three indicators are available, are divided into two groups: (a) small island developing States that are also least developed countries (Kiribati, Solomon Islands, Tuvalu, and Vanuatu); and (b) small island developing States that are not least developed countries (Fiji, Maldives, Micronesia (Federated States of), Palau, Papua New Guinea, Tonga and Samoa). The performance of each of these countries is compared with a benchmark based on the performance of a reference group of Asian developing countries that are not CSN, as described above. See annex I for more details. Figures 1.7 and 1.8 show the evolution of the three selected indicators for the two types of small island developing States.

As shown in figure 1.7, in 2015 the percentage of the population that had access to improved sanitation facilities remained low in the small island developing States that are also least developed countries, particularly in Solomon Islands and Kiribati. Access is higher in Vanuatu and Tuvalu, where the value of this indicator is close to that for the benchmark.

Access to mobile phones has been slowly improving over time, but this indicator also lags behind the benchmark in all four countries. In 2014, the number of mobile phone subscriptions per 100 people was around 60 for Solomon Islands and Vanuatu, which is about half the value of the indicator for the benchmark countries. The pace of progress has been much slower in Tuvalu and Kiribati.

The share of renewable energy in electricity generation is negligible in Kiribati and Solomon Islands, but in Vanuatu it has been comparable with the benchmark in recent years. The latest value of the indicator for Vanuatu was 16%, the same as the level of the benchmark countries. According to the National Energy Road Map 2013-2020 of Vanuatu, the country aspires to increase the share of renewables even more in the future, targeting 40% in 2015 and 65% by 2020 (Vanuatu, 2013).

Figure 1.8 shows the performance in the three indicators for a number of Asia-Pacific small island developing States that are not least developed countries. Among these countries, Palau and Maldives have achieved nearly 100% access to improved sanitation facilities in 2015, exceeding the benchmark. The value of this indicator is lowest for Papua New Guinea, where a large proportion of the population lives in rural areas, followed by Micronesia (Federated States of). Access to sanitation is slightly lower but close to the benchmark in Fiji, Samoa and Tonga.

Access to mobile phones is highly uneven among this group of countries. For Papua New Guinea, Tonga and Samoa, access has been increasing over time. Progress has been somewhat slower in Micronesia (Federated States of). The best performer has been Maldives, with a mobile phone penetration rate greatly exceeding the benchmark, followed by Fiji and Palau.

The share of renewable energy in electricity generation is negligible in Maldives and Tonga, while it is close to the benchmark in Palau. The countries that rely most intensely on renewables for electricity generation are Fiji, Papua New Guinea and Samoa. More details on these countries' experiences with renewable energy are provided in the following subsection.

Table 1.5 compares the latest readings of the three selected indicators for small island developing States. It also provides a comparison with the benchmark of the respective reference groups of Asian developing countries that are not CSN. The observations and implications drawn therefrom for the two groups of Asia-Pacific small island developing States can be summarized as follows:

(a) **Small island developing States that are also least developed countries:** This group of countries lags far behind the other group of small island developing States of the region in all of the three areas analysed in this section. Both access to sanitation and access to mobile phones are considerably limited in these countries compared with the other group of small island developing States or the reference group of countries. None of the three countries in this group with data on electricity generation shows any development in the

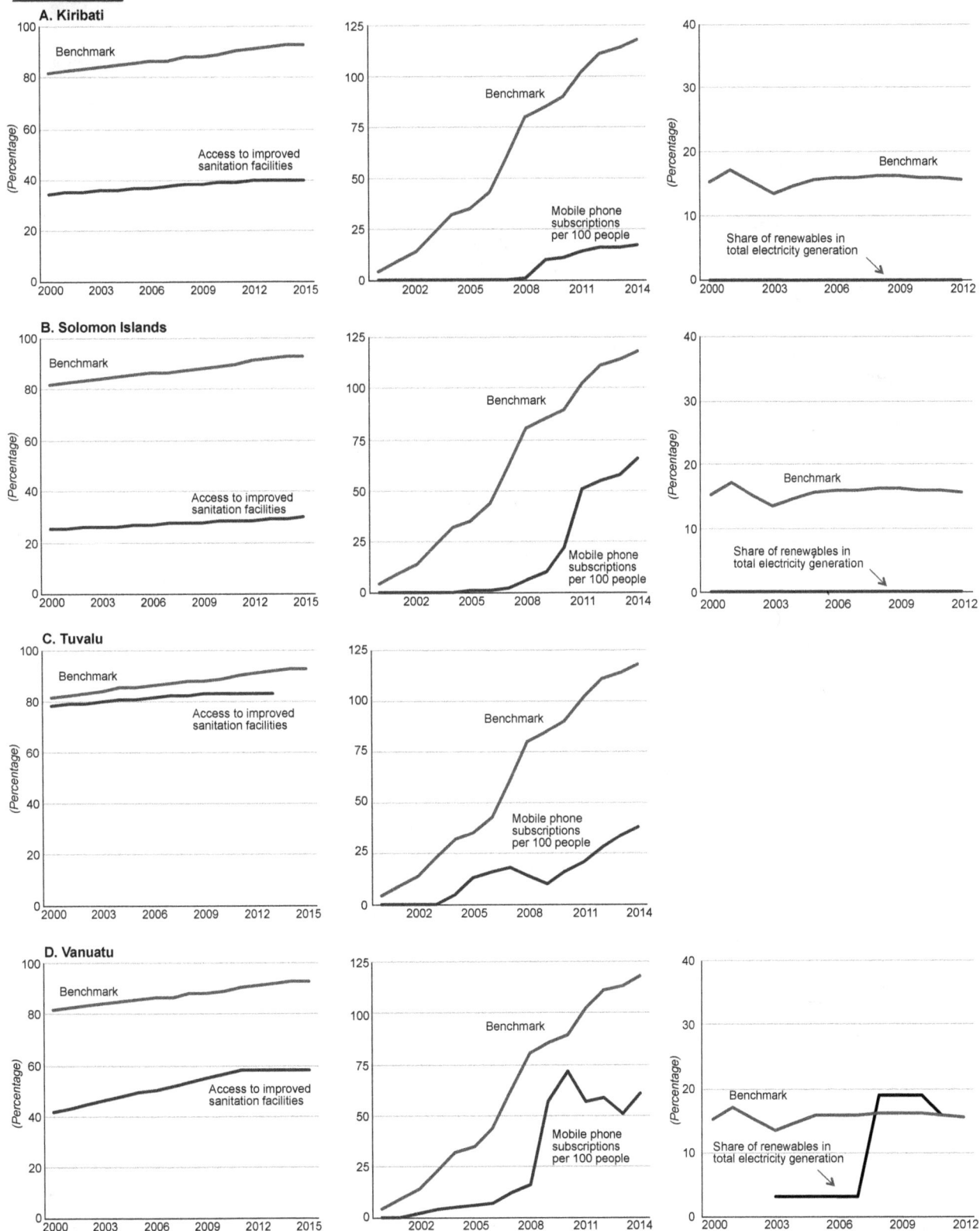

Figure 1.7 Selected structural indicators of small island developing States that are also least developed countries

A. Kiribati

B. Solomon Islands

C. Tuvalu

D. Vanuatu

Source: ESCAP calculations based on data from various sources.

Note: See annex I.

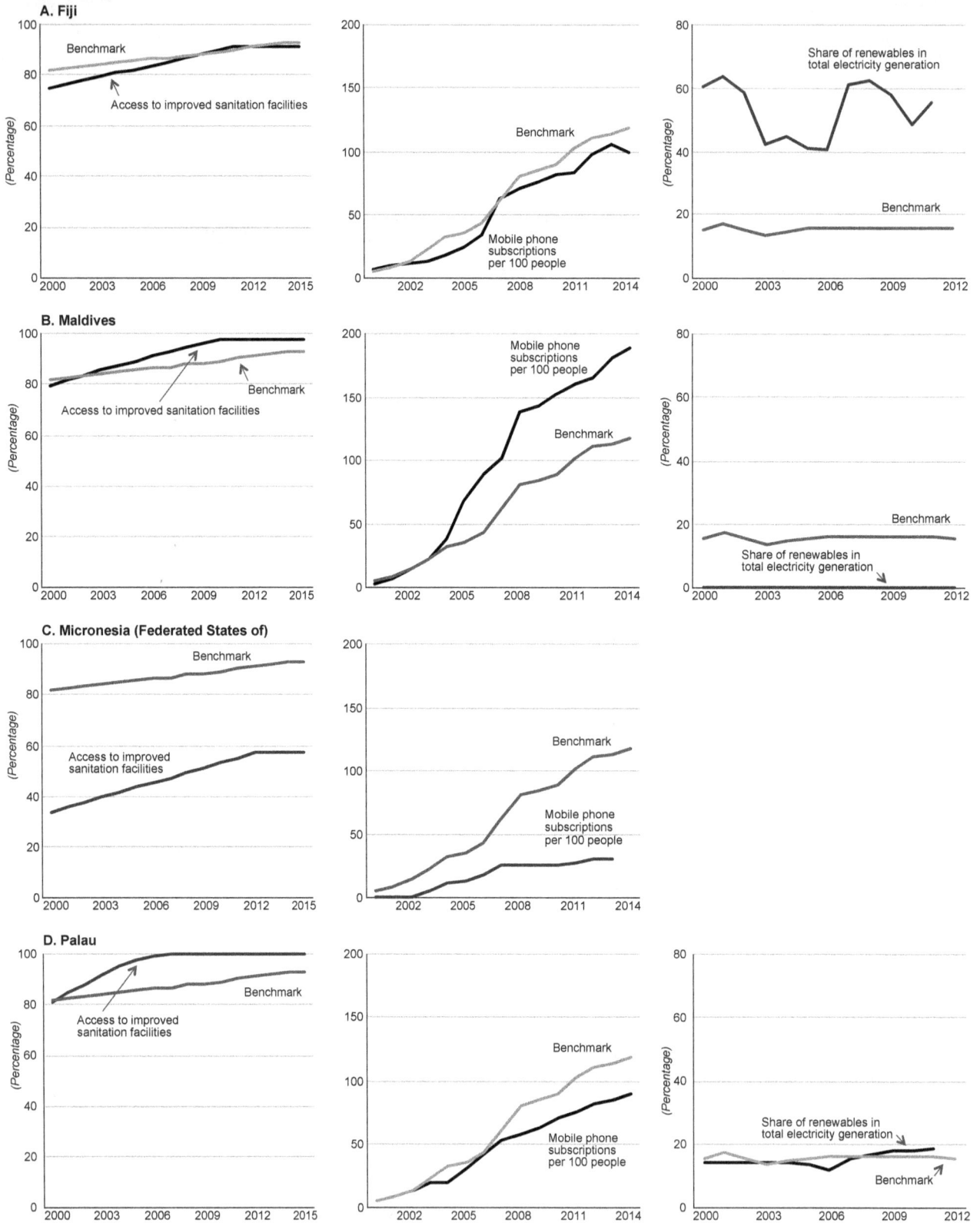

Figure 1.8 Selected structural indicators of small island developing States that are not least developed countries

A. Fiji

B. Maldives

C. Micronesia (Federated States of)

D. Palau

Figure 1.8 (continued)

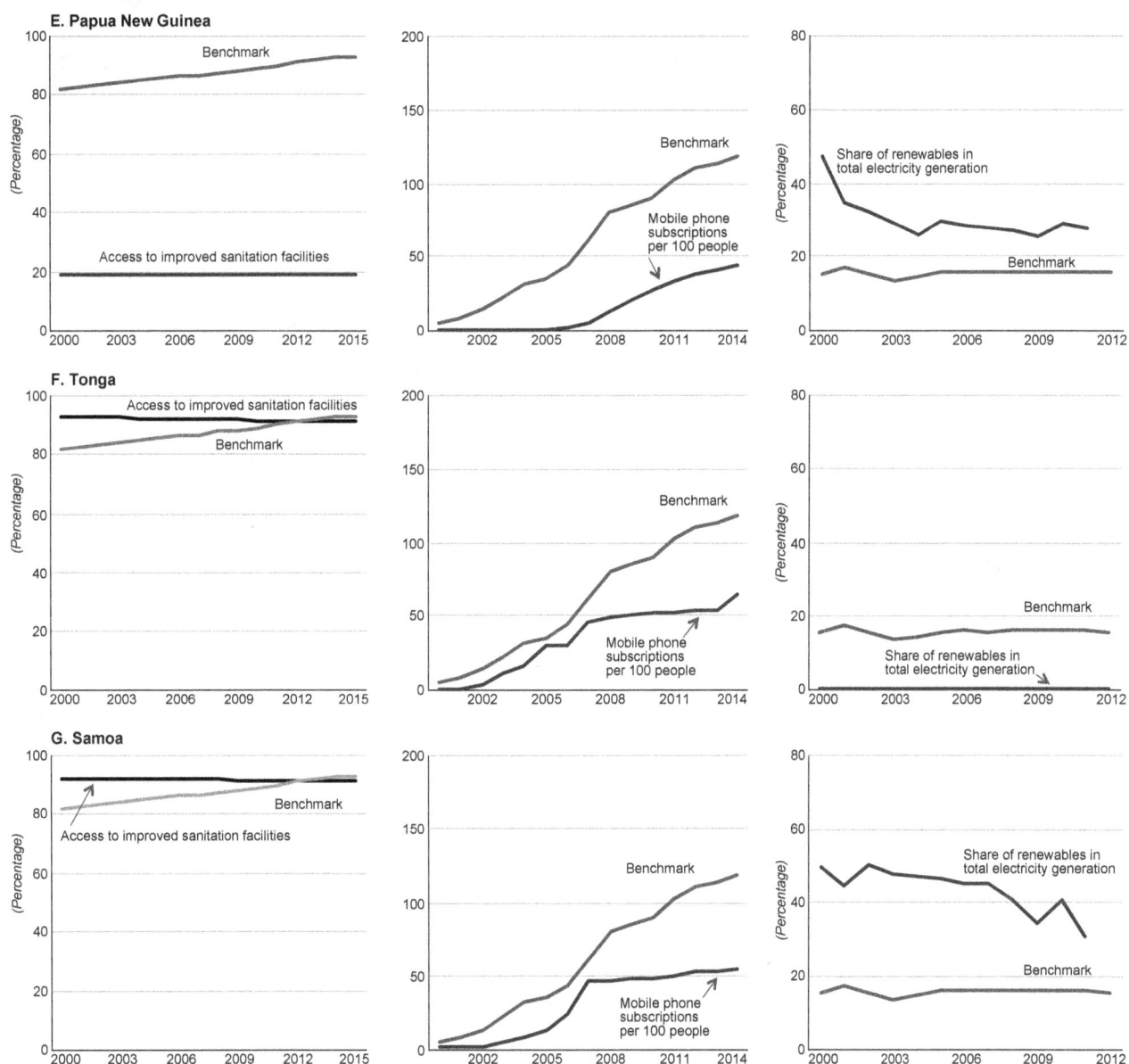

E. Papua New Guinea

F. Tonga

G. Samoa

Source: ESCAP calculations based on data from various sources.

Note: See annex I.

Table
1.5

Indicators of small island developing States, latest data available

Country	Improved sanitation facilities (share of population with access, 2015)	Mobile phone subscriptions per 100 people (2014)	Share of renewables in total electricity generation (2012)
Small island developing States that are also least developed countries			
Group average	52.7	45.5	0.0
Kiribati	39.7	17.4	0.0
Solomon Islands	29.8	65.8	0.0
Tuvalu	83.3	38.4	-
Vanuatu	57.9	60.4	0.0
Small island developing States that are not least developed countries			
Group average	78.2	82.0	27.8
Fiji	91.1	98.8	67.6
Maldives	97.9	189.4	0.1
Micronesia (Federated States of)	57.1	30.3	-
Palau	100.0	90.6	-
Papua New Guinea	18.9	44.9	32.8
Tonga	91.0	64.3	0.0
Samoa	91.5	55.5	38.3
Benchmark	**93.0**	**118.1**	**16.6**

Source: ESCAP calculations based on data from various sources.
Note: See annex I.

area of renewables. In this sense, the challenges they face are not only related to geographic remoteness from global markets but are also interconnected with more fundamental issues, such as lack of adequate sanitation facilities and communication and energy infrastructure;

(b) **Small island developing States that are not least developed countries:** In this group of countries, access to sanitation is generally comparable with the reference group. The notable exception to this observation is Papua New Guinea, where the geography is extremely rugged, which has been a serious impediment to infrastructure development. With regard to renewable energy, three of the five countries in this group with data on electricity generation rely strongly on renewables. Nevertheless, the selected indicators to track progress offer only a partial view of these economies' pathways to sustainable development, owing to the unavailability of time series data in most of these areas.

3.2. Selected experiences with renewable energy in the Pacific

Pacific leaders have recognized the "crippling effect" on their small and fragile economies of heavy reliance on imported fuel (DESA, 2010), and reducing this

dependence has become a priority for most countries (United Nations and others, 2011). Finding alternative low carbon renewable sources of energy and improving energy efficiency can together generate substantial economic savings as well as environmental and social benefits, including increasing energy security for the poor. To this end, most Pacific small island developing States have adopted ambitious goals for replacing a high percentage of diesel-fuelled electricity generation with renewable energy. While hydropower and small-scale biofuels are emerging as attractive alternatives, solar power remains the most practical option in most countries, especially in meeting the energy and electrification needs of rural and outer island communities. This transition is not without its challenges and constraints, in particular the high initial costs of renewable energy technology, ensuring that the technology is appropriate for small tropical island conditions, capacity issues and difficulties accessing international finance and investment (SPREP, 2011).

Fiji

Fiji has developed comprehensive national energy policies for renewables, ranging from setting up renewable energy targets, portfolio standards, concession bidding, subsidies, research and development and public awareness-raising campaigns. As a result, Fiji has made significant progress in improving access to modern energy and increasing the share of renewable energy sources in electricity generation. The Fiji Electricity Authority, the sole operator of the national grid, currently provides access to approximately 90% of the population (ADB, 2015).

Fiji has stood out in the Pacific region for having the highest use of renewable energy in its grid-based generation mix and, over the last 10 years, it has developed a diversified mix of hydro, biofuel, wind, solar and biomass power. Today, more than 60% of electricity comes from renewables, with hydroelectricity accounting for roughly 55% of renewable generation. Consequently, Fiji has both the lowest oil dependency and electricity tariffs among Pacific island countries (IRENA, 2014).

The National Energy Policy, first endorsed in 2006 and most recently updated in 2014, has guided the overall development of the energy sector in Fiji. The policy includes a target of around 99% of electricity generation from renewables by 2030 (Fiji, 2014). It requires frequent assessments of the country's renewable resources, including available sites and technologies, and it encourages investment in grid-connected renewable generation. The policy also prioritizes an increase in renewable energy providers outside the main grid operator, particularly in small-scale grid generation, through implementing economically efficient feed-in tariffs.[11] The Government has also been promoting the development of other indigenous local energy resources, such as ethanol production.

A number of incentives have been introduced to encourage private investment and reduce the risks for small-scale renewable energy generation connected to the grid. These include zero fiscal and import duties on renewable energy equipment, duty-free imports of plant and chemicals for biofuel manufacture, a 10-year tax holiday for new activities related to the processing of agricultural commodities into biofuels, and a 5-year tax holiday for new activities related to renewable energy projects and cogeneration power projects.[12]

The main challenges to further increasing investment in renewable generation in Fiji are related to legislative and regulatory issues. For example, an effective independent power producer framework that would attract private capital into renewable-energy-based power generation is still lacking. An enabling framework for private sector participation would also have to address barriers for small-scale, decentralized grid-connected renewable-energy-based generation. At present, the inefficient feed-in tariffs and lack of net metering provisions or incentive programmes

hinder such generation by households and small and medium-sized enterprises. Geographical and environmental factors are also important, as the cost of transportation is a deterrent to the development of renewable energy systems in the country's outer islands, and tropical cyclones can damage hydropower systems, wind farms and terrestrial solar farms.

Papua New Guinea

Electricity in Papua New Guinea is often unreliable and relatively expensive. Only about 13% of the population had access to electricity in 2010; nearly 90% cooked mainly with fuel wood while 3% used liquefied petroleum gas or electricity. The lack of reliable power has constrained growth in urban areas and contributed to poverty in rural areas. To address this deficiency, the National Electrification Roll-out Plan aims at increasing the population's access to electricity to 41% by 2020 and 70% by 2030.

Currently, Papua New Guinea has about 580 megawatts (MW) of installed generation capacity, 40% of which comes from hydropower plants, 37% from diesel generators, 14% from gas and 9% from geothermal sources. Of these 580 MW, Papua New Guinea Power, the national utilities company, manages 300 MW and the remaining 280 MW are supplied by the private sector, particularly large mines and plantations (ADB, 2015). The generation of electricity by the private sector includes a larger share of renewables compared with Papua New Guinea Power.

The country's current state of underdevelopment in power generation provides it with a unique opportunity to develop and build up a clean, efficient, cost-effective and sustainable generation system. Through the Papua New Guinea Development Strategic Plan 2010-2030, the Government has targeted a share of 52% of electricity generation to come from hydropower and an additional 25% to come from thermal and other sources of renewable energy by 2030 (Papua New Guinea, 2010a; 2011). Additionally, through Vision 2050, the Government has targeted (a) 100% rural electrification and (b) 100% power generation from renewable energy sources by 2050 (Papua New Guinea, 2010b).

The potential for renewable energy in Papua New Guinea is enormous. For instance, high and frequent rains combined with the rugged, mountainous terrain provide opportunities for expanding hydropower plants. Challenges for the development of renewable energy include limited demand in remote rural areas and the lack of a regulatory framework to encourage the development of a competitive electricity market. In addition, to support the achievement of the targets of Vision 2050, it will be necessary to gradually phase out fiscal policies favouring conventional energy as opposed to renewables.

Samoa

Despite a broad spectrum of renewable options in Samoa, roughly 70% of the country's energy capacity comes from petroleum products. Total installed grid power capacity in 2012 was 42 MW, of which 30 MW came from diesel generators, 11 MW from hydropower and 1 MW from biofuels (ADB, 2015). Reliance on petroleum products has developed out of the mismatch between the considerable growth in demand for energy and the lack of investment in maintaining and upgrading the country's legacy hydropower plants. Additionally, periodic droughts and floods have led to hydropower being perceived as a less stable source of energy (IRENA, 2014). The reliance on fossil fuel imports combined with oil price fluctuations have contributed to unpredictability in energy production costs and high electricity prices for consumers in Samoa. The Electric Power Corporation, the State-owned, sole provider of electricity, has passed on the costs of imported fuel to consumers by introducing a variable monthly surcharge (IRENA, 2014).

Despite its current dependency on fossil fuels, Samoa is committed to expanding sustainable renewable energy generation. Under the National Infrastructure Strategic Plan of 2011, a number of feasibility studies and pilot projects are underway to help the country decide which large-scale renewable energy projects are most worth pursuing. In addition, the promotion of electricity generation from proven renewable energy technologies is the key strategy of the Samoa Energy Sector Plan (2012-2016) and the Strategy for the Development of Samoa 2012-2016 has targeted increasing renewable energy for energy services (Samoa, 2012a; 2012b). Furthermore, Samoa is aiming for 100% of its electricity generation to come from renewables by 2030 (Samoa, 2015).

As of 2015, eight solar farms, one wind farm and three hydropower stations were in operation. In addition to building a second wind farm and three more hydropower stations, there are also plans underway to rebuild three hydroelectric plants that were destroyed by Cyclone Evans in 2012. Private investment in renewable energy infrastructure will be essential to meeting these targets, particularly through investment and cooperation with independent power producers. Through the Electricity Act of 2012, the private sector has been allowed to build and operate renewable energy power plants and sell electricity to the grid. Currently, the Electric Power Corporation has power purchase agreements with six independent power producers.

In order for Samoa to meet these ambitious targets, a number of challenges need to be overcome. Given that the introduction of independent power producers has only alleviated some of the financial burden associated with developing renewable energy generation, improvements in transmission and distribution infrastructure still need to be financed by the Government. Furthermore, the existing renewable generation infrastructure needs to be refurbished and properly maintained, which requires substantial investment in both improving existing infrastructure and fostering local technical capacity.

3.3. Renewable energy to enhance access to electricity in rural communities

As discussed above, hydropower is a key source of renewable energy in Fiji, Papua New Guinea and Samoa. Although a reliance on hydropower has increased energy security on these islands, it has also made their power systems vulnerable to the seasonal variations of annual hydrological cycles and extreme weather events. Severe droughts, El Niño and El Niño Southern Oscillation can all adversely affect the capacity of hydropower to be a reliable source of power and warrants the scaling up of non-hydro renewable sources, such as wind, solar, tidal energy, biomass and geothermal options, where possible (IRENA, 2015). However, diversifying the sources for generating electricity must be carefully planned through appropriate assessment of grid specifications, supply technologies and demand characteristics. Similar to hydropower, wind, solar, biomass and tidal energy not only fluctuate seasonally and daily, but are also unpredictable. The variability of these sources creates challenges for integrating them into electricity supply systems due to grid stability issues. While there is no one-size-fits-all solution, a recent study by the International Energy Agency (2014) has shown that through appropriate power system planning and regulatory and policy measures, levels of these variable sources can be integrated at a small, incremental cost.

Energy security and diversification of the energy mix have been major drivers for renewable policies and targets in the Pacific islands. Although the Pacific small island developing States are endowed with various renewable energy sources, they remain highly dependent on expensive fuel imports to meet their energy requirements. Therefore, increasing renewable energy investments has been seen as a means to mitigate the financial risks associated with oil price fluctuations by diversifying energy supplies. As renewable energy technologies offer considerable potential in the region for replacing oil-based power generation, most of the targets that Pacific small island developing States have set are focused on increasing investments and installations in the electricity sector, as discussed above.

The geographic isolation of Pacific islands not only prevents their connection to intercontinental grids but also constrains rural electrification based on centralized power systems. This underscores the need to invest in renewable energy technologies in rural areas that are not connected to the grid. The lack of focus on rural energy access combined with, inter alia, the high upfront costs associated with rural electrification and the limited government resources dedicated to rural electrification has kept the pace of rural development slow in the Pacific.[13]

A key concern related to the ambitious targets of Pacific small island developing States is that many of them favour investment in the electricity grid over rural electrification. The inherent danger of their ambitious targets is that low levels of demand for power in rural areas could lead to the bulk of renewable investment going into urban areas that already have access to electricity (Dornan, 2014). The focus of many targets on centralized grid systems also implies that they are less geared towards directing greater investment towards the development and utilization of off-grid, decentralized energy solutions that are especially suited for rural and, in particular, remote and hard-to-access areas where extensions of centralized grid connections are less feasible. Installation of off-grid systems is crucial in countries such as Kiribati, Micronesia (Federated States of), Papua New Guinea, Solomon Islands and Vanuatu, where geography and population dispersion hinder the expansion of centralized grid systems. In addition to installation, investment must also be directed towards advancing technical capacity in operating and maintaining off-grid electrification projects.

Green growth through renewables in the Pacific islands is not just about increasing renewable energy installations, it is also about creating a conducive environment for the development of renewables, which includes rehabilitating existing energy sources, accelerating the utilization of emerging energy technologies and developing an innovative approach to financing renewable energy solutions. Additionally, it also involves achieving universal access to affordable, reliable, sustainable and modern energy for all, which

in turn requires that the right indicators be set to incentivize the energy sector and that policy discourses shift from focusing on output to prioritizing access.

Such a shift would enable national policies and financing to be more reflective of a balanced approach to energy needs, supplies and services. The ability of targets and policies to achieve universal energy access is largely dependent on an ability to assess the level of energy access. The Global Tracking Framework, a multi-agency effort led by the International Energy Agency and the World Bank, which has been adopted by the Sustainable Energy for All programme, has developed a multi-tier energy framework to track global and national progress on energy access, renewable energy and energy efficiency in a more holistic and comprehensive way than current methods allow.

The renewable energy targets of the Pacific small island developing States present opportunities for widening electricity access, reducing poverty and improving the quality of life in the region. Given the progress that Fiji, Papua New Guinea and Samoa have made towards increasing the share of renewables in their electricity generation mix, the following discussion reviews some of the specific policy initiatives and investment-related issues concerning renewables in these countries and then subsequently provides a discussion of the lessons that can be learned from these three case studies.

3.4. Lessons for energy reform in the Pacific small island developing States

Facilitating energy sector reform through the expansion of renewable, sustainable clean energy in small island developing States will require overcoming a number of challenges. As illustrated by the above country experiences, a number of factors related to financial constraints, weak institutional mechanisms and regulatory frameworks, the availability of technology and technical capacity, as well as geographic constraints and environmental vulnerabilities have limited the development of renewable energy resources in small island developing States.

The substantial planning and investments shifts entailed in moving from high- to low-carbon investment require an enabling, robust and predictable regulatory environment and economic framework to stimulate and support effective private sector activities. A widespread deployment of the most relevant renewable energy technologies that fit with the unique geographic and environmental vulnerabilities of small island developing States depends heavily on the availability of financing. While the financial assistance of donors and development partners will be essential in implementing proposed renewable energy projects and in improving existing infrastructure and technologies, it is also imperative that Governments take concrete measures to designate the right market signals and provide the necessary incentives to curtail the risks involved in climate-friendly investments. ,

A significant scaling up of renewable energy generation capacity in small island developing States requires supportive legal and regulatory frameworks to address planning restrictions, grid access and an efficient use of independent power producers. It also requires the removal of barriers to investment in renewable technologies and that private sector and household investment in such technology be stimulated. Governments can accelerate such investments through creating incentives that promote an increased prevalence of renewable energy in the resource mix by means of implementing fiscal policies that favour investment in renewables over traditional fossil fuels, developing clear standard specifications for renewable energy components and providing accessible funding schemes for renewable uptake.

Additionally, feed-in-tariff schemes can also be an important way for Governments to encourage uptake of renewable and low-carbon energy by offering long-term contracts and guaranteed pricing to small-scale producers of renewable energy. Such schemes generally offer a guaranteed payment to renewable energy producers per unit of energy output. They also make it easier for producers to obtain credit to invest in renewable power by providing a guaranteed income stream that reduces risks associated with lending to energy producers.

A number of common challenges impeding renewable energy deployment in small island developing States can be identified:

(a) The renewable electrification targets that many small island developing States have set require that they develop adequate storage capacity for electricity. While this is expensive, it is considered necessary as it would allow renewables to become a stable source of power and also enable them to provide sufficient generating capacity during peak hours;

(b) Limited availability of energy data and lack of adequate data on the potential of hydropower,

geothermal, ocean energy, wind and biomass constrain policy formulation as well as energy planning, financial planning and renewable system project development in many small island developing States;

(c) Limited public awareness and knowledge of renewable energy and energy efficiency options combined with high upfront costs for renewable technology and lack of access to credit have acted as barriers to renewable uptake, especially for households and communities;

(d) Lack of local technical capacity in installing, operating and maintaining renewable systems remains a critical hindrance to the scaling up of renewable energy technologies in small island developing States. As the case studies above demonstrated, a particular challenge is the poor maintenance of legacy renewable systems. Capacity development and training activities are critical to accelerating the uptake of renewables and sustaining their generating capacities in the long term.

In addition to these challenges, certain geographic factors as well as environmental conditions and vulnerabilities also necessitate that the policies, programmes and projects that small island developing States pursue to expand renewable energy uptake be uniquely designed and customized to meet their individual capacity needs and available resources. Fiji, Papua New Guinea and Samoa have all set ambitious, yet appropriate, renewables targets that are cost effective given the abundant availability of low-cost renewable resources such as hydropower, geothermal and biomass in each country. However, such ambitious targets may not be feasible in countries with limited access to low-cost renewable energy sources. For example, while wind power is available in low islands and atolls, such as Tuvalu, Tonga and Vanuatu, low wind speeds combined with the need to ensure that wind turbines are cyclone proof make it expensive. Some other considerations warranting the need for carefully planning and diligently assessing policies, programmes and projects include: land availability; the extent of adequate transport facilities to reach remote villages and outer islands; whether and how energy systems on outer islands can be managed; and whether the terrain as well as population densities make grid extensions and their subsequent upkeep economically feasible.

CONCLUDING REMARKS

The present chapter tracked selected indicators of Asia-Pacific CSN in order to capture the progress of the region's least developed countries, landlocked developing countries and small island developing States towards the agreed goals and objectives of their respective programmes of actions. The tracking provides useful insights to policymakers on areas on which to focus policies and regional cooperation efforts to address structural impediments to sustainable development.

Least developed countries have been making remarkable progress towards meeting the criteria for graduation. However, the high level of economic vulnerability, especially for the small island developing States, casts doubts on the ability of these countries to sustain their development gains in the long term. In addition, this suggests the need for a framework that goes beyond current smooth graduation transition arrangements.

A key challenge for landlocked developing countries is to diversify beyond primary commodities and to advance in transit reforms in order to reduce their vulnerability to external shocks, which are also primary concerns of their programme of action. In this regard, an indicator-based mechanism for monitoring the pace of change in areas of concern of these countries will be useful for countries looking to adjust their policies based on their progress; it will also support the negotiation and review processes of the Vienna Programme of Action.

Small island developing States experience major challenges associated with their small size and remoteness from major markets, which are compounded by inadequate domestic infrastructure. Consequently, they continue to face structural bottlenecks that hamper the development of adequate productive capacities, making sustainable development difficult and expensive. That is the case, for example, of the energy sector and the initiatives to reduce heavy reliance on imported fuel. Finding renewable sources of energy and improving energy efficiency can generate much needed economic, environmental and social benefits. However, these alternatives are coupled with the high initial cost of technology, the challenge to find solutions that are appropriate for small tropical island conditions and the difficulties in accessing international sources of finance and investment.

Endnotes

[1] See annex I for details.

[2] The calculations shown in this section are only intended for analytical purposes. The only official data used to assess eligibility for graduation are those prepared by the Committee for each of its triennial reviews.

[3] E/2012/32 and E/2013/20.

[4] A/RES/70/78.

[5] The group of non-CSN developing countries is used in the sections on landlocked developing countries and small island developing States to provide a benchmark. See annex I for the list of countries that are included in this reference group. The data for these countries are for 2013.

[6] The significant contribution of export instability to the economic vulnerability index partly reflects the greatest weight (one quarter) assigned to this component in its overall calculation. See annex I for details.

[7] As noted below and explained in annex I, remoteness is partly based on physical geography (distance to markets) and partly based on economic geography (the geographical distribution of international trade).

[8] More generally, future research will consider the provision of incentives and support measures to least developed countries — including grants, concessional aid, capacity-building and technology transfer — to facilitate their progress towards sustainable development both before and after graduation.

[9] See ESCAP (2015) for the explanation of the choice of indicators. The shares of top-10 export commodities in total exports used in last year's report have been replaced this year by the export product concentration index because the required data to construct the first indicator were unavailable for some countries.

[10] The benchmark is constructed as the median value of each indicator for a group of up to 17 non-CSN developing countries. See annex I for details.

[11] Feed-in tariffs are a policy mechanism designed to accelerate investment in renewable energy technologies by providing renewable energy producers a fee above the retail rate of electricity. However, the feed-in-tariff for non-firm power in 2013 of $0.07 per kilowatt-hour was too low to stimulate household and private sector investment in renewables.

[12] Available from www.investmentfiji.org.fj.

[13] The upfront costs of rural electrification are related to the installation of distribution lines, wires and additional generating capacity. See Dornan (2014) for more discussion.

FROM THE GLOBAL PROGRAMMES OF ACTION TO THE 2030 AGENDA

As mentioned in chapter 1, the global programmes of action were instituted to address the unique development challenges and vulnerabilities of the least developed countries, landlocked developing countries and small island developing States. The Istanbul Programme of Action aims to overcome the structural challenges of least developed countries through building their human and productive capacities, enabling graduation from the least developed country category. The Vienna Programme of Action for landlocked developing countries targets the enhancement of competitiveness, expansion of trade and diversification through strengthening partnerships between landlocked and transit countries. The

Samoa Pathway calls for international cooperation to support the small island developing States in overcoming their particular vulnerabilities and the compound effects of climate change. The priority areas of each of these programmes of action are listed in table 2.1.

Although the actions in each programme of action are specific to their respective priority areas of CSN, they are ultimately expected to support the sustainable development of the least developed countries, landlocked developing countries and small island developing States, as is clear from the quotations below:

A successful renewed and strengthened global partnership that effectively addresses the special needs of least developed countries will contribute to the cause of peace, prosperity and sustainable development for all.[1]

The overarching goal of the new Programme of Action is to address the special development needs and challenges of landlocked developing countries arising from landlockedness, remoteness and geographical constraints in a more coherent manner and thus contribute to an enhanced rate of sustainable and inclusive growth, which can contribute to the eradication of poverty by moving towards the goal of ending extreme poverty...[2]

Table 2.1   Priority areas of the global programmes of action for countries with special needs

Istanbul Programme of Action - 8 priorities and 251 actions
Priority 1: Productive capacity
Priority 2: Agriculture, food security and rural development
Priority 3: Trade
Priority 4: Commodities
Priority 5: Human and social development
Priority 6: Multiple crises and other emerging challenges
Priority 7: Mobilizing financial resources for development and capacity-building
Priority 8: Good governance at all levels

Vienna Programme of Action - 6 priorities and 88 actions
Priority 1: Fundamental transit policy issues
Priority 2: Infrastructure development and maintenance
Priority 3: International trade and trade facilitation
Priority 4: Regional integration and cooperation
Priority 5: Structural economic transformation
Priority 6: Means of implementation

Samoa Pathway - 16 priorities and 133 actions
Priority 1: Sustained and sustainable, inclusive and equitable economic growth with decent work for all
Priority 2: Climate change
Priority 3: Sustainable energy
Priority 4: Disaster risk reduction
Priority 5: Oceans and seas
Priority 6: Food security and nutrition
Priority 7: Water and sanitation
Priority 8: Sustainable transportation
Priority 9: Sustainable consumption and production
Priority 10: Management of chemicals and waste, including hazardous waste
Priority 11: Health and non-communicable diseases
Priority 12: Gender equality and women's empowerment
Priority 13: Social development
Priority 14: Biodiversity
Priority 15: Invasive alien species
Priority 16: Means of implementation, including partnerships

...we recognize that there is an urgent need to strengthen cooperation and enable strong, genuine and durable partnerships at the subnational, national, subregional, regional and international levels to enhance international cooperation and action to address the unique and particular vulnerabilities of small island developing States so as to ensure their sustainable development.[3]

Because of their ultimate goal of contributing to sustainable development, the programmes of action should be seen as instrumental for the implementation of the 2030 Agenda for Sustainable Development. Indeed, the 2030 Agenda not only supports the implementation of the programmes of action but also states that they are an integral part of it.[4]

In addition, although the Goals and targets of the 2030 Agenda are integrated, indivisible, global in nature and universally applicable, the Agenda recognizes that their implementation should take into account different national realities, capacities and levels of development, while respecting national policies and priorities.[5] As such, the 2030 Agenda suggests that Governments set their own national targets and decide how to incorporate them in national development

planning processes, policies and strategies. In other words, the 2030 Agenda gives countries policy space to adapt the Goals in the way they deem most suitable.

The present chapter considers two elements for the discussion of the adaptation of the 2030 Agenda at the national level. It first discusses the complementarities between the Agenda and the global programmes of action. While the 2030 Agenda includes 17 Sustainable Development Goals and 169 associated targets (table 2.2), it does not include specific policy actions that countries can take to achieve the Goals. However, the detailed actions contained in the global programmes of action, which aim at addressing the structural challenges of least developed countries, landlocked developing countries and small island developing States to help them achieve sustainable development, can also be instrumental in the implementation of the 2030 Agenda. The next section, thus, considers how exactly such actions contribute to meeting the targets and Goals of the Agenda.

Second, the chapter discusses current perceptions of experts and practitioners from 38 Asia-Pacific countries (of which 25 are CSN) on how they believe

Table 2.2   The 2030 Agenda and the Sustainable Development Goals

2030 Agenda - 17 Sustainable Development Goals and 169 associated targets

Goal 1: End poverty in all its forms everywhere
Goal 2: End hunger, achieve food security and improved nutrition and promote sustainable agriculture
Goal 3: Ensure healthy lives and promote well-being for all at all ages
Goal 4: Ensure inclusive and equitable quality education and promote lifelong learning opportunities for all
Goal 5: Achieve gender equality and empower all women and girls
Goal 6: Ensure availability and sustainable management of water and sanitation for all
Goal 7: Ensure access to affordable, reliable, sustainable and modern energy for all
Goal 8: Promote sustained, inclusive and sustainable economic growth, full and productive employment and decent work for all
Goal 9: Build resilient infrastructure, promote inclusive and sustainable industrialization and foster innovation
Goal 10: Reduce inequality within and among countries
Goal 11: Make cities and human settlements inclusive, safe, resilient and sustainable
Goal 12: Ensure sustainable consumption and production patterns
Goal 13: Take urgent action to combat climate change and its impacts
Goal 14: Conserve and sustainably use the oceans, seas and marine resources for sustainable development
Goal 15: Protect, restore and promote sustainable use of terrestrial ecosystems, sustainably manage forests, combat desertification, and halt and reverse land degradation and halt biodiversity loss
Goal 16: Promote peaceful and inclusive societies for sustainable development, provide access to justice for all and build effective, accountable and inclusive institutions at all levels
Goal 17: Strengthen the means of implementation and revitalize the Global Partnership for Sustainable Development

their countries should prioritize and sequence the achievement of the Goals in their countries. The 160 respondents of the survey also identified unfinished elements of the agenda of the Millennium Development Goals that need to be carried on into the 2030 Agenda, as well as institutional arrangements, sources of finance and the roles of different stakeholders. The results of the survey are presented in the second section of this chapter.

1. MAPPING THE PROGRAMMES OF ACTION ONTO THE 2030 AGENDA

To map a global programme of action onto the 2030 Agenda, each action of a programme of action is matched to a single target of the 2030 Agenda based on: (a) similarity in wording; (b) similarity in meaning; or (c) similarity of objective. If none of these criteria are met, the action is considered as "not matching at the target level", in which case it is matched to the Goal to which it contributes the most. Box 2.1 contains examples of the criteria used for matching actions to Goals and targets. Given the integrated nature of the 2030 Agenda, many actions contribute to more than one Goal. However, the mapping exercise matches the actions with one target or one Goal only as illustrated in figure 2.1.[6]

The main results of the mapping exercise are shown in table 2.3 and figure 2.2. Table 2.3 shows the distribution of the actions across the three pillars of sustainable development plus governance and means of implementation. The social pillar refers to actions related to Goals 1-6, the economic pillar corresponds to Goals 7-10, the environmental pillar comprises Goals 11-15, and governance and means of implementation include actions categorized under Goals 16-17.

The distribution of actions reveals that the Istanbul Programme of Action covers all three pillars of sustainable development while placing greater emphasis on the social pillar (table 2.3). The Samoa Pathway also covers the three pillars of sustainable development, but with its focus on the environmental pillar. In sharp contrast, the Vienna Programme of Action is focused just on the economic pillar. All three programmes of action cover governance and means of implementation.

For simplicity, the results of this exercise hereafter reported are aggregated at the Goal level. Figure 2.2 further details the distribution of actions across the 17 Sustainable Development Goals. The values on top of the bars are the number of actions that contribute to each Goal, and the percentages on the vertical axis represent the share of the actions that contribute to each of the Goals.

The figure also shows the distribution of actions matching specific targets (red portion of the bars) and those matching Goals but with no specific targets (blue portion of the bars). Confirming the overall picture shown in table 2.3, the figure shows

Figure 2.1 Mapping the actions of a programme of action onto the Sustainable Development Goals and their targets

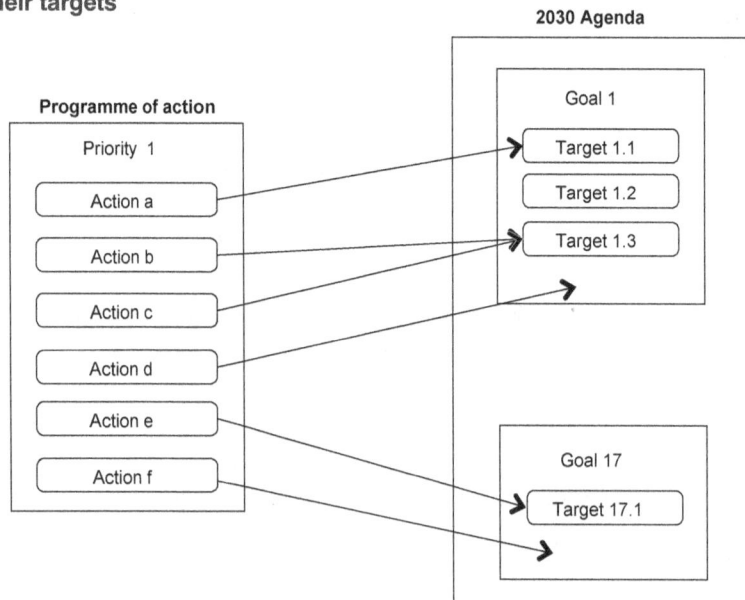

Source: ESCAP.

Box 2.1	Criteria used for mapping actions onto the Goals and their targets

Similarity of wording

The Istanbul Programme of Action includes the action "Strengthen the capacity of domestic financial institutions to reach out to those who have no access to banking, insurance and other financial services, including through leveraging the contribution of, among others, micro-finance, micro-insurance, and mutual funds, in creating and expanding financial services targeted to poor and low-income populations, as well as small- and medium-size enterprises". Target 8.10 of the 2030 Agenda aims to "Strengthen the capacity of domestic financial institutions to encourage and expand access to banking, insurance and financial services for all". The action and the target are matched based on the similarity of their wording.

Similarity of meaning

The Samoa Pathway supports the action "to engage in national and regional efforts to sustainably develop the ocean resources of small island developing States and generate increasing returns for their peoples". Target 14.7 aims "by 2030, increase the economic benefits to small island developing States and least developed countries from the sustainable use of marine resources, including through sustainable management of fisheries, aquaculture and tourism". Although the wording is different, the action and the target have a similar meaning. Thus, they are considered a match.

Similarity of objective

When it is not possible to match actions with targets based on the wording or meaning, a third criterion is used based on the objective they are both referring to. The Vienna Programme of Action calls on development partners to "promote energy efficient investments in landlocked developing countries and facilitate the green economic transformation", while target 7.b aims to "…expand infrastructure and upgrade technology for supplying modern and sustainable energy services for all in developing countries, in particular least developed countries, small island developing States and landlocked developing countries, in accordance with their respective programmes of support". The Vienna Programme of Action also calls on development partners "[t]o support the efforts of landlocked developing countries to improve their productive capacities and create economic diversification", while target 8.2 aims to "achieve higher levels of economic productivity through diversification…". Given the similarity of the objectives of the actions and targets, they are considered a match.

Matching at the Goal level only

Finally, some actions of the programmes of action do not bear any similarity to the targets, and in this case the actions are only matched at the Goal level. For instance, the Istanbul Programme of Action calls on least developed countries to "[d]iversify export products and markets to non-traditional destinations", the Vienna Programme of Action calls on landlocked developing countries "[t]o promote a better business environment so as to assist national firms to integrate into regional and global value chains" and the Heads of State and Government in the Samoa Pathway strongly support the efforts of the small island developing States "to develop cultural and creative industries, including tourism, that capitalize on their rich heritage and have a role to play in sustainable and inclusive growth". Although there are no corresponding targets in the 2030 Agenda that relate to these actions, they clearly contribute to Goal 8 (Promote sustained, inclusive and sustainable economic growth, full and productive employment and decent work for all).

---

that while the Istanbul Programme of Action and the Samoa Pathway cover virtually all the Goals, the Vienna Programme of Action focuses exclusively on Goals 7-10 (economic pillar) and 17 (means of implementation).[7] Most of the actions of the three programmes match the specific targets of the Goals.

The actions of the Istanbul Programme of Action cover the 17 Goals, with greater emphasis on Goal 2 (zero hunger), Goal 8 (decent work and economic growth), Goal 16 (peace, justice and strong institutions) and Goal 17 (partnerships for the Goals). These Goals reflect priority areas of the Istanbul Programme of

Distribution of actions by pillar of sustainable development

	Social pillar (Goals 1-6)	Economic pillar (Goals 7-10)	Environmental pillar (Goals 11-15)	Governance and means of implementation (Goals 16-17)	Total
Istanbul Programme of Action	75 (30%)	57 (23%)	32 (13%)	87 (34%)	251 (100%)
Vienna Programme of Action	0 (0%)	57 (65%)	0 (0%)	31 (35%)	88 (100%)
Samoa Pathway	35 (26%)	22 (17%)	49 (37%)	27 (20%)	133 (100%)

Source: ESCAP.

Notes: The first line in each cell is the number of actions; the second line is the percentage of the total number of actions. See Isgut and others (forthcoming) for details.

Action (tables 2.1 and 2.2). For instance, Goal 8 is closely related to productive capacities (Priority 1), trade (Priority 3) and commodities (Priority 4); Goal 2 clearly refers to agriculture, food security and rural development (Priority 2); Goal 16 reflects good governance at all levels (Priority 8) and Goal 17 closely matches mobilizing financial resources for development and capacity-building (Priority 7). Of the 251 actions of the Istanbul Programme of Action, 208 actions (83%) match a specific Goal target.

The actions of the Vienna Programme of Action are all clearly concentrated on Goal 7 (affordable and clean energy), Goal 8, Goal 9 (industry, innovation and infrastructure), Goal 10 and Goal 17. These Goals are also closely related to the programme's priorities as regards infrastructure development and maintenance (Priority 2), international trade and trade facilitation (Priority 3) and structural economic transformation (Priority 5). Out of 88 actions, 60 (68%) are closely related to specific targets under these Goals.

Besides the fair distribution across most of the 17 Goals, the majority of the actions of the Samoa Pathway fall under Goal 5 (gender equality), Goal 13 (climate action), Goal 14 (life below water), Goal 15 (life on land) and Goal 17. Out of a total of 133 agreed actions, 95 (71%) closely relate or match Goal targets.

The results of the mapping exercise can be also described by the distribution of actions within each Goal. Table 2.4 shows for each Goal the percentage of associated targets that are covered by actions of the three global programmes of action. The actions of the Istanbul Programme of Action cover at least one of the associated targets for all 17 Goals. Overall, 12 Goals have a coverage of 50% or higher. Goal 7 and Goal 13 have all their targets covered under the programme. As for the Vienna Programme of Action, although its actions are heavily concentrated on Goals 7-10 and 17, only Goals 7 and 8 have their associated targets covered by 50% or more. The

Distribution of actions within the Sustainable Development Goals

(Percentage)

	Sustainable Development Goal																
	1	2	3	4	5	6	7	8	9	10	11	12	13	14	15	16	17
Istanbul Programme of Action	86	75	38	50	67	63	100	50	63	50	30	18	100	20	25	58	84
Vienna Programme of Action	0	0	0	0	0	0	60	25	63	10	0	0	0	0	0	0	32
Samoa Pathway	0	50	23	20	67	50	40	33	25	0	30	36	100	100	58	33	26

Source: ESCAP.

Note: The numbers in the tables are the percentages of targets of the Goals that are covered by the actions of the respective global programmes of action. The numbers in bold represent those that are 50% or more.

Figure 2.2

Distribution of actions across the Sustainable Development Goals

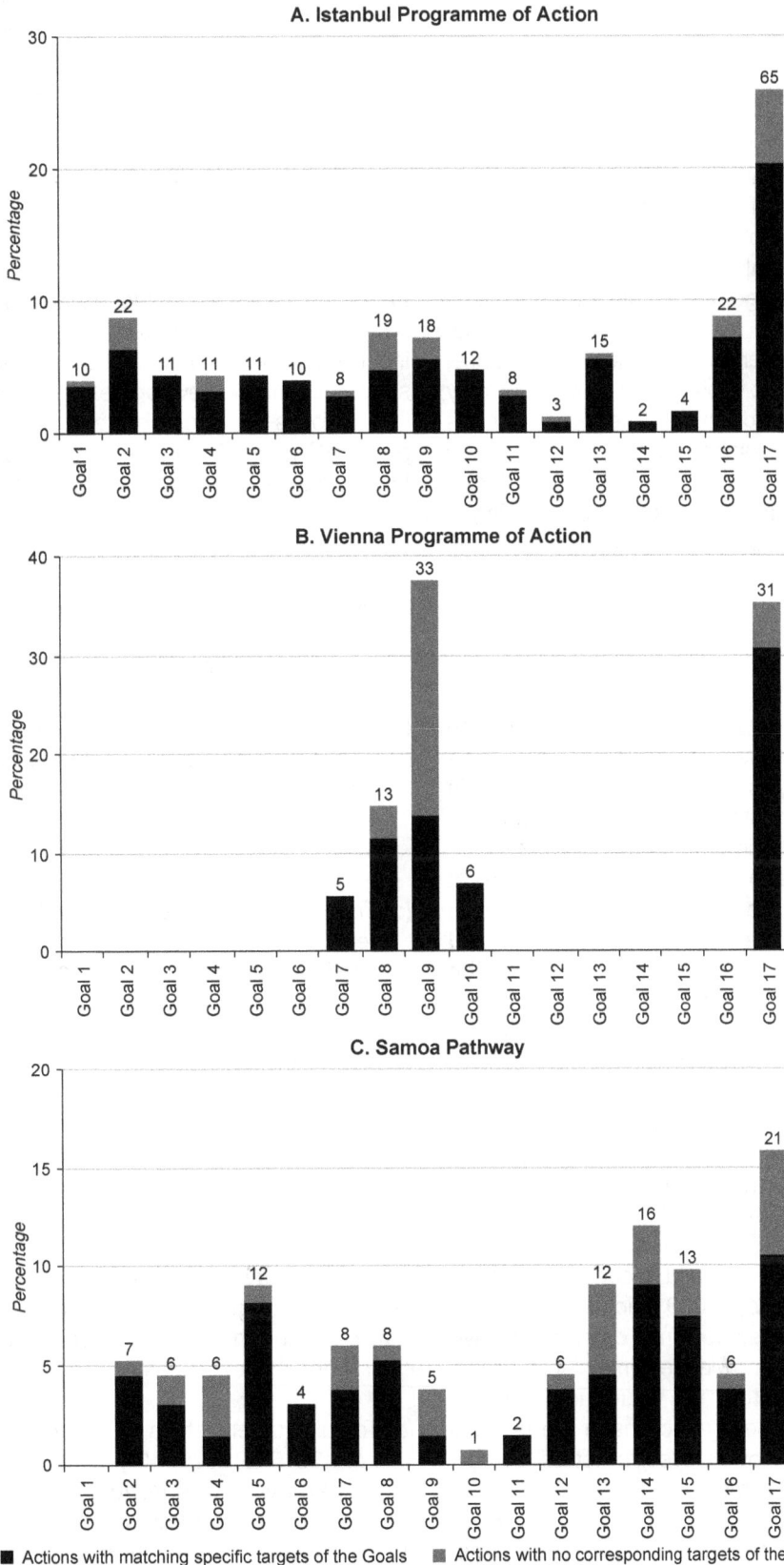

A. Istanbul Programme of Action

B. Vienna Programme of Action

C. Samoa Pathway

■ Actions with matching specific targets of the Goals   ■ Actions with no corresponding targets of the Goals

Source: ESCAP.

Notes: The numbers on top of the bars denote the numbers of actions of the global programmes of action that are categorized under corresponding Goals. See Isgut and others (forthcoming) for details.

Samoa Pathway thoroughly spans the targets under Goals 13 and 14. It also covers 50% or more of the targets under Goals 2, 5, 6 and 15, while none of the targets are covered for Goals 1 and 10.

These results partly confirm the findings shown in table 1.7 and figure 1.10 on the wide coverage of the Istanbul Programme of Action and the Samoa Pathway across the Goals, as well as a strong focus on the economic pillar of sustainable development by the Vienna Programme of Action (table 2.3 and figure 2.2). However, the results also reveal that a large number of actions categorized under certain Goals do not necessarily imply a wide coverage within that Goal. The Vienna Programme of Action, for instance, has 33 actions related to Goal 8, but they cover only five of its eight associated targets. The reason for this discrepancy is that the global programmes of action have a strong focus on areas in which their target countries have structural vulnerabilities, requiring a more thorough and detailed set of actions, as further discussed below.

1.1 Complementarities between the programmes of action and the 2030 Agenda

The mapping exercise, by identifying overlaps between actions in the programmes of action and the Goals and their targets, reveals that by pursuing actions in their respective programmes of action, the region's least developed countries, landlocked developing countries and small island developing States can, at the same time, make progress towards implementation of the 2030 Agenda. The programmes of action and the 2030 Agenda are complementary in that the former provide very specific guidance within their respective time frames and are customized to the specific circumstances of each category of country on how to achieve the Goals. In some areas related to the specific structural vulnerabilities of the CSN, their respective programmes of action include many relevant actions that facilitate the achievement of Goals and associated targets. For instance, target 2.3 under Goal 2 (zero hunger) aims at doubling the agricultural productivity and incomes of small-scale food producers by 2030, including through secure and equal access to land, other productive resources and inputs, knowledge, financial services, markets and opportunities for value addition and non-farm employment. Several actions in the Istanbul Programme of Action provide specific details on how to reach this target. Examples include:

(a) Strengthen institutions, including cooperatives, to boost small-holder farmer food production,

agricultural productivity and sustainable agricultural practices;

(b) Make rural markets work better for the poor by linking small-scale farmers to markets throughout the food chains, including the provisions of price and other relevant information and improving sanitary and phytosanitary services;

(c) Enhance land tenure security, access to irrigation systems, credit, other farm inputs and markets for small-holder farmers.[8]

As another example, target 9.1 under Goal 9 (industry, innovation and infrastructure) aims at developing quality, reliable, sustainable and resilient infrastructure, including regional and transborder infrastructure, to support economic development and human well-being, with a focus on affordable and equitable access for all. The Vienna Programme of Action supports this target through many actions such as the following:

(a) To develop and implement comprehensive national policies for infrastructure development and maintenance encompassing all modes of transportation and ensure that they are well coordinated with the transit countries in the areas where transit infrastructures intersect;

(b) To collaborate to promote sustainable and resilient transit systems through, inter alia, regular upgrading and maintenance, development of corridors along transit highways ...and promoting economies of scale for transport systems through intermodal transport development...;

(c) To endeavour, at the bilateral, subregional and regional levels, to gradually liberalize road transport services, taking into account specific circumstances in landlocked and transit developing countries.[9]

In addition, the Vienna Programme of Action emphasizes cooperation between landlocked developing countries and neighbouring transit countries, which are not explicitly mentioned as part of the Global Partnership for Sustainable Development proposed by the 2030 Agenda.

The specificity of actions to achieve Goals and associated targets also characterizes the Samoa Pathway for small island developing States, as is clear from the examples below:

(a) To take urgent steps to establish, for the period from 2015 to 2025, 10-year targets and strategies to reverse the spread and severity of non-communicable diseases;[10]

(b) To enable cooperation among small island developing States on diseases by using existing international and regional forums to convene joint biennial meetings of ministers of health and other relevant sectors to respond in particular to non-communicable diseases;

(c) For States that have not done so, considering becoming parties to and ensuring an enabling environment for the implementation ...of the multilateral environmental agreements on chemicals and waste...;[11]

(d) Leveraging the expertise of, inter alia, the Global Sustainable Tourism Council, the Global Observatories on Sustainable Tourism of the World Tourism Organization, the Global Partnership for Sustainable Tourism and other United Nations bodies, as well as the 10-year framework of programmes on sustainable consumption and production patterns, to provide platforms for the exchange of best practices and direct and focused support to their national efforts.[12]

In addition to the specificity and comprehensiveness of the programmes of action on the specific aspects of the 2030 Agenda of interest to CSN, the simultaneous implementation of the relevant programme(s) of action and the 2030 Agenda could lower administrative and logistical costs, for instance, by building common data platforms, monitoring mechanisms and reporting systems (United Nations, 2016). A relevant point was brought up during the Forty-Sixth Pacific Islands Forum, calling for "a regional process for the follow up and review of the SDGs and [Samoa] Pathway that would seek to reduce the burden of reporting at the country level" (Pacific Islands Forum Secretariat, 2015). A focus on the implementation of common

aspects of both agendas can also be beneficial for national planning purposes, as well as for coordinating the support of international development partners.

2. VIEWS ABOUT THE ADAPTATION OF THE 2030 AGENDA

Adapting the Goals to national realities is not a trivial undertaking. It first requires a good understanding of countries' needs, strengths and challenges to decide which Goals and associated targets should be prioritized and sequenced. It also requires conducting extensive consultations to raise public awareness and gather broad support for national implementation plans for the Goals. It is also likely to require reforms to policymaking and budgetary institutions to enhance their coordination and effectiveness, as well as improvements in data collection and reporting to monitor progress. The United Nations Development Group (2015) proposes eight elements, grouped into three stages, when adapting the Goals to national contexts (figure 2.3).

The purpose of this section and the following chapter is to contribute to discussions on the adaptation of the Goals to national contexts. The present section presents the results of a survey among experts and practitioners from across the developing countries of the Asia-Pacific region aimed at understanding how perceptions on the prioritization, sequencing and implementation challenges of the Goals vary across countries.

Figure 2.3   **Elements in adapting the 2030 Agenda to national contexts**

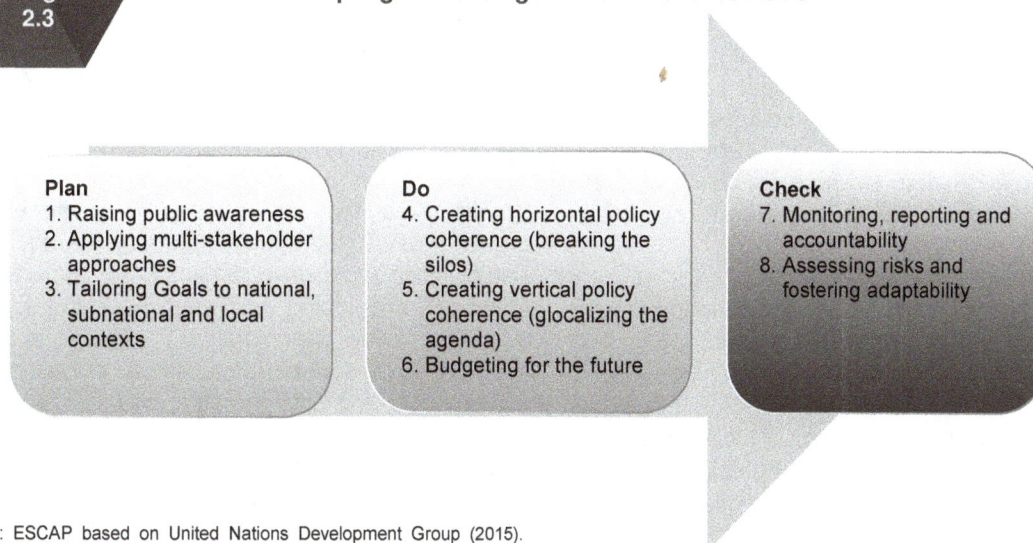

Plan
1. Raising public awareness
2. Applying multi-stakeholder approaches
3. Tailoring Goals to national, subnational and local contexts

Do
4. Creating horizontal policy coherence (breaking the silos)
5. Creating vertical policy coherence (glocalizing the agenda)
6. Budgeting for the future

Check
7. Monitoring, reporting and accountability
8. Assessing risks and fostering adaptability

Source: ESCAP based on United Nations Development Group (2015).

2.1. The survey

Analyses of countries' experiences in implementing the Millennium Development Goals together with the review of initial national efforts to integrate and align Sustainable Development Goals with national plans, programmes and policies suggest six emerging principles for the adaptation of the latter set of Goals into national contexts:[13]

(a) Prioritization and sequencing of the Goals and targets of the 2030 Agenda, adapted to national circumstances;

(b) Identification of the unfinished agenda of the Millennium Development Goals that needs to be carried on into the 2030 Agenda and establishment of the benchmarks for the Sustainable Development Goal indicators;

(c) Attainment of coherence in the national development programme by exploiting complementarities and synergies across Goals and targets;

(d) Assessment of a country's needs with regard to means of implementation;

(e) Understanding how systemic issues, such as global economic governance, affect national implementation of the Goals;

(f) Identification of the specific roles of internal and external development partners of national Governments.

In order to gather information about countries' views on some of these principles, ESCAP conducted a survey of experts and practitioners from across the Asia-Pacific region. The survey was distributed throughout the secretariat's network of experts via e-mail, inviting them to share their views. The questionnaire, which is available in annex II, included multiple-choice and open-ended questions on a number of issues related to adapting the 2030 Agenda at the national level, including, among others, Goal prioritization and sequencing, unfinished Millennium Development Goals, institutional arrangements, sources of finance and the roles of different stakeholders. Between 18 November 2015 and 17 February 2016, a total of 160 respondents from 38 Asia-Pacific countries completed the survey.

With 95 respondents from 25 CSN and 65 respondents from 13 developing countries that are not CSN, the survey is broadly representative of the region's views on implementing the 2030 Agenda. See annex II for a list of participating countries. The respondents are mostly from Government (39%) and research institutes and academia (29%), followed by civil society organizations and non-governmental organizations (NGOs) (21%) and the private sector (8%).[14] The vast majority of the respondents indicated that they were familiar with the Goals. It should be pointed out that the survey represents the views of experts and practitioners in their own capacities and not the official position of their institutions or Governments.

2.2 Results

The results of the survey provide information on national perspectives regarding the following issues: prioritization and sequencing of the Sustainable Development Goals and the unfinished agenda of the Millennium Development Goals; key implementation challenges; financing; systemic concerns; and the roles of domestic and international development partners. The responses of experts from CSN are grouped into three mutually exclusive groups: (a) least developed countries; (b) landlocked developing countries that are not least developed countries; and (c) small island developing States that are not least developed countries.

Prioritization

Because countries differ as regards levels of income, geographic and demographic factors, resource endowments and governance and administrative capacities, it is both expected and desirable that the pathways they choose to implement the Sustainable Development Goals reflect their national characteristics. As such, countries may seek to fast-track a limited number of Goals and targets over the others.

The survey asked experts and practitioners to identify which of the 17 Goals they considered most relevant in their respective countries on a scale from 1 to 4, with 1 indicating "very low" and 4 indicating "very high". The responses were aggregated into four groups representing the social (Goals 1-6), economic (Goals 7-10) and environmental (Goals 11-16) dimensions of sustainable development together with governance and means of implementation (Goals 16-17).

Results reveal that the top priority of the experts from least developed countries is related to the social pillar of sustainable development, while experts from landlocked developing countries are more focused on the economic pillar (table 2.5). The small island developing States place, on average, priority to both the economic and environmental pillars. This pattern of prioritization is similar to the areas of focus of the three global programmes of actions that are analysed in the previous section, suggesting that the focus of experts is consistent with the priorities of the respective

| Table 2.5 | Goal priority scores by country group and pillar of sustainable development |

	Social pillar (Goals 1-6)	Economic pillar (Goals 7-10)	Environmental pillar (Goals 11-15)	Governance and means of implementation (Goals 16-17)
Asia-Pacific CSN	**3.28**	3.18	2.91	3.10
Least developed countries	**3.38**	3.15	2.90	3.15
Landlocked developing countries	2.98	**3.28**	2.87	**3.06**
Small island developing States	2.90	**3.23**	**3.00**	2.87
Non-CSN developing Asia	**3.30**	3.20	3.07	3.12

Source: ESCAP.

Notes: As noted above: 1 represents "very low", 2 "low", 3 "high" and 4 "very high". The numbers in the table are simple averages of priority scores assigned to each Goal, aggregated over four groups representing the three pillars of sustainable development plus governance and means of implementation. The numbers in bold represent the highest scores by country group. In cases where the differences in scores between the highest and the second highest (or third highest) were statistically insignificant at the 5% level, the second (and third) highest scores were also highlighted in bold.

global programmes of action. This argument will be further detailed in the following subsection.

Figure 2.4 shows the percentage of survey respondents that identified the respective Goals as "very high" priority for their countries. Results for the Asia-Pacific CSN show that Goal 1 (no poverty) is perceived as top priority for most of the experts, closely followed by Goal 8 (decent work and economic growth), Goal 2 (zero hunger), Goal 4 (quality education) and Goal 3 (good health and well-being). The high priority accorded to these Goals suggests that the objectives of poverty and hunger elimination, economic growth and employment, access to good health services and quality education and improved infrastructural services are closely interrelated and may be best achieved by considering them as a package.

Interestingly, reducing inequality (Goal 10) was not accorded a high priority by CSN, in spite of its close relationship with poverty reduction and the provision of basic social services. Also, the low priority accorded to Goal 14 (life below water) is partly due to the fact that 42 out of 95 CSN respondents are from landlocked developing countries (see annex II). It may be further noted that the identified priority Goals varied across the professional affiliations of the respondents, irrespective of their country (not shown in the figure). For example, academics accorded the highest priority to quality education (Goal 4), NGOs to climate action (Goal 13), the private sector to economic growth and employment (Goal 8) and Governments to Goals 1-4 and 8.

| Figure 2.4 | Percentage of survey respondents assigning "very high" priority to each Goal in countries with special needs |

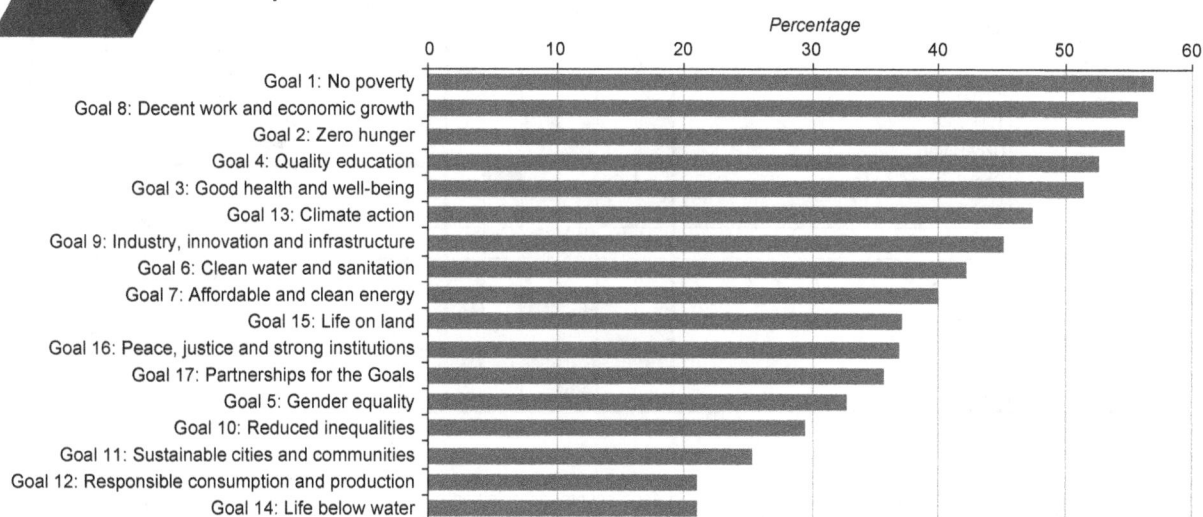

Source: ESCAP.

Sequencing

The average scores for all country groups shown in table 2.5 are around 3 for all three pillars of sustainable development, indicating that the experts consulted perceived all pillars as "high" priority. However, from a practical point of view, it is not possible to pursue all the Sustainable Development Goals simultaneously, even if all have high priority. To further refine our understanding of how countries expect to adapt the 2030 Agenda to their national contexts, the survey asked experts to select up to five Goals that they thought their countries should focus on the initial period of implementation, between 2016 and 2020.

The results are summarized in figure 2.5. The coloured cells represent the top-five Goals selected as an initial priority in each country. The figure shows a concentration by country groups on specific Goals.

The Goals most selected by experts from least developed countries are Goal 1 (no poverty), Goal 2 (zero hunger), Goal 3 (good health and well-being) and Goal 4 (quality education). In contrast, most experts from landlocked developing countries preferred Goal 4 (quality education), Goal 7 (affordable and clean energy), Goal 8 (decent work and economic growth) and Goal 9 (industry, innovation and infrastructure). Finally, the top choices from experts from small island developing States were rather spread across the Goals, including Goal 3 (good health and well-being), Goal 9 (industry, innovation and infrastructure) and Goal 13 (climate action).

Additional results (not included in the table) by type of respondent show that academics and researchers prioritized implementation of Goal 1 (no poverty) and Goal 4 (quality education). Government officials agree with Goal 1 but add good health (Goal 3),

Figure 2.5 — Initial Goal priorities by country

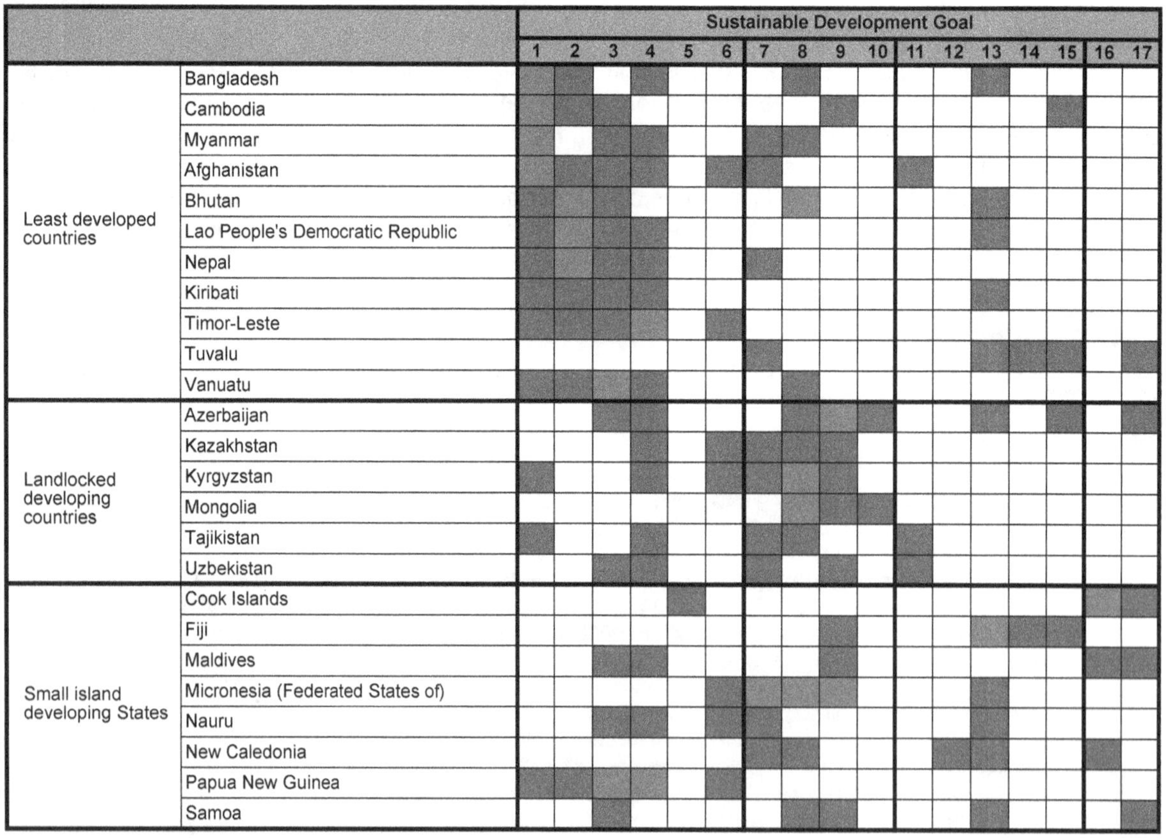

Country group	Country	\multicolumn{17}{c}{Sustainable Development Goal}
		1 · 2 · 3 · 4 · 5 · 6 · 7 · 8 · 9 · 10 · 11 · 12 · 13 · 14 · 15 · 16 · 17
Least developed countries	Bangladesh	
	Cambodia	
	Myanmar	
	Afghanistan	
	Bhutan	
	Lao People's Democratic Republic	
	Nepal	
	Kiribati	
	Timor-Leste	
	Tuvalu	
	Vanuatu	
Landlocked developing countries	Azerbaijan	
	Kazakhstan	
	Kyrgyzstan	
	Mongolia	
	Tajikistan	
	Uzbekistan	
Small island developing States	Cook Islands	
	Fiji	
	Maldives	
	Micronesia (Federated States of)	
	Nauru	
	New Caledonia	
	Papua New Guinea	
	Samoa	

Sources: ESCAP.

Notes: For each country, the Goals selected to answer question 3 in the survey (see annex II) were ranked according to how many respondents selected them. Each row of the figure shows the top-five choices in each country as coloured cells, with the orange cells indicating the top position in the ranking. In some countries there were ties in the rankings. When a tie occurred for the top position, the country has more than one orange cell. Ties at the bottom of the ranking may result in countries having more than five coloured cells. In cases where a country had only one respondent, blue cells were used for the five selected Goals.

while NGOs support the elimination of hunger (Goal 2) and climate action (Goal 13), and the private sector unequivocally supports economic growth and employment (Goal 8). Figure 2.5 also shows that Goal 5 (gender equality), Goal 10 (reduced inequalities), Goal 12 (responsible consumption and production) and Goal 14 (life under water) were given very little priority by experts from CSN.

Table 2.6 summarizes the information shown in figure 2.5 by country group and the three pillars of sustainable development plus governance and means of implementation. The table shows very clearly that experts from least developed countries prioritize Goals in the social pillar (58%) in the initial years of implementation, experts from landlocked developing countries prioritize Goals in the economic pillar (67%) and experts from small island developing States have balanced preferences across pillars (32% for all pillars).

The results contained in figure 2.5 and table 2.6 show a remarkable resemblance to the distribution of actions across Goals under the Istanbul Programme of Action, the Vienna Programme of Action and the Samoa Pathway as shown in table 2.3. This reinforces the importance of such programmes of action as frameworks for the implementation of the Sustainable Development Goals in least developed countries, landlocked developing countries and small island developing States. However, in spite of the similarities of countries within each of these groups, it is important to keep in mind that they differ in many ways. In that regard, the analytical framework proposed in chapter 3 provides guidance for the implementation of the Goals, taking into account the unique challenges and structural impediments of individual countries.

Unfinished businesses as regards the Millennium Development Goals

Although the final assessment of the delivery of the Millennium Development Goals is yet to come, it is well acknowledged that the record of achievements has been quite uneven across countries and time periods (Bhattacharya and others, 2013; LDC IV Monitor, 2014). Indeed, the closing record of the Millennium Development Goal period, which is not likely to be available for another year or so due to lags in producing the relevant statistics, is largely going to define some of the benchmarks for the implementation of the Sustainable Development Goals. Thus, a closer and updated appreciation of Millennium Development Goal delivery will be particularly necessary to identify the "unfinished business" of the Millennium Development Goals and to develop an approach to deal with it within the framework of the 2030 Agenda.

More than 90% of respondents from CSN acknowledged that there is an "unfinished" Millennium Development Goal agenda, which has to be addressed upfront during the period between 2016 and 2020. For the respondents from least developed countries, eradication of extreme poverty and hunger (Goal 1) remained the most important unfinished Millennium Development Goal, while for those from CSN that are not least developed countries and other developing Asian economies, environmental sustainability (Goal 7) was the most important (table 2.7). For experts from small island developing States, gender equality (Goal 3) was another important unfinished Millennium Development Goal.

| Table 2.6 | Initial Goal priorities by country group and pillar of sustainable development |

(Percentage)

	Social pillar (Goals 1-6)	Economic pillar (Goals 7-10)	Environmental pillar (Goals 11-15)	Governance and means of implementation (Goals 16-17)
Asia-Pacific CSN	41	35	17	16
Least developed countries	58	20	16	5
Landlocked developing countries	31	67	13	8
Small island developing States	32	32	32	32

Source: ESCAP.

Note: The table shows the percentages of cells in figure 2.5 that are coloured over the total number of cells for each country group and the four groups representing the three pillars of sustainable development together with governance and means of implementation. On average, the percentages should be around 30%, representing 5 selected Goals out of 17 for each country.

Table
2.7

Unfinished Millennium Development Goals by country group

(Percentage)

	Millennium Development Goal							
	Goal 1	Goal 2	Goal 3	Goal 4	Goal 5	Goal 6	Goal 7	Goal 8
Asia-Pacific CSN	**69**	48	45	39	42	40	**64**	49
Least developed countries	**79**	54	42	44	46	41	61	56
Landlocked developing countries	**44**	22	22	11	33	33	**56**	11
Small island developing States	40	40	**73**	33	27	40	**87**	40
Non-CSN developing Asia	45	40	45	29	25	32	**78**	38

Source: ESCAP.

Notes: The numbers in the table are the percentages of survey respondents who consider the respective Millennium Development Goals as unfinished business. The numbers in bold represent the highest percentages by country group. In cases where the differences in percentages between the highest and the second highest (or third highest) were statistically insignificant at the 5% level, the second (and third) highest percentages were also highlighted in bold. The full list of Millennium Development Goals is: eradicate extreme poverty and hunger (Goal 1); achieve universal primary education (Goal 2); promote gender equality and empower women (Goal 3); reduce child mortality (Goal 4); improve maternal health (Goal 5); HIV/AIDS, malaria and other diseases (Goal 6); ensure environmental sustainability (Goal 7); and Global Partnership for Development (Goal 8).

The views of the respondents on unfinished Millennium Development Goals are, for the most part, consistent with the responses on the priorities for the initial five-year period of implementing the 2030 Agenda as shown in figure 2.5 and table 2.6. For instance, experts from the least developed countries chose eradication of poverty and hunger (Goal 1) as the most important unfinished Millennium Development Goal, while also prioritizing implementation of Goals 1 and 2 of the 2030 Agenda for the initial stage of implementation. Similarly, the choice of Millennium Development Goal 7 on environmental sustainability as unfinished business by small island developing States coincides with their selection of Goal 13 (climate action) as their first priority for implementing the 2030 Agenda.

However, when it comes to gender equality and empowerment of women, there seems to be some apparent divergence between the responses on "sequencing" and "unfinished Millennium Development Goals" in the survey. For instance, for small island developing States, 73% of respondents recognized gender equality (Millennium Development Goal 3) as still to be delivered, while only 20% agreed on the idea of assigning initial priority to its corresponding Goal of the 2030 Agenda (Sustainable Development Goal 5).

Implementation challenges

The complexity of the 2030 Agenda raises several questions on how to implement it successfully and how to adapt its internationally agreed Goals and targets to national realities. This requires a clear understanding of the level of preparedness of countries for: (a) integrating the Goals into national planning processes, such as interfacing the Goals and targets with national development plans and programmes; (b) integrating the Goals into fiscal frameworks and budget processes; (c) establishing a suitable institutional mechanism that would lead the process within Government; (d) making arrangements between central and local Government to coordinate actions from different institutions at different levels; (e) ensuring adequate human capacities within Government and among policymakers; and (f) guaranteeing the availability of data and statistics to monitor and follow up progress towards meeting Goal targets.[15]

The results, shown in table 2.8, are reported as simple averages of scores on a scale of 1 to 4, with 1 indicating "not challenging" and 4 indicating "very challenging". As in the previous tables, the results are aggregated by type of CSN and for developing countries that are not CSN.

The top implementation challenges identified in CSN are, in descending order of importance: data availability; technical and administrative capacity; and coordination among various agencies and levels of Government. The availability of data and statistics is identified as most challenging to least developed countries and small island developing States. For developing countries that are not CSN, the main challenge is coordination, followed by the integration of the Goals into national budgets. For all groups of countries, the integration of the Goals into national plans is the least challenging task. Comparing responses from different types of stakeholders from CSN, it is interesting to note that those belonging to academia or NGOs emphasize intra-Government coordination as the main challenge, although government officials do not share such a view (not shown in the table).

Table 2.8 Main challenges regarding implementation of the Goals by country group

	Integration into national plans	Integration into annual budgets	Coordination across government agencies	Coordination across levels of Government	Technical and administrative capacities	Data and statistics
Asia-Pacific CSN	2.56	3.12	**3.19**	**3.18**	**3.32**	**3.37**
Least developed countries	2.58	3.20	**3.32**	**3.30**	**3.37**	**3.46**
Landlocked developing countries	2.11	**3.11**	2.78	2.89	**3.11**	2.56
Small island developing States	2.73	2.73	2.87	2.79	**3.20**	**3.47**
Non-CSN developing Asia	2.63	3.19	**3.37**	**3.36**	2.97	2.90

Source: ESCAP.

Notes: The numbers in the table represent simple averages of scores on a scale of 1 to 4, with 1 indicating "not challenging", 2 "somewhat challenging", 3 "moderately challenging" and 4 "very challenging". The numbers in bold represent the highest scores across the six challenges by country group. In cases where the differences in scores between the highest and the other scores were statistically insignificant at the 5% level, the other scores were also highlighted in bold. See annex II for the exact wording of the challenges of implementing the Goals in the questionnaire.

Financing of the Goals

One of the distinguishing features of the 2030 Agenda is the importance it accords to means of implementation (Goal 17), among which the mobilization of financial resources plays an important role. Thus, survey participants were asked to assign a degree of priority to various domestic and external sources of finance to be (further) developed for the implementation of the Goals, using a scale from 1 to 4, with 1 indicating "very low priority" and 4 indicating "very high priority".

Respondents from different country groups largely agreed on the relevance of domestic financial courses. According to table 2.9, the highest importance was assigned to enhancing government revenue and improving the quality of public expenditure. The third and fourth priorities were public-private partnerships and providing financial services to disadvantaged sectors of society. The development of domestic capital markets was the last priority for respondents from CSN, particularly for the small island developing States. This pattern also holds with regard to the

Table 2.9 Relevance of domestic financial sources for the Goals

	Asia-Pacific CSN				Non-CSN developing Asia
	Average	Least developed countries	Landlocked developing countries	Small island developing States	
Domestic public resources – national government revenue	**3.45**	**3.45**	**3.33**	**3.53**	**3.52**
Domestic public resources – local government revenue	2.85	2.96	2.67	2.47	3.12
Improved management of domestic public expenditures	**3.48**	**3.48**	**3.44**	**3.53**	**3.49**
Commercial banks (public and private, including subsidiaries of foreign banks)	2.88	2.93	2.89	2.67	2.66
National development banks	3.04	3.01	3.22	3.07	2.95
Affordable financial services for disadvantaged and low-income segments of society (financial inclusion)	3.14	3.22	2.56	3.13	3.29
Domestic capital markets	2.80	2.86	2.89	2.47	2.75
Public-private partnerships	3.32	**3.38**	3.00	**3.20**	**3.35**

Source: ESCAP.

Notes: The numbers in the table represent simple averages of scores on a scale of 1 to 4, with 1 indicating "very low priority", 2 "low priority", 3 "high priority" and 4 "very high priority". The numbers in bold represent the highest scores for sources of finance by country group. In cases where the differences in scores between the highest and the second highest (or third highest) were statistically insignificant at the 5% level, the second (and third) highest scores were also highlighted in bold.

potential role to be played by commercial private banks in financing the Goals.

Among the external sources of finance, respondents from CSN indicated that multilateral development banks, including the regional development banks, need to play the key role in financing the Goals (table 2.10). An important role is also expected from foreign direct investment (FDI) and official development assistance (ODA). The respondents allocated a relatively modest role to the international capital market and blended finance when it comes to financing the Goals externally. Within subgroups of CSN, FDI is listed as the first priority for external financing in least developed countries. Multilateral development banks, together with ODA, have been accorded the highest importance in the small island developing States. Except for respondents from the private sector, government officials, NGO staff and academics thought that the role of international capital markets in providing resources for Goal delivery would be quite limited (not shown in the table).

Sequencing the sources of financing

When respondents from CSN were asked to prioritize all domestic and foreign sources of finance during the initial five years of the 2030 Agenda, the aggregate view was that national government revenues along with ODA, closely followed by improved management of public expenditure, multilateral development banks and FDI, were the main priorities (figure 2.6). While developing countries that are not CSN agreed on the first priority of national government revenues, they selected as second and third priorities two other sources of domestic resource mobilization — improved management of public expenditure and public-private partnerships.

Financial inclusion is accorded a relatively low priority by respondents in both CSN and developing countries that are not CSN, but it is twice as high in the latter group of countries. Both domestic and external capital markets are accorded the least priority as sources of finance for the Goals in the two groups of countries.

Additional results (not included in the table) by type of respondent show that government officials and respondents from NGOs ranked government revenues first, followed by ODA and improved public expenditure. Respondents from academia agreed in ranking government revenues first, with ODA and improved quality of public expenditure tied in second place. Private sector respondents ranked improved quality of public expenditure first, followed by public-private partnerships and FDI.

It is remarkable that although CSN accord more importance to traditional external sources of finance such as ODA, multilateral development banks and FDI, their most important priority is enhancing national government revenues. These views contrast with the prominent role accorded to ODA in the Millennium Development Goals. To be sure, ODA has been critical in fostering development in certain areas, such as health and education, transport and communication, a recent study by Overseas Development Institute and others (2015) shows that domestic resources, government revenue in particular, should play a leading role — with FDI and ODA occupying marginal positions — in financing the Goals.

Global systemic issues

Survey respondents from CSN expressed the view that success in implementing the Goals depends on

| Table 2.10 | Relevance of external financial sources for the Goals |

	Asia-Pacific CSN				Non-CSN developing Asia
	Average	Least developed countries	Landlocked developing countries	Small island developing States	
ODA	**3.40**	**3.39**	3.22	**3.53**	2.88
Multilateral development banks, including regional development banks (such as the World Bank and Asian Development Bank)	**3.51**	**3.51**	**3.33**	**3.60**	3.20
FDI	**3.40**	**3.43**	**3.67**	3.13	3.03
International capital markets	2.53	2.51	2.67	2.53	2.58
Blended finance	2.98	2.96	2.89	3.13	2.95

Source: ESCAP.

Note: See notes to table 2.9.

Figure 2.6

Percentage of survey respondents assigning "very high" importance to each source of finance

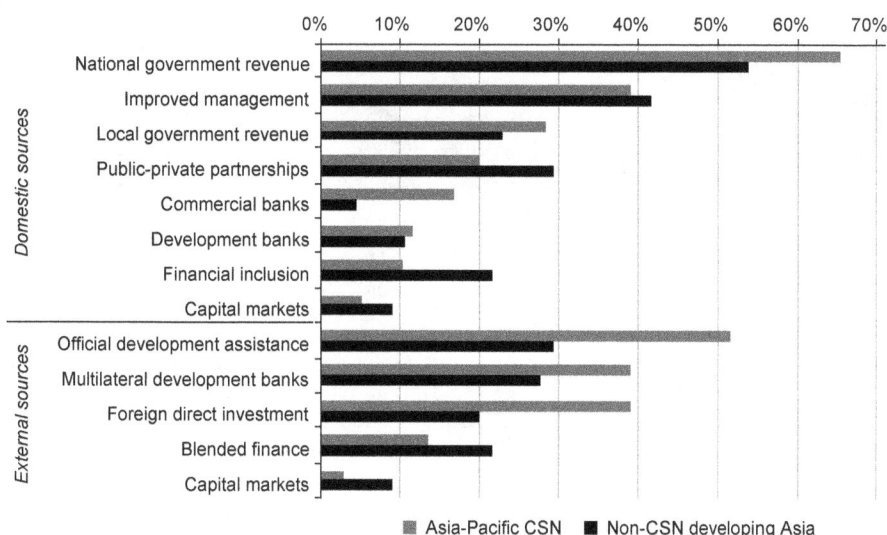

■ Asia-Pacific CSN   ■ Non-CSN developing Asia

Sources: ESCAP.

the following systemic factors, in descending order of importance: stability of commodity prices; sustained growth of the world economy; and transfer of technology and intellectual property rights (table 2.11). Respondents from developing countries that are not CSN broadly agreed with that ranking but added stability of global financial markets as almost as important as global economic growth. Additional results (not included in the table) by type of respondent show that responses by government officials concurred with the importance of commodity price stability, financial stability and

global economic growth. NGO representatives added climate negotiations, while the private sector highlighted multilateral trade negotiations.

Stakeholders' engagement

As table 2.12 suggests, respondents to the survey from both CSN and developing countries that are not CSN ranked the domestic private sector, particularly its small and medium-sized enterprises, and public representatives, such as parliamentarians and local

Table 2.11   Perceptions of global systemic issues by country group

(Percentage)

	Asia-Pacific CSN				Non-CSN developing Asia
	Average	Least developed countries	Landlocked developing countries	Small island developing States	
Global economic growth	**54**	48	**78**	67	**54**
Multilateral trade negotiations	49	**54**	33	40	44
Global financial stability	49	46	56	**60**	**53**
Transfer of technology and intellectual property rights	**51**	**54**	25	53	50
Climate negotiations	48	48	13	**67**	40
Stability of global commodity prices (of food, fuel, minerals, etc.)	**63**	57	**89**	73	62

Source: ESCAP.

Notes: The numbers in the table are the percentages of survey respondents who stated that the respective global systemic issues were "very important" for their countries. The numbers in bold represent the highest percentages across the six issues by country group. In cases where the differences in percentages between the highest and the other percentages were statistically insignificant at the 5% level, the other percentages were also highlighted in bold.

Table
2.12

Engaging the development actors by national Government

(Percentage)

	Asia-Pacific CSN				Non-CSN developing Asia
	Average	Least developed countries	Landlocked developing countries	Small island developing States	
Foreign private sector	31	30	11	47	25
Domestic private sector – small and medium enterprises	**70**	**72**	**78**	53	**58**
Domestic private sector – others	47	46	44	54	46
NGOs	42	35	**56**	67	47
Civil society organizations	43	36	44	**73**	**56**
Public representatives (such as parliamentarians and local government members)	**68**	**64**	67	87	67
Media	46	40	**67**	60	54

Source: ESCAP.

Notes: The numbers in the table are the percentages of survey respondents who stated that the engagement of the respective development actors is "very important" for their countries. The numbers in bold represent the highest percentages across the six issues by country group. In cases where the differences in percentages between the highest and the other percentages were statistically insignificant at the 5% level, the other percentages were also highlighted in bold.

government members, as the main actors to be engaged by Governments for the implementation of the Goals. Respondents from small island developing States also highlighted the role of NGOs and civil society organizations. The important role of the media was recognized by respondents from landlocked developing countries.

Role of the United Nations

The survey also explored the role of the United Nations, along with its specialized agencies, in implementing the Goals. The clustered responses presented in table 2.13 clearly reveal the wide-ranging role that the United Nations is expected to play in supporting adaptation of the Goals at the national level. The interventions include effective engagement with national Governments, support for capacity-building and resource mobilization, addressing risk management and fostering accountability. Respondents from least developed countries mentioned the needs of these countries for incentives and assistance for a smooth and sustainable graduation process, and those from small island developing States emphasized the need for technical and institutional support.

Role of other international development partners

The majority of the respondents considered that the main role of multilateral development banks and bilateral donors in supporting realization of the 2030 Agenda would be to provide enhanced financial resources. They expect them to provide more financial support, particularly, for infrastructure projects. Many respondents also mentioned the need for these development partners to provide more capacity-building and technical support, with a focus on small and medium-sized enterprises. Some respondents suggested that development banks and bilateral donors should be more active in the area of monitoring and evaluation of progress towards the achievement of the Goals. A significant number of respondents asked for improved partnerships, coordination and cooperation among the agencies themselves as well as with national Governments. Some respondents also called for a more effective accountability framework for international development cooperation.

Summary of the results

The survey results suggest that the views of experts and practitioners from CSN on the priorities for the initial stages of implementation of the 2030 Agenda vary consistently across least developed countries, landlocked developing countries and small island developing States. While experts from least developed countries express a strong preference for prioritizing the social pillar of sustainable development, experts from landlocked developing countries focus on the economic pillar, and those from small island developing States expressed a preference for a balanced prioritization of the social, economic and environmental pillars.

Table 2.13	Role of the United Nations in implementing the Goals

Engagement with Government	• Create awareness about Goals and support coordination among government agencies and officials; encourage regular consultations to ensure that Goals are prioritized by government officials • Encourage national and local Governments to remain committed to implementing the Goals through strong advocacy • Help Governments to integrate the Goals in the national budget along with a results-based management framework
Capacity-building	• Provide in-country training to broaden knowledge regarding how to go about achieving the Goals • Assist, gather and disseminate technical knowledge and international best practices • Support capacity-building, the transfer of technology and human resource development for data collection and building reliable statistical systems and help create a digital library
Resource mobilization	• Help countries to raise the necessary finance from external sources as well as assist in mobilizing domestic resources • Provide budget support to effectively implement the Goals • Play a major role in providing technical and financial support, specifically in building capacity for local Governments to follow through with implementing the Goals
Monitoring and accountability	• Play a supportive role with more assistance in supervision and evaluation of project feasibility and sustainability • Continuously monitor and hold Governments and other relevant accountable during the 15-year lifetime of the 2030 Agenda • Help countries to build a functional delivery framework with time-bound targets for line ministries • Help to ensure that accountability in the management of public resources concerning both national Governments and international development partners • Provide substantive assistance to build a participatory national monitoring system
Risk management	• Respond to countries in cases of emergency or "urgent need" • Provide leadership in addressing, among others, climate change, treatment of refugees and health hazards
CSN-specific instruments	• Pay special attention to small island developing States in terms of support for technology transfer and capacity-building; provide the necessary financial and institutional support; and help build partnerships with advanced peer countries to deliver on the Goals • Support countries after graduating from least developed country status through technical assistance • Ensure continuity and sustainability of the accountability framework of the Goals in the context of changes in CSN Governments • Carry out independent monitoring and evaluation and prepare progress reports specifically on CSN

Source: ESCAP.

These priorities are consistent with their views on the unfinished Millennium Development Goals, which should also be tackled at an early stage of implementing the 2030 Agenda, particularly for least developed countries.

Survey respondents noted that national Governments will have to play a lead role in implementing the Goals, for which coordination — both horizontal and vertical — among different government agencies will be a critical challenge. Respondents also pointed out that bringing about changes in budgetary processes to mainstream the Goals will be more difficult than reflecting the Goals in national plans.

Respondents from both CSN and developing countries that are not CSN identified enhancing national government revenue collection as the most important source of finance to prioritize in the first stage of implementing the Goals. In CSN, ODA was the second most important source of finance, followed by management of public expenditure, multilateral development banks and FDI. Respondents expressed a desire for Governments to engage with the private sector, particularly small and medium-sized enterprises, and public representatives, such as parliamentarians and local Governments, in efforts to implement the Goals.

Respondents pointed out that the successful delivery of the Goals will depend on the availability of an enabling global economic environment characterized by stable international commodity and financial markets and by the sustained expansion of the global economy. They expect the United Nations system and other development partners to play a critical role in supporting countries to adapt the Goals to their national realities.

As is clear from the discussion of the survey results, the first stage in the process of adapting the Goals should be to identify the priorities and sequencing in order to achieve the Goals and targets of the 2030 Agenda that are most appropriate to each country's unique circumstances. The analytical framework proposed in the next chapter provides a potentially useful tool for that purpose.

CONCLUSIONS AND THE WAY FORWARD

The mapping exercise and the survey results described in the present chapter have provided key elements for the discussion of the adaptation of the 2030 Agenda to the unique circumstances, capacities and levels of development of the Asia-Pacific CSN.

The mapping exercise reveals a great overlap between the actions of each programme of action and the targets of the 2030 Agenda. Indeed, the vast majority of the 17 Sustainable Development Goals are already covered by the Istanbul Programme of Action and the Samoa Pathway and, to a lesser extent, by the Vienna Programme of Action.

The Istanbul Programme of Action covers all three pillars of sustainable development, while placing greater emphasis on the social pillar. The Samoa Pathway also covers the three pillars of sustainable development, but with its focus on the environmental pillar. In sharp contrast, the Vienna Programme of Action is focused just on the economic pillar. All three programmes of action cover governance and means of implementation.

Moreover, all the actions of the programmes of action contribute in some degree to the achievement of the Goals of the 2030 Agenda, either through actions that are very similar and closely match the related targets or through actions that are relevant in the context of CSN and relate to the Goals.

Understanding such complementarities between the global programmes of action and the 2030 Agenda allows policymakers to design an effective and coherent policy. It also reinforces the importance of addressing the special vulnerabilities of CSN as a condition for the progress towards sustainable development.

The survey of experts furthers the understanding of the priorities and challenges of CSN. It is evident that experts and development practitioners in Asia-Pacific CSN demonstrated a reasonable level of understanding regarding the need for an integrated approach to prioritization of different Goals and targets. They also recognized that, given the resource and capacity constraints, some of the Goals and targets have to be given a head start.

Most importantly, the opinion of experts on the prioritization and sequencing of the Goals coincides with the focus areas set forth in the programmes of action of their respective country groups. This reinforces the importance of such programmes of action as frameworks for achieving the Goals. Therefore, Government can be guided by the specific actions agreed in such programmes to prepare national plans for the adaptation of the 2030 Agenda to their unique circumstances.

Taking note of the above-mentioned lessons and to take the process forward, it may be suggested that national exercises might be undertaken in CSN to achieve the following:

(a) Identification of the Goal priorities within a time frame and their interface with national policies, plans, programmes and budgetary practices;
(b) Assessment of the preparedness of national administrative mechanisms to pursue Goal implementation and the ability to provide necessary coordination and leadership in this regard;
(c) Estimation of the resources required — both financial and non-financial — for the first five years along with the necessary international support measures;
(d) Preparation of a capacity development plan to address the governance challenges of implementation and the data deficit so as to ensure proper monitoring of progress.

ESCAP may consider providing, inter alia, the necessary technical support to develop further the elements of the proposed framework and operationalize such a framework so as to effectively promote the process of adapting the 2030 Agenda in CSN by overcoming the attendant changes.

Endnotes

[1] See A/CONF.219/3/Rev.1, para. 8.

[2] See A/CONF.225/L.1, para. 21.

[3] See A/RES/69/15, para. 21.

[4] See A/RES/70/1, para. 64.

[5] See A/RES/70/1, para. 55.

[6] Complete details of this exercise are available in Isgut and others (forthcoming).

[7] Although the Samoa Pathway does not have any actions directly matching the targets under Goal 1, poverty eradication is recognized in the document as one of the overarching objectives of sustainable development and it is addressed in a number of its priorities.

[8] See A/CONF.219/3/Rev.1, para. 60.

[9] See A/CONF.225/L.1, para. 32.

[10] See A/RES/69/15, para. 75(c).

[11] See A/RES/69/15, para. 71(b).

[12] See A/RES/69/15, para. 30(e).

[13] See Bhattacharya and Rezbana (forthcoming) for further elaboration.

[14] The areas of expertise of the respondents are distributed as follows: economics and development (56%); social sectors (11%); trade, investment and finance (9%); environment and disasters (8%); agriculture and natural resources (4%); transport, information and communications technologies (ICT) and energy (4%); and others (7%).

[15] See Bhattacharya and others (2016) for further details.

3

PATHWAYS TO ENHANCE CAPACITIES FOR SUSTAINABLE DEVELOPMENT

The 2030 Agenda is an ambitious and holistic agenda for development that encompasses a broad spectrum of economic, social and environmental issues. Building upon the Millennium Development Goals, the 2030 Agenda includes a more diverse and comprehensive set of aspirational Goals applicable to all countries, be they developing or developed (United Nations, 2015). However, unlike the Millennium Development Goals, the specific targets for the Goals rarely include measurable outcomes, making their implementation more amenable to adaptation to country-specific circumstances, capacities and aspirations. While this flexibility is highly desirable, it also demands a deeper level of stakeholder engagement and country ownership in deciding which areas of the 2030 Agenda can be most productively prioritized and effectively implemented, taking into account the unique level of development, capacities and comparative strengths of each country.

This is a difficult task because the attainment of the Goals and targets of the 2030 Agenda are characterized by interdependencies, including synergies and trade-offs. For example, there seems to be a close relationship between Goal 1 (no poverty), Goal 2 (zero hunger), Goal 3 (good health and well-being) and Goal 8 (decent work and economic growth). Devising policies that move forward the 2030 Agenda in these four areas in a holistic and coordinated way could take advantage of potential synergies among them, resulting in much more effective implementation. On the other hand, a popular view holds that there is a trade-off between Goal 8 and Goals 11-15 related to environmental sustainability. Such a trade-off needs to be taken into account for a balanced and effective implementation of the Goals associated with the three pillars of sustainable development. This suggests that a clear understanding of the interdependencies, synergies and trade-offs across Goals and targets is essential for the successful implementation of the 2030 Agenda (UN-OHRLLS, 2012).

The interdependencies among the Goals and related targets are not new. They have been recognized by the United Nations, political leaders and scientists in academia for a long time (ICSU and ISSC, 2015). For example, at the United Nations Conference on Human Environment (Stockholm Conference) in 1972, the Indian Prime Minister, Indira Gandhi, advocated an integrated approach to development: "The population explosion, poverty, ignorance and disease, the pollution of our surroundings, the stockpiling of nuclear weapons and biological and chemical agents of destruction are all parts of a vicious circle. Each is important and urgent but dealing with them one by one would be wasted effort" (United Nations, 2015). Similarly, the Brundtland Commission's definition of sustainable development as "development that meets the needs of the present without compromising the ability of future generations to meet their own needs" underlies an integrated view of development in which issues such as economic growth, intra- and intergenerational equity and environmental sustainability influence and reinforce each other and evolve in tandem.

The purpose of the present chapter is to propose an analytical framework to facilitate the understanding of complementarities, synergies and trade-offs across Goals and their targets at the national level, taking into account each country's unique level of development, capacities and structural characteristics. The framework allows for the identification of optimal strategies of implementation of the Goals, including specific recommendations for the prioritization and sequencing necessary to achieve each Goal. The

framework is based on the premise that it is possible to conceptualize the Goals as a complex system composed of countries and degrees of attainment of a number of indicators representative of the 17 Goals and their associated targets. By allowing a systematic evaluation of the benefits of alternative policies and pathways for progress towards the achievement of the Goals, it is expected that the proposed framework will contribute to deliberations on the design of plans and strategies for the adaptation of the 2030 Agenda to national contexts.

1. INDICATORS UTILIZED IN THE ANALYSIS

At the time of writing, the Inter-agency and Expert Group on Sustainable Development Goal Indicators was in the process of refining and fine-tuning the list of indicators that will be used to track progress for each of the 17 Goals and 169 targets, and data for these indicators will gradually become available in the coming years. Therefore, the indicators used for the analysis of this chapter, which are listed in annex III, were selected as follows:

(a) All the indicators used to track progress towards the Millennium Development Goals that overlap in meaning and scope with the Goals and related targets were included, provided that they have reasonable coverage across countries;

(b) Among the indicators tentatively agreed to be included in the final list of Goal indicators at the 2nd meeting of the Inter-Agency and Expert Group, those that have data readily available from official sources and do not overlap with indicators selected from the first criterion were added, again provided that they have reasonable coverage across countries;

(c) Other internationally comparable indicators that closely reflect the Goals and their targets and have reasonable coverage across countries were added to cover Goals for which relevant indicators could not be found using the first two criteria.

It is important to note that the analysis of the Goals as a complex system, which will be discussed below, requires as much information about the "system" as possible, including as many countries as possible and a wide variety of indicators relevant to the Goals. However, there is a trade-off between including more indicators and including more countries. Taking into account this trade-off, the final analysis was conducted on the basis of 82 indicators that broadly cover all 17

Goals, while providing decent data coverage across countries. The data set is based on the most recent data available for each country. The finalized data set includes data spanning from 2006 to 2014, with the majority of data points for 2010 or later years. The median number of indicators per Goal is 4, with a minimum of 2 for Goals 1 and 10 and a maximum of 10 for Goals 3 and 9. The correspondence between indicators and Goals is included in annex III.

After selecting the 82 indicators with reasonable country coverage, 120 out of 209 countries had missing data points. This presented a problem because the methods used in the analysis perform poorly with incomplete data sets. Instead of limiting our analysis to just the 89 countries for which a full data set was available, a multiple imputation technique was used to impute missing data. The technique was applied to countries with missing data for no more than 20 out of the 82 indicators.[1] After imputation, the number of countries in the data set increased to 174.

The use of imputation is particularly important to ensure the representativeness of the data used for the analysis. Among the 174 countries included in the data set, there were 22 Asia-Pacific CSN, including 9 least developed countries (Afghanistan, Bangladesh, Bhutan, Cambodia, the Lao People's Democratic Republic, Myanmar, Nepal, Solomon Islands and Vanuatu), 8 landlocked developing countries (Armenia, Azerbaijan, Kazakhstan, Kyrgyzstan, Mongolia, Tajikistan, Turkmenistan and Uzbekistan), and 5 small island developing States (Fiji, Maldives, Papua New Guinea, Samoa and Tonga).[2]

2. ATTAINMENT OF THE GOALS BY THE ASIA-PACIFIC COUNTRIES WITH SPECIAL NEEDS

A snapshot of the current status of Goal attainment by the Asia-Pacific CSN is obtained by averaging the values of indicators corresponding to each Goal, both for specific countries and for groups of countries. For that purpose, the values of each indicator were normalized to be between 0 and 100, where 100 is the 90th percentile and 0 is the 10th percentile of attainment across countries. See annex III for details.

When taking a broad look at how Asia-Pacific CSN are faring, it becomes evident that these countries are indeed lagging behind in many areas, some more than others (figure 3.1). Compared with the developing Asia-Pacific countries that are not CSN, the region's

CSN lag behind in areas related to health (Goal 3), water and sanitation (Goal 6), industry, innovation and infrastructure (Goal 9), institutions (Goal 16) and implementation (Goal 17). In particular, the weaknesses of Asia-Pacific CSN are evident for Goals 9 and 17, with attainment levels significantly lower than both the developing Asia-Pacific countries and the rest of the world.

However, it can also be seen that these countries have comparatively high levels of attainment in poverty, measured by the poverty headcount and gap ratio. In addition, Asia-Pacific CSN are performing relatively well in areas related to environmental sustainability (Goals 12-15). Yet, considering that, in general, indicators related to the environment are inversely related to economic growth and wealth, a key issue for the Asia-Pacific CSN is to devise a pathway for progress that does not relinquish their advantage in environmental aspects, while simultaneously improving upon other Goals that are dependent on economic development.

Comparing the least developed countries, landlocked developing countries and small island developing States, what is noticeable is that the three groups are to a large extent heterogeneous in their current status. The least developed countries in general are lagging behind the other two groups, yet they do have their comparative advantage in indicators related to climate action (Goal 13) and life below water (Goal 14). The landlocked developing countries are performing exceptionally well compared with the other two groups in many aspects; in particular, poverty (Goal 1), hunger (Goal 2), education (Goal 4), gender equality (Goal 5) and inequality (Goal 10). However, the landlocked developing countries are struggling with indicators related to sustainable consumption and production (Goal 12) as well as climate action (Goal 13).

The small island developing States are performing generally well in environment-related Goals (Goals 12-15), yet are struggling with sustainable energy (Goal 7), industry, infrastructure and technology (Goal 9) and implementation (Goal 17). Overall, the analysis suggests that taking group-specific circumstances into serious consideration is very important when devising plans of action for Goal implementation. This, however, is not enough, as the data also reveal significant variation within each CSN category at the national level, suggesting that country-specific circumstances are also of importance.[3]

(a) Comparison with developing Asia-Pacific countries that are not CSN and the rest of the world

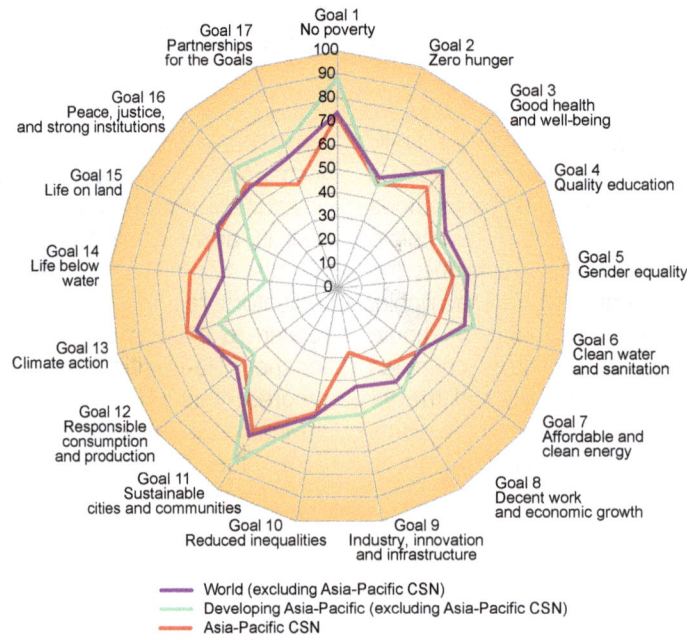

Legend:
- World (excluding Asia-Pacific CSN)
- Developing Asia-Pacific (excluding Asia-Pacific CSN)
- Asia-Pacific CSN

Source: ESCAP.

Notes: (a) The attainment for each Goal is normalized to be between 0 and 100, with 100 being the highest and 0 being the lowest level of attainment given the set of countries included in the analysis; and (b) developing Asia-Pacific countries in the sample, excluding Asia-Pacific CSN, are: Brunei Darussalam; China; Georgia; India; Indonesia; Malaysia; Pakistan; Philippines; Republic of Korea; Russian Federation; Singapore; Sri Lanka; Thailand; Turkey; and Viet Nam.

(b) Comparison across the three groups of CSN

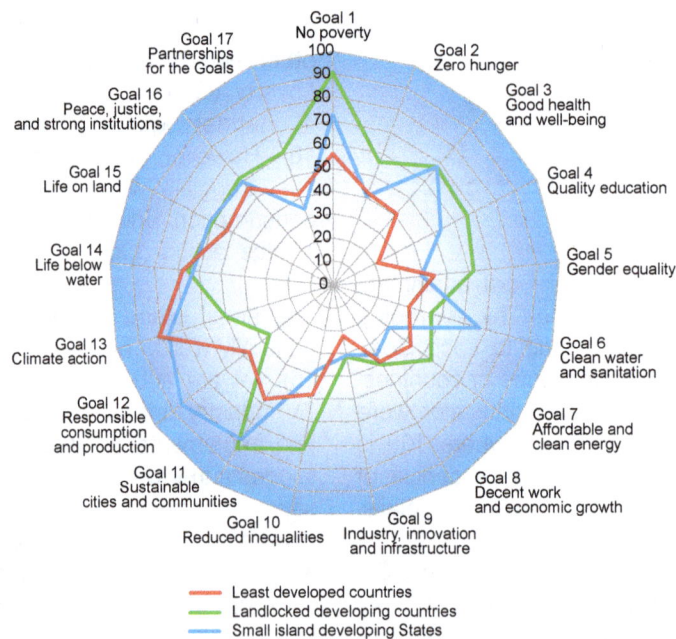

Legend:
- Least developed countries
- Landlocked developing countries
- Small island developing States

Source: ESCAP.

Notes: (a) The attainment for each Goal is normalized to be between 0 and 100, with 100 being the highest and 0 being the lowest level of attainment given the set of countries included in the analysis; and (b) the least developed countries are: Afghanistan; Bangladesh; Bhutan; Cambodia; Lao People's Democratic Republic; Myanmar; Nepal; Solomon Islands; and Vanuatu. The landlocked developing countries are: Armenia; Azerbaijan; Kazakhstan; Kyrgyzstan; Mongolia; Tajikistan; Turkmenistan; and Uzbekistan. The small island developing States are: Fiji; Maldives; Papua New Guinea; Samoa; and Tonga.

3. THE GOALS AS AN INTEGRATED, COMPLEX SYSTEM

An effective way to facilitate the understanding of the interdependencies, synergies and trade-offs across the Goals and targets of the 2030 Agenda at the national level is to view the set of Goals and countries as a complex system. In essence, a complex system is a nexus of diverse, multiple interconnected elements in which the whole is not equal to the sum of the parts (Simon, 1991). Academic researchers from various disciplines have been increasingly using complex systems for the analysis of economic phenomena and sustainable development.[4] ESCAP (2015) has conducted research on this topic with regard to measuring productive capacities in the Asia-Pacific region, where such capacities are measured using information on interlinkages among products and countries.[5]

In the present chapter, the Sustainable Development Goals system — or SDG system — is conceptualized as a network consisting of (a) the indicators relevant to each of the Goals, (b) the countries and (c) the linkages among and between countries and indicators. The following two subsections describe the SDG system.

3.1. The network of indicators

The advantage of viewing the indicators related to the Goals as a network is that it makes it clear how they are interlinked, revealing their synergies and trade-offs. The information provided by an indicator network can allow policymakers to devise plans of action that take advantage of the spillovers that are present among the indicators, while identifying potential trade-offs that need to be reconciled. The indicator network also allows for the identification of bottlenecks that act as barriers to the attainment of the broader 2030 Agenda.

The network of indicators is constructed so that each indicator is connected to another based on their "proximity". The proximity of two indicators from the perspective of a specific country is higher when the attainment of the country in the two indicators is similar. A high degree of proximity between two indicators can be interpreted as meaning that attainment of the two indicators requires similar capacities.[6] A graphical representation of this network for the Asia-Pacific CSN is shown in figure 3.2.[7]

The network of indicators suggests a clear core-periphery structure, with indicators related to health, hunger, infrastructure and poverty occupying a prominent space within the densely connected core. Life expectancy, infant mortality, food supply and agriculture value added are at the very centre of this core, since they represent essential needs that form the basis for higher attainment in other indicators. Poverty headcount, poverty-gap ratio, malnutrition, maternal and child mortality and years of schooling are also central for similar reasons. Infrastructure indicators regarding telephone, cellular and Internet subscriptions are also relatively central within this core. This is consistent with the new institutional economics viewpoint that facilitating information exchange is important in transforming the political economy of a society, resulting in lower transaction costs, alleviation of information asymmetries and thus a more sustainable socioeconomic development (Coase, 1998).

In figure 3.2, the size of each node is based on how "important" the corresponding indicator is within the network.[8] The importance of an indicator is based on two distinct characteristics: (a) how well connected each indicator is with the other indicators, in the sense of being close to many other indicators; and (b) how important the indicator is in serving as a "gatekeeper" between different portions of the network. Gatekeeper indicators represent indicators that a country must pass in order to cross between otherwise unconnected groups of indicators. From figure 3.2, it can be seen that most of the indicators within the broad core of the network are important in the sense that they are close to many other indicators. However, other indicators such as natural resource depletion or carbon dioxide (CO_2) emissions per \$1 GDP are also relatively important because of their role as gatekeepers.

The red nodes in figure 3.2 represent indicators for which average attainment by the Asia-Pacific CSN is below the 50th percentile for the 174 countries considered in the analysis. The figure shows that these countries have low levels of attainment in a number of important indicators, such as income (GDP per capita and GDP per capita at purchasing power parity), telephone and Internet access, gender and human inequality and years of schooling. Their relative centrality within the network suggests that an improved performance in these indicators could have positive spillover effects on the attainment of other relevant indicators.

The red links in figure 3.2 represent indicators that are relatively less connected to each other. They show that many of the indicators related to the environment

Figure 3.2 The network of indicators for Asia-Pacific countries with special needs

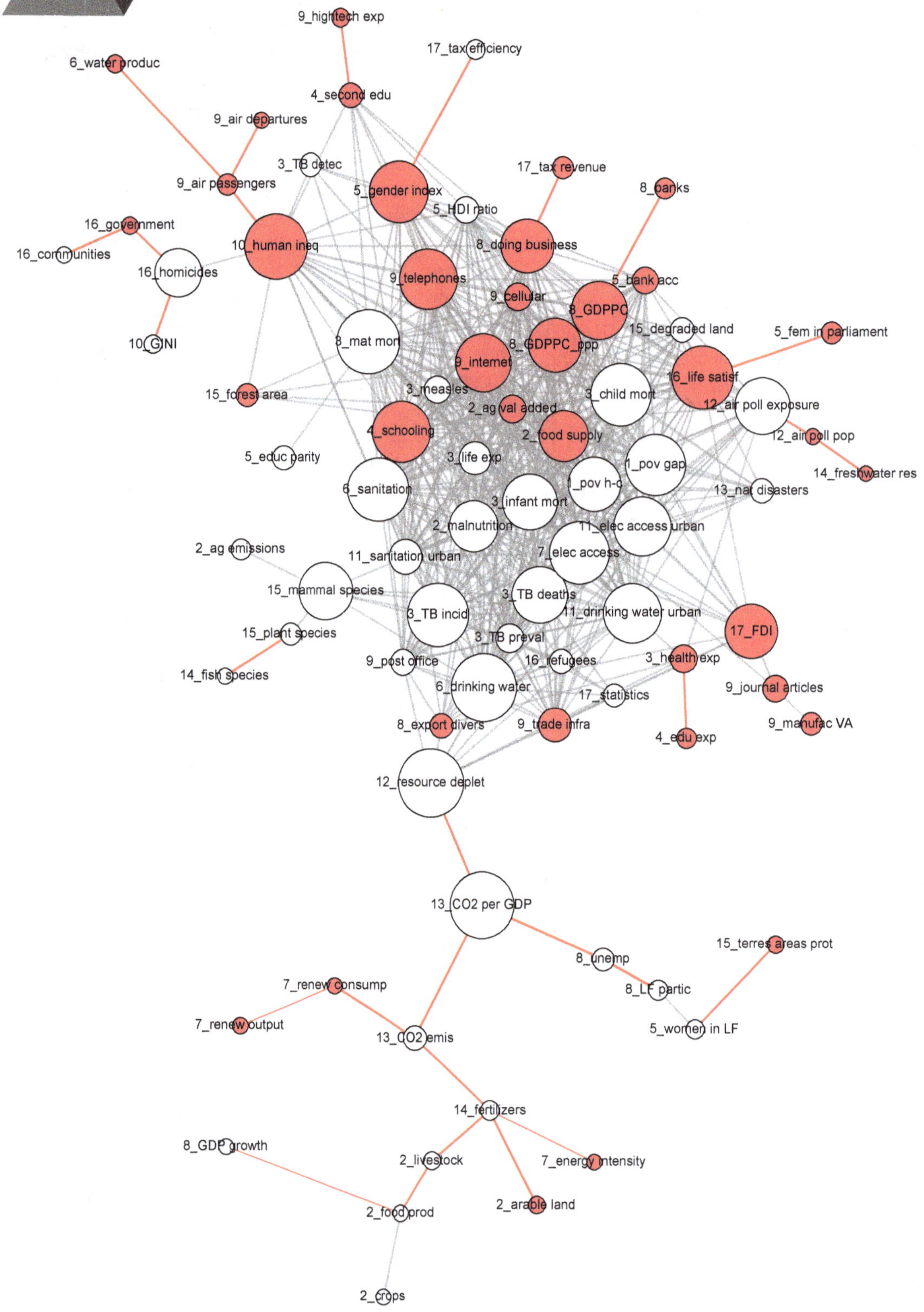

Source: ESCAP.

Notes: (a) The red links represent proximity values that are less than 0.75; (b) the size of nodes is based on the average of an indicator's weighted degree centrality and betweenness centrality (see annex III); and (c) red nodes are those for which the average attainment for Asia-Pacific CSN is below the 50th percentile of attainment across all the countries included in the analysis.

— such as CO_2 emissions per capita, consumption and production of renewable energy and fertilizer consumption — reside in the lower portion of the network and are not directly connected to the core. This could be interpreted as representing a trade-off between environmental and socioeconomic indicators. However, the two main gatekeeper indicators that connect this lower portion of the network and the upper core are resource depletion and CO_2 emissions per \$1 GDP. The figure suggests that addressing these two particular environmental indicators can facilitate the attainment by the Asia-Pacific CSN of other environmental indicators in the lower portion of the network.

Overall, the network representation for the Asia-Pacific CSN shows a dense core of highly interrelated socioeconomic indicators and a periphery that includes a number of environmental indicators. The representation shows that these countries have relatively low levels of attainment in a number of indicators that are both in the core and highly connected to other indicators. This suggests that implementing policies to improve the attainment of such indicators could have positive spillover effects, facilitating the attainment of other core indicators.

However, the representation also shows that a number of indicators related to environmental sustainability are in the periphery of the network. Because of their lower degree of connection to the socioeconomic indicators at the core of the network, the representation suggests that their attainment is less likely to benefit from positive spillover effects, further suggesting the existence of trade-offs between the achievement of the socioeconomic and environmental pillars of sustainable development.

3.2. The network of countries

Countries can also be linked together in a network, where the links are representative of how similar two countries are in attainment across the 82 indicators included in the analysis. Figure 3.3 shows a graphical representation of this network, which is constructed similarly to the network of indicators, with the size of the nodes based on each country's per capita income. The network shows distinct clusters of countries, with low-income countries at the bottom and developed economies at the top.

Countries belonging to different groups of Asia-Pacific CSN — least developed countries, landlocked developing countries and small island developing States — tend to be located close to each other in the network, suggesting that they have similar levels of attainment in the indicators. Eight of the nine least developed countries for which data are available (Bangladesh, Bhutan, Cambodia, Lao People's Democratic Republic, Myanmar, Nepal, Solomon Islands and Vanuatu) are, in fact, located next to each other, in the bottom-centre of the network. The other least developed country, Afghanistan, is located in the bottom-left of the network, close to least developed countries from other regions, such as Sudan and Haiti.

Of the five small island developing States in the database, four (Fiji, Samoa, Tonga and Maldives) are clustered in the middle-right portion of the network. The fifth one, Papua New Guinea, is located in the bottom-centre of the network, suggesting that this country's level of attainment across the indicators is similar to that of the region's least developed countries. The Asian landlocked developing countries are dispersed into three small clusters: (a) Armenia, Turkmenistan and Uzbekistan are located close to the Asia-Pacific small island developing States; (b) Mongolia and Tajikistan are in the bottom of the network, close to a number of Asian developing countries; and (c) Azerbaijan and Kazakhstan are located near the top of the network, close to countries such as Bahrain, Brunei, Qatar and the Russian Federation, which are all oil-exporting countries.

Although the data used to construct the countries' network are cross-sectional, the network can be interpreted as representing potential pathways for progress towards the Sustainable Development Goals. For instance, for the groups of Asia-Pacific least developed countries at the bottom-centre of the network, one pathway for progress would be to initially strive for levels of attainment across the indicators similar to Indonesia, Viet Nam, China and Thailand. At a later stage, they could try to achieve similar patterns of attainment to countries that are positioned higher up the network, such as Mexico, Slovakia, Dominican Republic, Albania and "the former Yugoslav Republic of Macedonia".

However, the countries' network also identifies obstacles to the development of lower income countries. The red links in figure 3.3 represent comparatively weaker links, in the sense that the two countries that share such links are less similar to each other in their attainment of the indicators. The figure shows that the majority of the weaker links reside in the bottom portion of the network. Examples of weak links in the figure include the link between Bangladesh and Indonesia — which separates the region's least

Figure 3.3 The network of countries, based on proximities

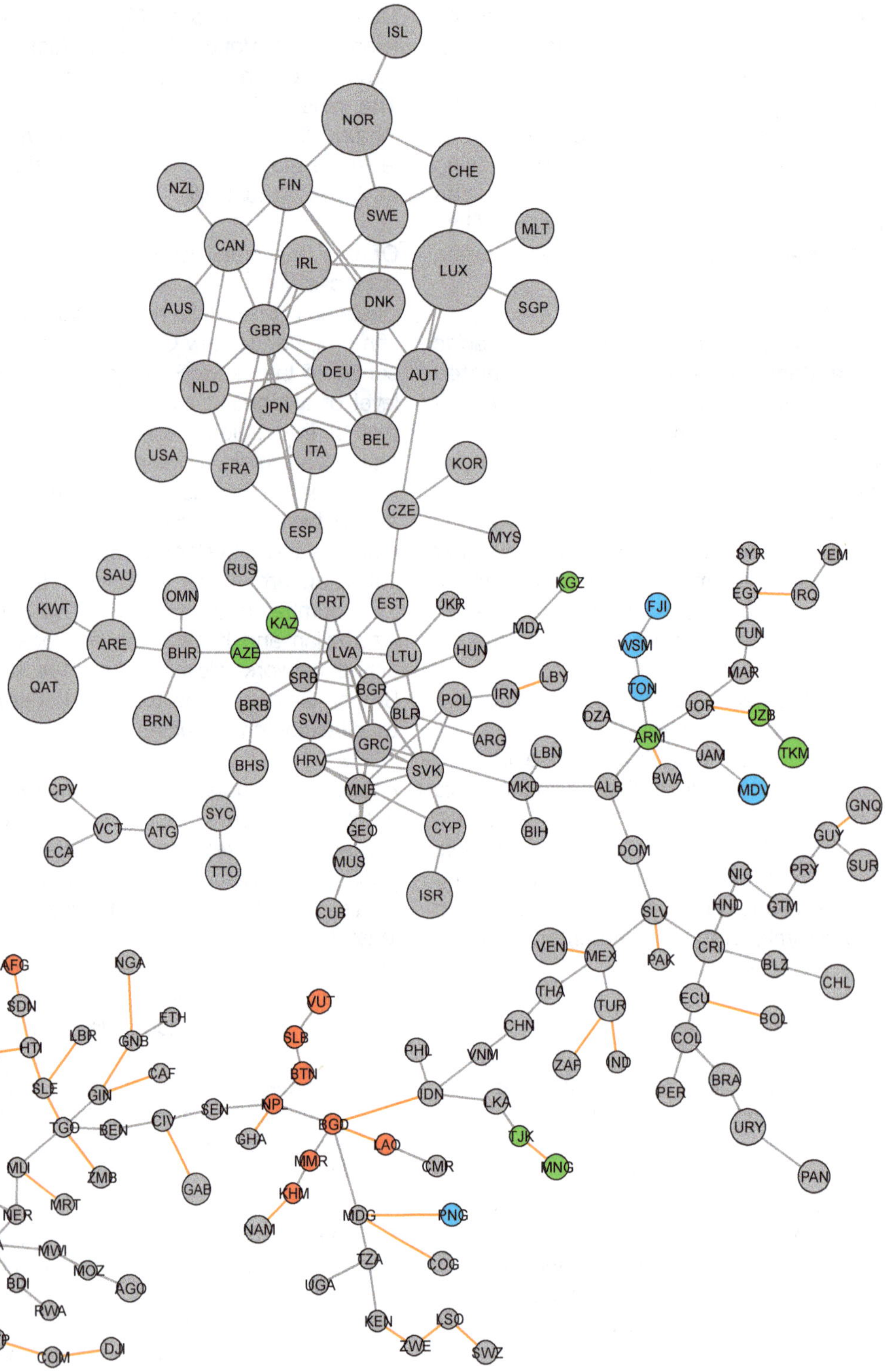

Source: ESCAP.

Notes: (a) The red links represent proximity values that are less than 0.75; (b) the size of a country is based on nominal GDP per capita (2014); and (c) red, green and blue countries are least developed countries, landlocked developing countries and small island developing States, respectively. Country names and codes are available in the explanatory notes.

developed countries from developing countries such as the Philippines, Viet Nam, Sri Lanka, China and Thailand — and the links of Afghanistan and Papua New Guinea with other least developed countries. Such weak links are indicative of structural differences between the countries connected by them. Addressing them would require targeted agendas, such as the Istanbul Programme of Action, and special measures of support by the international community aimed at reducing their structural impediments to sustainable development.

As mentioned above, the network of countries suggests that the region's least developed countries are a very homogeneous group with regard to their attainment across the 82 indicators included in the analysis. Their similarities as least developed countries are more important than possible differences associated with geographic characteristics such as being landlocked or a small island developing State. Remarkably, the similarities among the Asia-Pacific least developed countries were also noted in the analysis of perceived priorities for the implementation of the 2030 Agenda that were discussed in chapter 2. Also, the structural differences between small island developing States according to whether or not they are also least developed countries are consistent with the analysis of selected indicators related to the Samoa Pathway, which appeared in chapter 1. These observations reinforce the need for particular attention from the international community in supporting implementation of the 2030 Agenda in the least developed countries.

4. SUSTAINABLE DEVELOPMENT GOAL CAPACITIES

The attainment of the Sustainable Development Goals requires countries to possess specific capacities related to the effective implementation of socioeconomic and environmental policies, which are very difficult — if not impossible — to directly observe and measure. They could include a Government's capacities to design and implement policies, as well as capacities in the population at large to contribute to the attainment of the Goals. In the present report — in a similar fashion to ESCAP (2015) in the case of productive capacities — the SDG capacities of a country are measured using information provided by the SDG system.

Using the 82 indicators included in the analysis, the simplest way to construct a measure of SDG capacities for a particular country is to calculate the average level of attainment across all the indicators.

However, this measure is unsatisfactory because it does not take into consideration that different indicators are characterized by different degrees of complexity. For instance, it is reasonable to assume that it would take considerably more resources for a country to increase its number of articles published in scientific and technical journals than to increase the number of users of mobile phones.

We assume that the degree of complexity of an indicator is inversely related to the number of countries that have high attainment in it, that is if many countries are doing well in a particular indicator, its complexity is assumed to be lower. Thus, a more accurate measure of the SDG capacities of a country is a weighted average of the levels of attainment in the indicators, using each indicator's complexity as weights. As shown in annex III, the measurement of SDG capacities can be further refined using the method of reflections. The more refined measures of SDG capacities are higher if a country is doing well in indicators that other countries are struggling with, since this suggests that the country possesses unique capacities that others do not have.

Figure 3.4 compares the country rankings among Asia-Pacific countries, from raw attainment, the simple average of attainment across the 82 indicators, to more refined measures of SDG capacities. The figure shows that countries such as Kyrgyzstan and Tajikistan drop substantially in rank while others, such as Maldives and Turkmenistan, gain in rank. For Kyrgyzstan and Tajikistan, this is because their comparative advantage across Goals is in indicators related to affordable and clean energy (Goal 7) and life on land (Goal 15), which have relatively low complexity. Maldives gains significantly in rank because it is doing very well in indicators such as water productivity, measured as GDP divided by annual total water withdrawal, and mobile cellular subscriptions per 100, for which complexity is very high. The movement of Turkmenistan up the rankings can be explained by its strength in education-related indicators that go beyond measuring basic primary education, such as mean years of schooling or the proportion of the population with some secondary education, for which again complexity is comparatively high.

Figure 3.5 shows the SDG capacities of the Asia-Pacific CSN. It shows that four small island developing States are among the top six, while the nine least developed countries are among the bottom 11 CSN from the region in SDG capacities. Landlocked developing countries are seen to have heterogeneous levels of capacities, with five countries in the middle of the

Figure
3.4

Relationship between raw attainment across indicators and Sustainable Development Goal
capacities, country rankings, Asia-Pacific countries

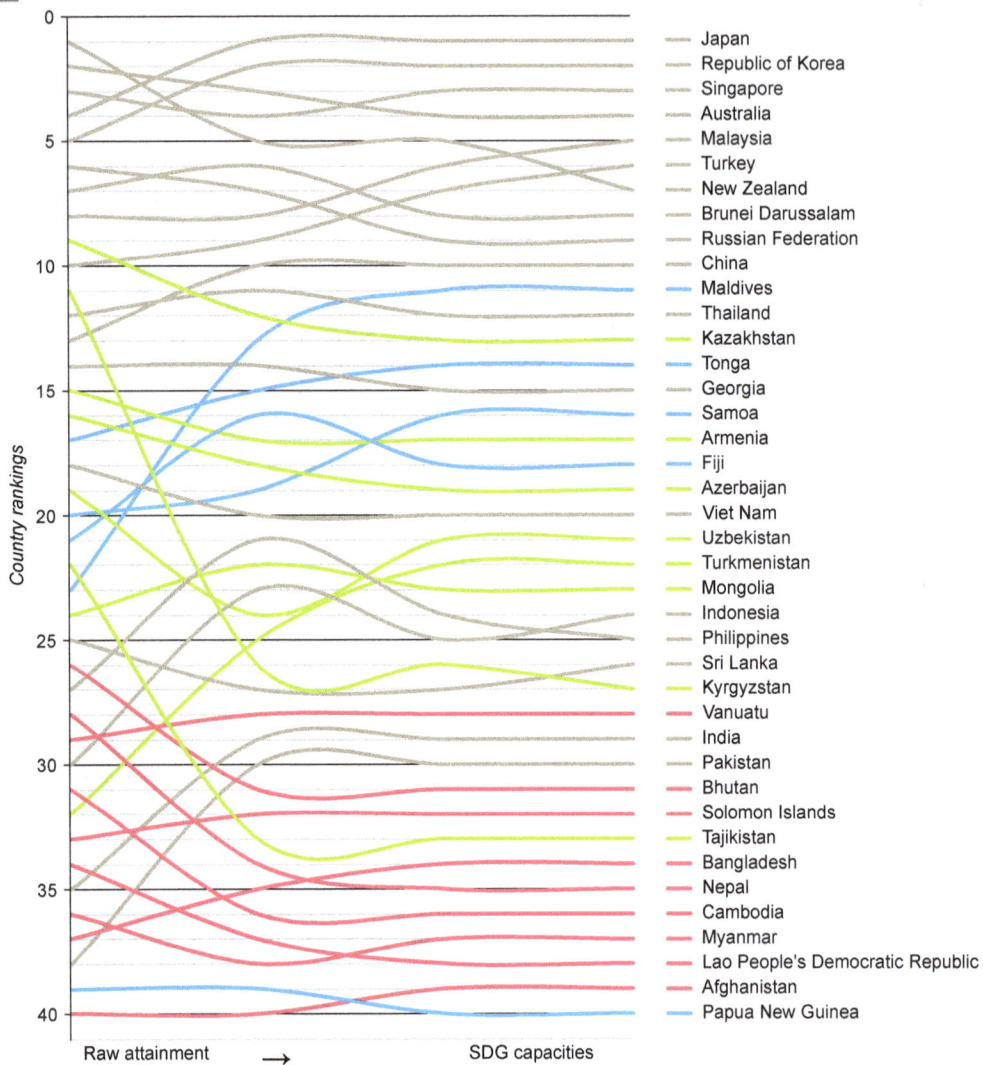

Source: ESCAP.

Notes: (a) The country rankings are for Asia-Pacific countries included in the analysis; (b) red, green, and blue lines represent least developed countries, landlocked developing countries and small island developing States, respectively.

distribution, two (Kazakhstan and Armenia) among the top five and one (Tajikistan) in the bottom half. In a similar fashion to the countries' network, Papua New Guinea is an outlier small island developing State. While the lower levels of SDG capacities of least developed countries reinforce the message of the countries' network that these countries need particular attention and support from the international community for the implementation of the 2030 Agenda, other countries that are not least developed countries will also need such support.

Figure 3.6 shows that SDG capacities are, to varying degrees, correlated with both income levels and the human development index, although the relationships are non-linear in both cases. The top panel of the figure shows that when comparing income levels measured by GNI per capita with SDG capacities, there is a tipping point at income levels of around $40,000 (roughly 4.6 on the logarithmic scale), where a further increase in income levels actually results in a decline in SDG capacity. The reason is that although the overall attainment levels across the indicators are high for high-income countries, these countries have lower attainment levels in indicators related to the environment, food production and sustainable energy. For example, Luxembourg and Qatar, the two highest income countries in the sample, have very

Figure 3.5   Sustainable Development Goal capacities, Asia-Pacific countries with special needs

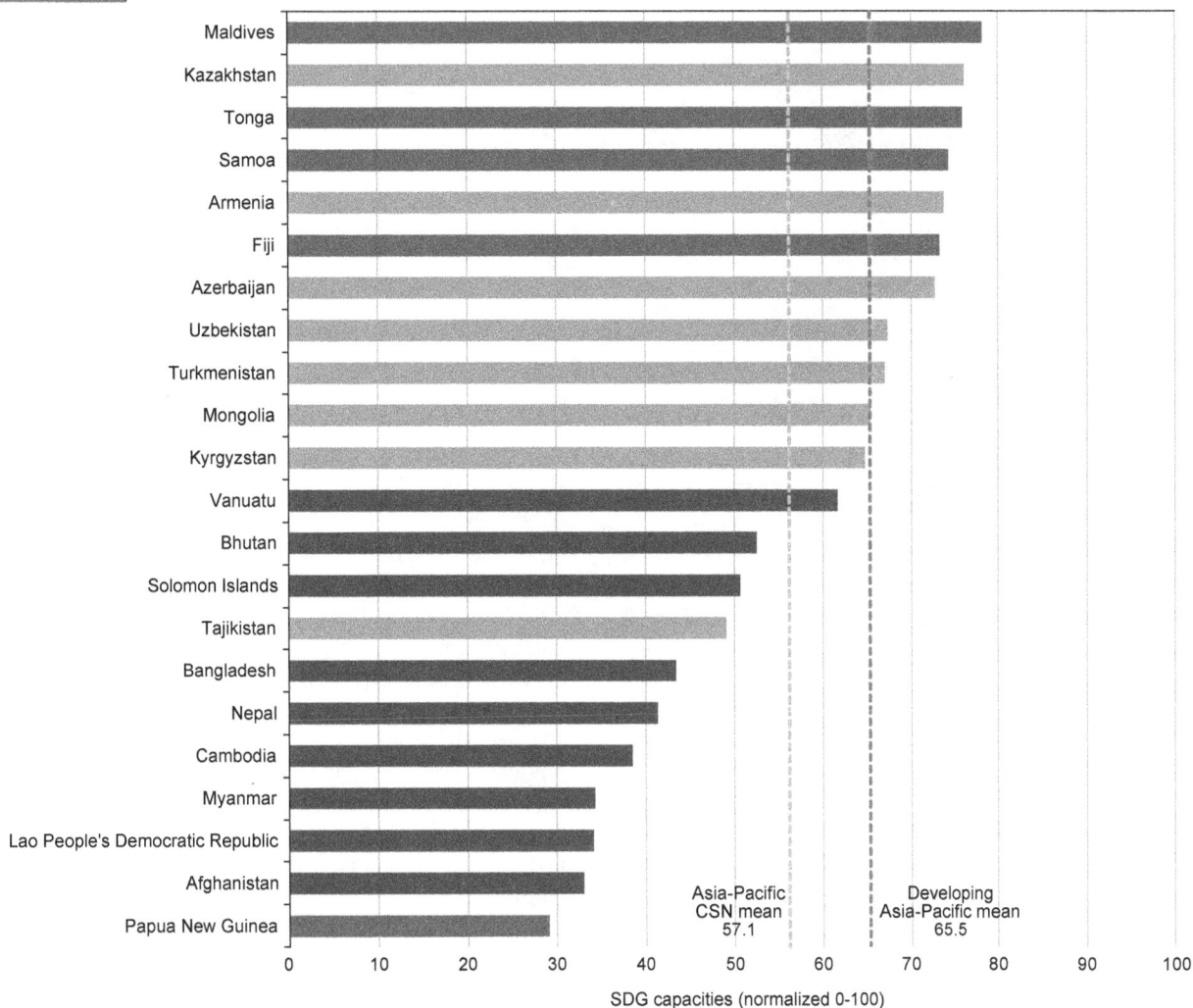

Source: ESCAP.

Notes: (a) The SDG capacities for each country are normalized so as to be between 0 and 100, with 100 being the highest and 0 being the lowest level of SDG capacities given the total set of countries included in the analysis; (b) developing Asia-Pacific countries in the analysis are all the regional ESCAP member States, with the exception of Australia, Japan and New Zealand; and (c) red, green, and blue bars represent least developed countries, landlocked developing countries and small island developing States, respectively.

poor attainment in indicators such as CO_2 emissions per capita, renewable energy consumption and output and air pollution from particulate matter, all of which are considerably lower than even the least developed country average.

Because per capita income refers to only one of the three pillars of sustainable development, a better way to gauge the appropriateness of the proposed measure of SDG capacities is by comparing it with the human development index, which includes life expectancy and education in addition to per capita income. Not surprisingly, the figure shows that SDG capacities correlate more with the human development index than

with income per capita. What is more interesting is that the relationship between the human development index and SDG capacities is also characterized by diminishing returns: for higher index levels, a unit increase has less of an impact on SDG capacities compared with a unit increase at lower index levels. This result could also be caused by the absence of environmental indicators in the human development index, along with a poorer performance in such indicators for countries with higher levels of human development.

In sum, the figure is reassuring in that the proposed measure of SDG capacities is highly correlated to

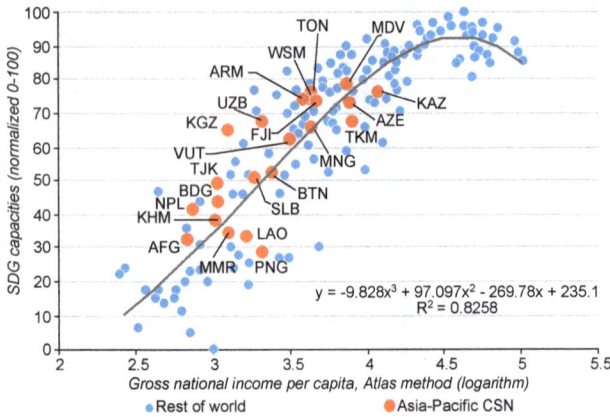

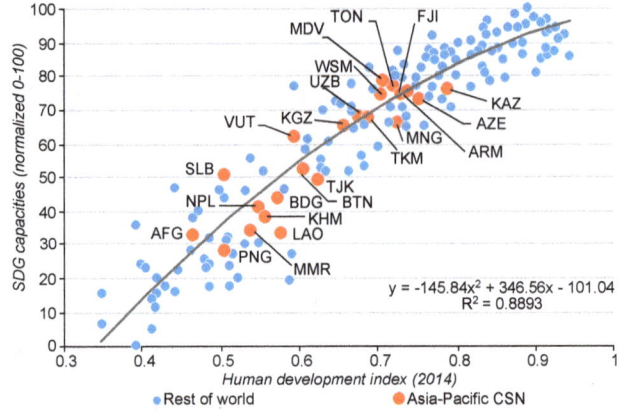

Source: ESCAP.

Notes: The SDG capacities for each country are normalized so as to be between 0 and 100, with 100 being the highest and 0 being the lowest
level of capacity observed within the total set of countries included in the analysis. Country codes are available in the explanatory notes.

existing measures of economic and socioeconomic progress. However, considering that the 2030 Agenda is multidimensional and applies to countries of all levels of income, SDG capacities is more relevant because it is constructed from a broad set of indicators covering not only the three pillars of sustainable development but also governance and means of implementation.

5. OPTIMAL PATHWAYS FOR IMPLEMENTING THE GOALS

Because the proposed measure of SDG capacities is directly related to the levels of attainment in all the indicators associated with the Goals and targets, it provides a synthetic way for countries to assess their progress towards the achievement of the 2030 Agenda.[9] However, SDG capacities can also be useful as a planning tool to guide countries on the prioritization and sequencing of the attainment of indicators over time. For that purpose, the value of the SDG capacities measure could be calculated for a small increase in the value of a number of indicators, one at a time, selecting the indicator that yields the largest increase in SDG capacities. Iterating this calculation many times can produce an "optimal" pathway for progress towards the achievement of the Goals.[10]

This calculation is country-specific, as it depends both on the specific levels of attainment of a country in each of the indicators and on the position of the country in the SDG system. The latter provides critical information about both the interlinkages, synergies

and trade-offs between indicators and the degree of complexity of each indicator. This information facilitates the selection of those indicators that will contribute the most to increasing SDG capacities. For instance, it seems intuitive to assume that it will be more costly for a country to make progress in an indicator characterized by a high degree of complexity compared with making progress in a less complex indicator, which could represent a "low hanging fruit".

The level of attainment of a country in a particular indicator also provides useful information for the selection of indicators to prioritize because of the existence of diminishing returns. For example, when seeking to decrease CO_2 emissions, small changes in behaviours, such as increased use of public transport, cycling or walking, can bring about large reductions. However, as emissions are lowered, more significant investments are required for further decreases, for example, in significant behavioural and urban development and social planning solutions such as transit-oriented development. Similarly, the provision of various services, ranging from the Internet to education, is subject to agglomeration economies, as the same investment in infrastructure can reach significantly more people in densely populated areas, such as large cities, than in sparsely populated rural areas. This suggests that it would be effective for countries to prioritize indicators in which their level of attainment is low.

In sum, a country-specific, optimal pathway for the implementation of the Goals can be derived by choosing to improve the attainment of those indicators that contribute the most to increasing a country's SDG capacities. By constraining the set of indicators eligible for improvement based on the criteria described above, the derived optimal pathway is specific to the current situation, capacities and levels of development of each country. The following section illustrates results from the derivation of optimal pathways for the implementation of the 2030 Agenda in a least developed country (Bangladesh), a landlocked developing country (Kazakhstan) and a small island developing State (Fiji).[11] The final section

of the chapter compares the benefits of the derived optimal pathways with alternative scenarios.

5.1. Pathways for Goal implementation: Bangladesh, Kazakhstan and Fiji

Tables 3.1 to 3.3 lay out the suggested priority areas for Bangladesh, Kazakhstan and Fiji based on the objective of maximizing SDG capacities. The results are aggregated into three five-year phases: 2016-2020, 2021-2025 and 2026-2030. The priority levels

Table 3.1   Top priority indicators for the implementation of the 2030 Agenda in Bangladesh

First phase (2016-2020)		
Goal	Indicator	Priority level (%)
4. Quality education	Education index (years of schooling)	12.1
4. Quality education	Secondary education	11.5
10. Reduced inequalities	Human inequality (health, education and income)	10.6
9. Industry, innovation and infrastructure	Internet users	10.1
9. Industry, innovation and infrastructure	Trade and transport-related infrastructure	8.3
5. Gender equality	Gender inequality (health, empowerment and labour)	8.0
8. Decent work and economic growth	GDP per capita	7.8
2. Zero hunger	Food supply	7.5
8. Decent work and economic growth	Commercial banking	6.3
Other		17.8
Second phase (2021-2025)		
Goal	Indicator	Priority level (%)
8. Decent work and economic growth	Ease of doing business index (regulations)	17.2
3. Good health	Infant mortality	12.1
6. Clean water and sanitation	Water productivity	10.0
2. Zero hunger	Food supply	5.5
16. Peace, justice and strong institutions	Overall life satisfaction index	5.5
9. Industry, innovation and infrastructure	Trade and transport-related infrastructure	5.2
8. Decent work and economic growth	GDP per capita	4.8
4. Quality education	Education index (years of schooling)	4.5
4. Quality education	Secondary education	4.5
10. Reduced inequalities	Human inequality (health, education and income)	4.1
Other		26.6
Third phase (2026-2030)		
Goal	Indicator	Priority level (%)
16. Peace, justice and strong institutions	Overall life satisfaction index	12.1
6. Clean water and sanitation	Improved sanitation	9.7
3. Good health	Health index (life expectancy)	8.3
9. Industry, innovation and infrastructure	Internet users	7.2
9. Industry, innovation and infrastructure	Air transportation	6.9
9. Industry, innovation and infrastructure	Scientific and technical journal articles	6.6
2. Zero hunger	Agriculture value added	5.2
3. Good health	Infant mortality	4.8
4. Quality education	Secondary education	4.8
10. Reduced inequalities	Human inequality (health, education and income)	4.8
Other		29.7

Source: ESCAP.

Notes: Priority levels for the indicators are calculated as the percentage of steps in each phase for which the indicator is chosen as a priority relative to the total number of steps in each phase. See annex III for details.

for each indicator are calculated as the percentage of steps in each phase for which the indicator is chosen as a priority, relative to the total number of steps in each phase.[12]

The first characteristic of the optimal pathways for the implementation of the 2030 Agenda in the countries shown in tables 3.1-3.3 is a large concentration in a relatively small number of indicators. Although the top indicators for each country and phase shown in the tables represent 10% or less of the total number of indicators in the data, a small number of indicators concentrate around 80% of the steps taken by each country in each phase. This suggests a very strategic approach for the achievement of the Goals, with a heavy policy focus on selected areas of great importance to the country. A second characteristic of the optimal pathways is sequencing,

in the sense that the priorities vary from phase to phase. A third characteristic is that the results are dependent on each country's level of capacities and position in the SDG system, tending to emphasize "low hanging fruits" or indicators in which the country underperforms compared with other countries with similar levels of SDG capacities.

In the case of Bangladesh, the optimal pathway emphasizes improvements in education as the top priority area in the first phase (2016-2020), with 23.6% of the improvements directed towards increasing years of schooling and the percentage of the population with secondary education. This is consistent with the fact that Bangladesh is underperforming in Goal 4 (quality education), as shown in figure A.1 in annex III. Additional priority areas in the first phase include two inequality indicators representing

Table 3.2   **Top priority indicators for the implementation of the 2030 Agenda in Kazakhstan**

First phase (2016-2020)		
Goal	Indicator	Priority level (%)
9. Industry, innovation and infrastructure	Trade and transport-related infrastructure	23.7
2. Zero hunger	Agriculture value added	13.1
9. Industry, innovation and infrastructure	Air transportation	11.6
9. Industry, innovation and infrastructure	Scientific and technical journal articles	11.6
5. Gender equality	Gender inequality (health, empowerment and labour)	11.1
8. Decent work and economic growth	Commercial banking	10.6
9. Industry, innovation and infrastructure	Internet users	10.1
Other		8.1
Second phase (2021-2025)		
Goal	Indicator	Priority level (%)
8. Decent work and economic growth	Commercial banking	22.4
8. Decent work and economic growth	Ease of doing business index (regulations)	8.5
9. Industry, innovation and infrastructure	Air transportation	8.5
9. Industry, innovation and infrastructure	Scientific and technical journal articles	8.5
2. Zero hunger	Food supply	7.9
2. Zero hunger	Agriculture value added	6.7
8. Decent work and economic growth	GDP per capita	6.7
9. Industry, innovation and infrastructure	Fixed-telephone users	6.7
Other		24.2
Third phase (2026-2030)		
Goal	Indicator	Priority level (%)
6. Clean water and sanitation	Water productivity	34.5
3. Good health	Infant mortality	9.7
9. Industry, innovation and infrastructure	Air transportation	9.1
8. Decent work and economic growth	Ease of doing business index (regulations)	7.3
8. Decent work and economic growth	GDP per capita	6.7
2. Zero hunger	Agriculture value added	6.1
10. Reduced inequalities	Human inequality (health, education and income)	6.1
Other		20.6

Source: ESCAP.

Note: See note in table 3.1.

Table 3.3 Top priority indicators for the implementation of the 2030 Agenda in Fiji

First phase (2016-2020)		
Goal	**Indicator**	**Priority level (%)**
5. Gender equality	Gender inequality (health, empowerment and labour)	19.9
9. Industry, innovation and infrastructure	Trade and transport-related infrastructure	15.7
9. Industry, innovation and infrastructure	Fixed-telephone users	13.9
9. Industry, innovation and infrastructure	Internet users	12.0
8. Decent work and economic growth	GDP per capita	10.6
2. Zero hunger	Agriculture value added	8.3
Other		19.4
Second phase (2021-2025)		
Goal	**Indicator**	**Priority level (%)**
8. Decent work and economic growth	Commercial banking	12.2
9. Industry, innovation and infrastructure	Fixed-telephone users	11.1
2. Zero hunger	Food supply	10.0
9. Industry, innovation and infrastructure	Trade and transport-related infrastructure	9.4
10. Reduced inequalities	Human inequality (health, education and income)	8.3
8. Decent work and economic growth	GDP per capita	7.8
9. Industry, innovation and infrastructure	Scientific and technical journal articles	7.8
4. Quality education	Secondary education	7.2
5. Gender equality	Gender inequality (health, empowerment and labour)	6.7
Other		19.4
Third phase (2026-2030)		
Goal	**Indicator**	**Priority level (%)**
4. Quality education	Secondary education	15.8
8. Decent work and economic growth	Ease of doing business index (regulations)	14.7
2. Zero hunger	Agriculture value added	12.1
8. Decent work and economic growth	GDP per capita	10.0
9. Industry, innovation and infrastructure	Scientific and technical journal articles	7.8
9. Industry, innovation and infrastructure	Trade and transport-related infrastructure	7.2
9. Industry, innovation and infrastructure	Internet users	6.1
10. Reduced inequalities	Human inequality (health, education and income)	5.0
Other		21.3

Source: ESCAP.

Note: See note in table 3.1.

18.6% of the improvements, and two infrastructure indicators, representing 18.4% of the improvements. In the second phase (2021-2025), the top priority indicator for Bangladesh is ease of doing business (17.2%), followed by infant mortality (12.1%) and water productivity (10%). The two education indicators that are so highly prioritized in the first phase receive a lower, but still important, priority in the second phase (9.0%), further highlighting the urgency for Bangladesh to invest heavily in education early on.

In the third phase (2026-2030), overall life satisfaction becomes the top indicator on which Bangladesh should focus (12.1%), followed by improved sanitation (9.7%) and life expectancy (8.3%). Three infrastructure and innovations indicators — the Internet, air transportation and scientific and technical journal articles – represent 20.7% of the improvements in the third phase. The top priority of overall life satisfaction in this phase is consistent with the strong investments in education recommended for phase 1 and in ease of doing business in phase 2, as it is well documented that life satisfaction is positively related to human capital and governance.[13]

The top priority indicators for Kazakhstan differ greatly from and are much more concentrated than those for Bangladesh. In the first phase, three indicators related to transport and telecommunications infrastructure represent as much as 45.5% of the improvements. This heavy concentration on connectivity is understandable in light of the country's status of landlocked developing country. Some of these indicators, including scientific and technical journal articles (11.6%) and agriculture value added (13.1%) are of relatively high complexity, reflecting the high SDG capacities of Kazakhstan. In the second phase, the priority on transport and telecommunications infrastructure drops significantly, reinforcing the importance for the country to invest heavily and early on in this area. The top indicator in this phase is commercial banking (22.4%), for which the current level of attainment of Kazakhstan is currently very low, below the 2nd percentile, even less than Bangladesh, which stands at the 15th percentile. Expanding commercial banking thus seems like a reasonable "low hanging fruit" for Kazakhstan to choose.

In the third phase, the optimal pathway for progress in Kazakhstan identifies water productivity, measured as GDP per cubic metre of total freshwater withdrawal, as the key area for improvement, with a priority level of 34.5%. Such results highlight the specific circumstances of Kazakhstan, which has an attainment level for water productivity close to the 3rd percentile and the fact that the country has traditionally experienced water deficits, relying heavily on neighbouring Kyrgyzstan for the bulk of its water supply. The emergence of water productivity as a driving factor in the latter phase may signal the need for Kazakhstan to diversify its output base, which is dominated by oil production, to other less water-intensive sectors as the economy develops toward maturity.[14]

The optimal pathway of Fiji has some similarities with that of Kazakhstan. For instance, both countries assign a high priority to transport and telecommunications infrastructure in the first phase, totalling 41.6% of the improvements in the case of Fiji. This could be explained by the high cost of international trade, which characterizes both landlocked developing countries and small island developing States. Interestingly, the composition of this initial high investment in infrastructure is different for both countries, with Fiji assigning a significantly larger role to telecommunications. This may be due to Fiji's larger distance from international markets, which may make the cost of international trade in services lower compared with merchandize trade. Another similarity is the top priority of commercial banking in the second phase in Fiji, although with a lower level of priority (12.2%) than in the case of Kazakhstan. These similarities could be related to the fact that both countries have similar and relatively high levels of SDG capacities, which enables them to focus on relatively complex indicators such as banking. A peculiarity of Fiji is the strong priority accorded to gender inequality (19.9%) in the first phase. This could be due to the fact that the current level of attainment of Fiji in the gender inequality index is around the 25th percentile, substantially lower than other countries with similar levels of SDG capacities.

Figures 3.7 to 3.9 illustrate the relative importance of each Goal during subsequent phases of development for Bangladesh, Kazakhstan and Fiji. For Bangladesh, Goal 4 (quality education), Goal 8 (decent work and economic growth) and Goal 9 (industry, innovation and infrastructure) are important early on. Both for

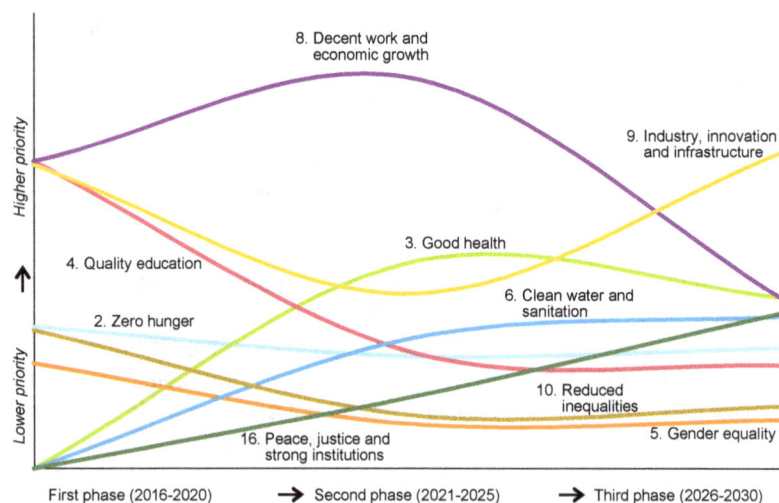

Figure 3.7 Priority Goals for the implementation of the 2030 Agenda in Bangladesh

First phase (2016-2020) → Second phase (2021-2025) → Third phase (2026-2030)

Source: ESCAP.

Figure 3.8   Priority Goals for the implementation of the 2030 Agenda in Kazakhstan

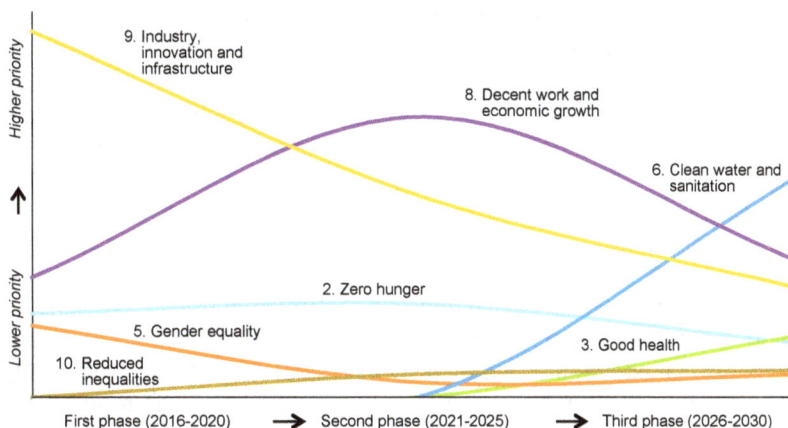

Source: ESCAP.

Figure 3.9   Priority Goals for the implementation of the 2030 Agenda in Fiji

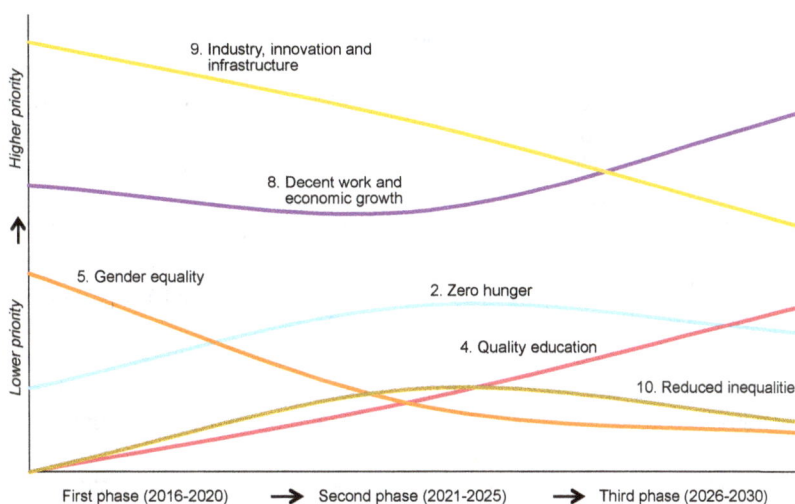

Source: ESCAP.

Kazakhstan and Fiji, Goal 9 (industry, innovation and infrastructure) is extremely important early on, but its importance quickly diminishes in later phases, giving way to other Goals such as clean water and sanitation for Kazakhstan and economic growth and quality education for Fiji. For Bangladesh, the U-shaped curve for Goal 9 is representative of the relative importance of basic infrastructure early on and the increasing importance of innovation and industry in the latter phases and as such is consistent with patterns for infrastructure development highlighted for Kazakhstan and Fiji. As mentioned above, the optimal pathway for Bangladesh assigns high priority to core social Goals such as education and health, which

is understandable given its relatively less developed status and lower level of endowed SDG capacity.

5.2. Identifying bottlenecks in developing Sustainable Development Goal capacities

The optimal pathways, illustrated in the previous section for the cases of Bangladesh, Kazakhstan and Fiji, are built so that they focus on improving the indicators in the most effective manner. This implies, as previously discussed, a preference for indicators in which the country is lagging behind compared with other countries with similar SDG capacities, for instance to take advantage of agglomeration economies, as well as for indicators that are relatively less complex and thus easier to make progress faster on them. The discussion in the previous section provided some examples of these choices. The present section complements the previous discussion by showing graphically the progress of the three countries in the implementation of the 2030 Agenda in their respective indicators networks.

In the indicator networks for Bangladesh, Kazakhstan and Fiji shown in figures 3.10 to 3.12, the red nodes represent indicators in which the countries are performing better than other countries with similar levels of SDG capacity (their "peers") at present.[15] The green nodes represent indicators in which the country is progressing from below the mean for the peer group at present to above the mean in 2030. These indicators are prioritized in the optimal pathway, indicating that improving their attainment is effective for the country. Finally, the white nodes represent indicators that are still below the average for the country's peers by 2030. These are indicators for which the country may have found difficulties in making much progress, either because of their complexity or because of the absence of synergies with other nearby indicators in the network. Some of the white nodes are large, representing indicators that are "important" within the network because of the number and strength of their connections with other indicators or because of their positions as "gatekeepers" between separate clusters of indicators. We refer to them as bottlenecks.

Figure 3.10 shows that the optimal pathway of Bangladesh for the implementation of the 2030 Agenda includes improvements in indicators that are near other indicators in which Bangladesh is already performing better than its peers. These indicators, which are mostly clustered in the bottom portion of the network, include the gender index, GDP per capita, average years of schooling and human inequality. The top portion of the network shows a cluster of indicators in which Bangladesh will not be able to outperform its peers by the year 2030. These include high-complexity indicators such as tax revenue, the percentage of high-tech exports and export diversification as well as some indicators broadly related to health and infrastructure. The depiction of the optimal pathway of Bangladesh also shows a number of bottlenecks, represented by large white nodes. These include poverty headcount, poverty gap ratio, the prevalence of tuberculosis and urban sanitation.

Figure 3.11 shows that the optimal pathway of Kazakhstan includes improvements in indicators such as Internet usage, scientific journal articles, the

business environment and agriculture value-added, for which complexity is relatively high. Much like Bangladesh, however, by 2030 Kazakhstan is still predicted to need improvements in indicators clustered at the top portion of the network. Considering that Kazakhstan has a high initial level of SDG capacity and will have significantly higher levels of SDG capacities by 2030 by following the optimal pathway, the indicators in which Kazakhstan will fail to improve its performance are more related to the country's specific circumstances than to the complexity of the indicators themselves.

Kazakhstan currently has attainment levels at the very bottom, close to the 1st percentile, in indicators such as natural resource depletion, CO_2 emissions per capita and per $1 GDP and renewable energy consumption. While Kazakhstan is expected to outperform its peers in some indicators in the top cluster, such as commercial banking and water productivity, the network representation suggests that tackling bottlenecks, such as drinking water provision, increased life expectancy and preventing tuberculosis, would further augment the process of developing SDG capacities.

Figure 3.12 shows that the main bottleneck to the implementation of the 2030 Agenda in Fiji is access to electricity. The importance of electricity access for Fiji and other Pacific island economies, which was discussed in chapter 1, can be seen by its role as a gatekeeper between the top and bottom portions of the network and by its strong relationships with many other indicators. The figure shows that most of the progress of Fiji by 2030 is expected to take place in the lower portion of the network. This suggests that addressing this important bottleneck will be necessary for Fiji to make progress in the upper portion of the network.

The network representations for the three countries suggest that indicators broadly related to environmental sustainability are less central to the development of SDG capacities than socioeconomic indicators. For Bangladesh, indicators related to Goals 13 (climate action), Goal 14 (life below water) and Goal 15 (life on land) are located in the periphery and are only connected to the core of the network through relatively weak links. The same is true for Kazakhstan, where indicators such as protected terrestrial areas, renewable energy output, air pollution and renewable internal freshwater resources are located at the edge of the network, and for Fiji.

It should be noted that the three countries, with the exception of Kazakhstan for natural resources and CO_2 emissions indicators, have relatively high initial levels

Figure 3.10 Progress across indicators in Bangladesh

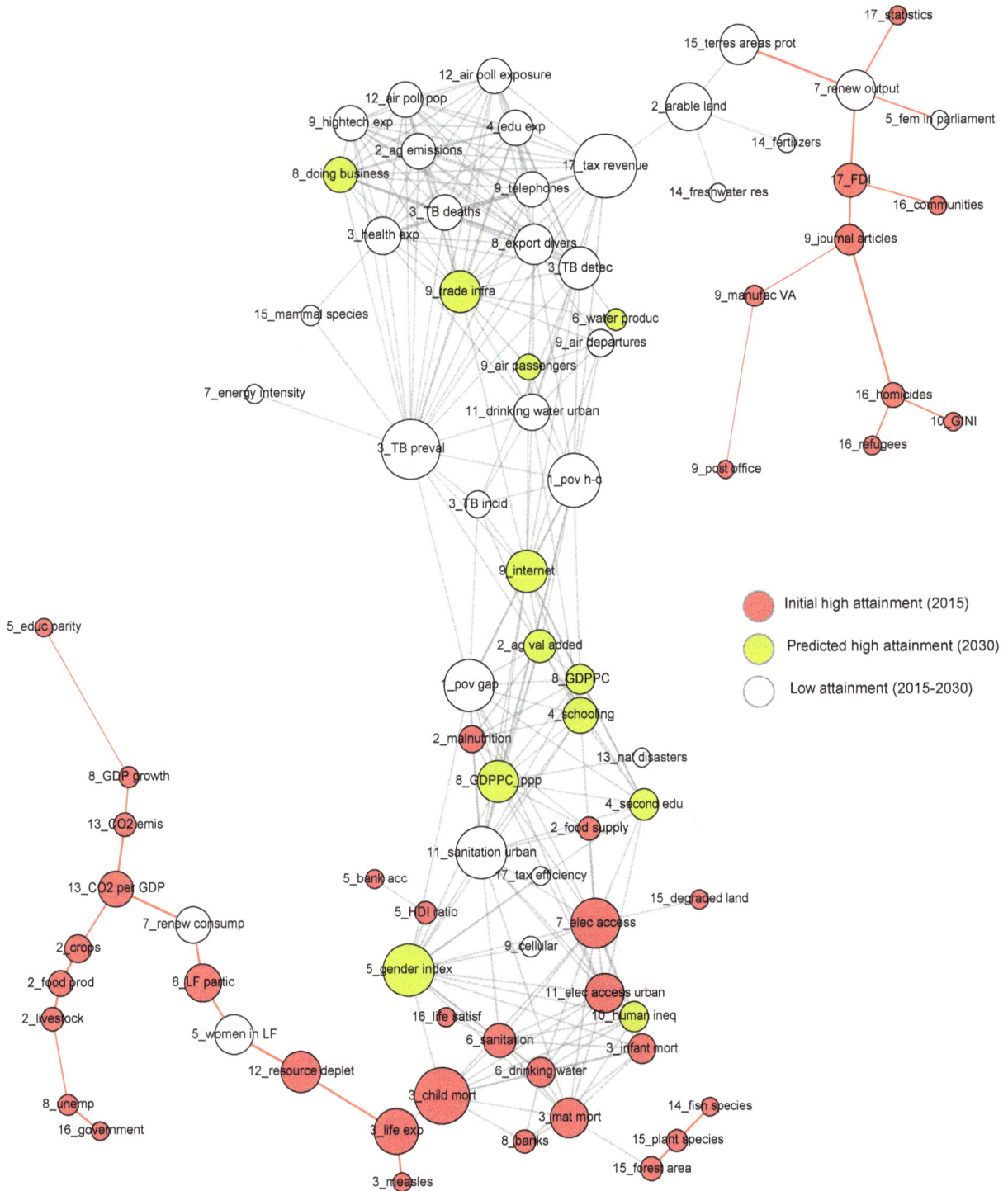

Source: ESCAP.

Notes: (a) The red links represent proximity values that are less than 0.75; (b) the size of indicators is based on the average of weighted degree and betweenness centrality; and (c) indicators are coloured based on the level of attainment of Bangladesh compared with its peers, identified as those countries with similar levels of SDG capacity. Red indicators are those in which Bangladesh exhibits higher attainment levels compared with its peers at the present, while green indicators are those in which Bangladesh is predicted to exhibit higher attainment levels relative to its peers in 2030 if it follows the optimal pathway. See annex III.

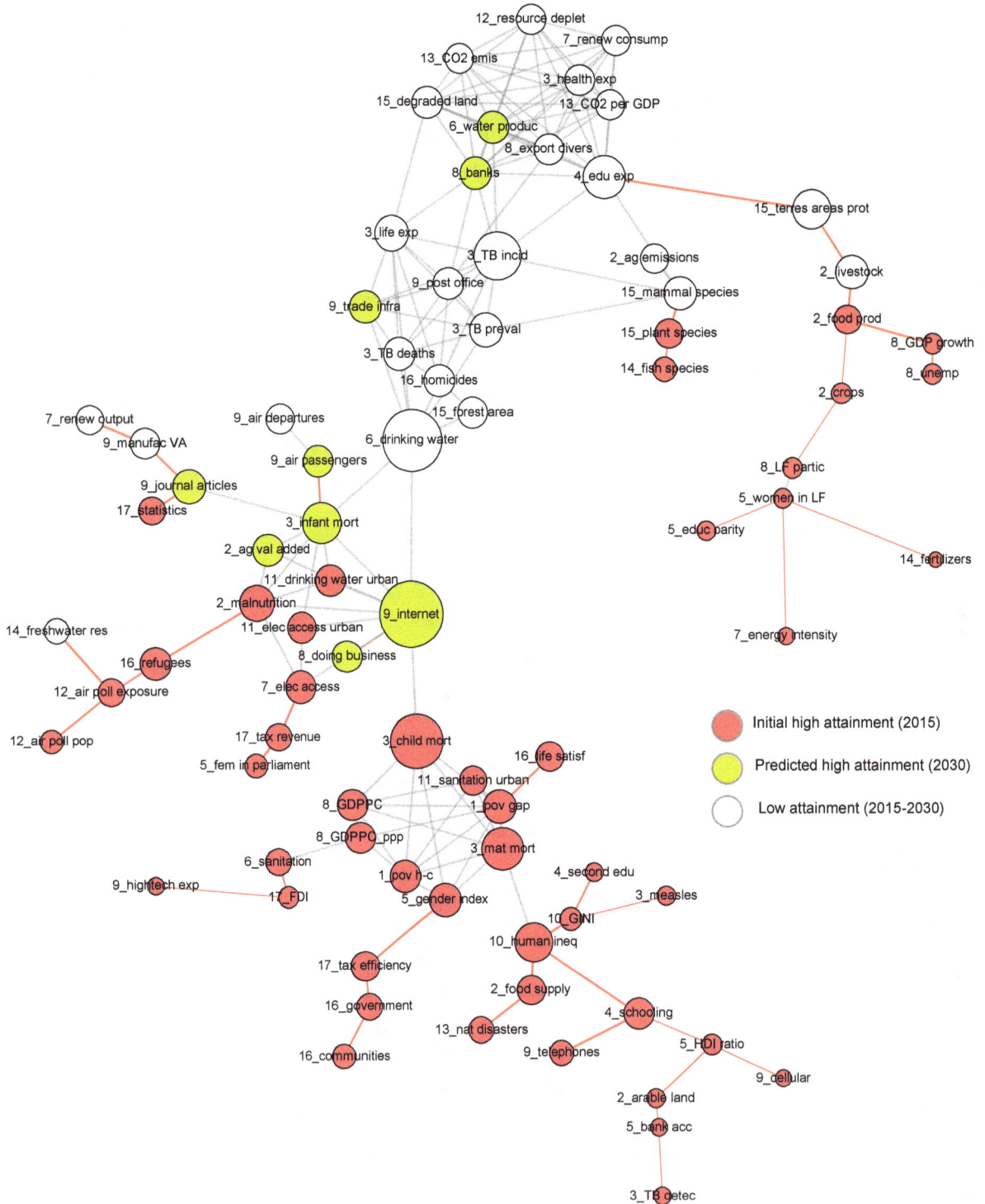

Figure 3.11 Progress across indicators in Kazakhstan

Legend:
- Initial high attainment (2015)
- Predicted high attainment (2030)
- Low attainment (2015-2030)

Source: ESCAP.

Note: See notes for figure 3.10.

Figure
3.12

Progress across indicators in Fiji

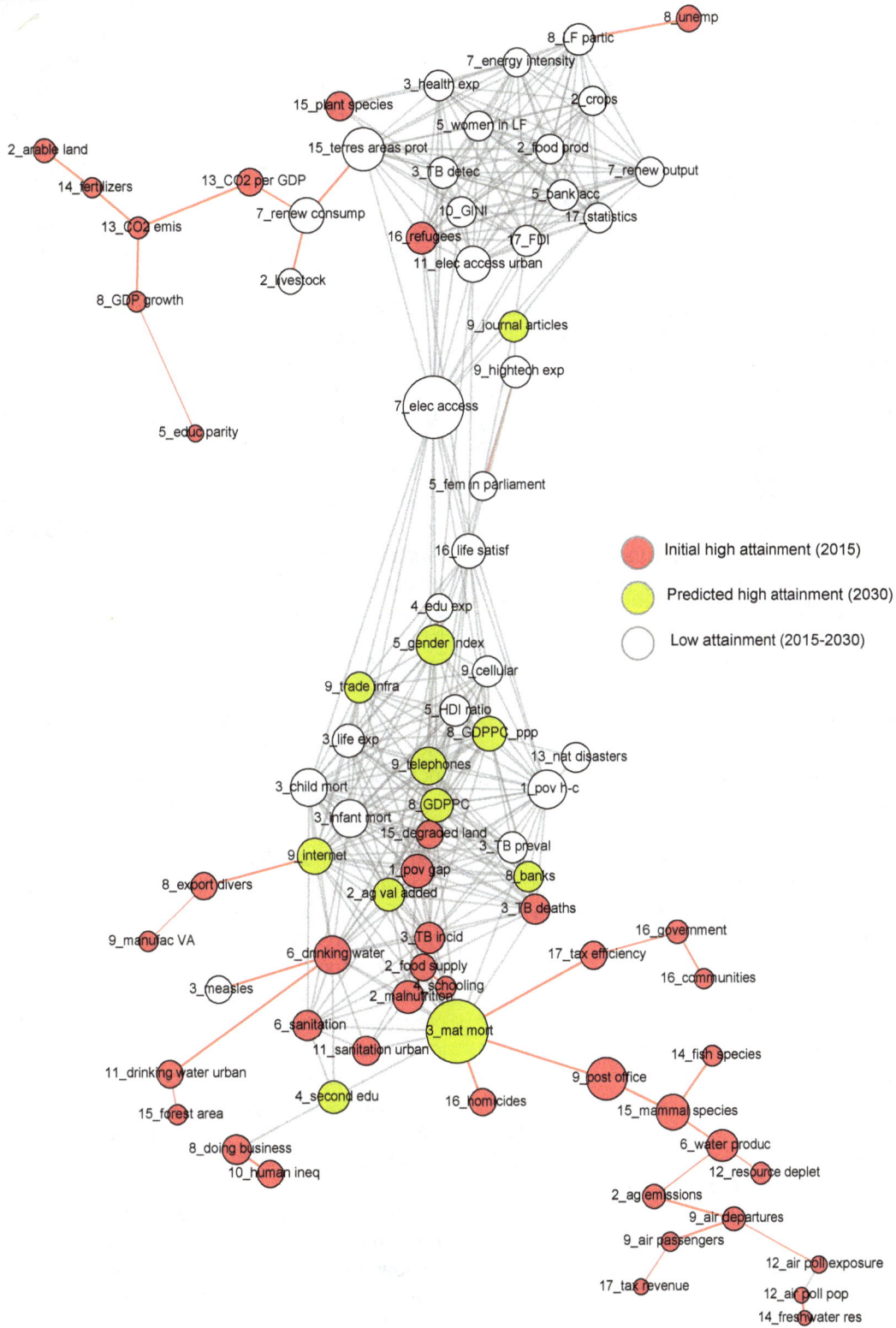

Legend:
- Initial high attainment (2015)
- Predicted high attainment (2030)
- Low attainment (2015-2030)

Source: ESCAP.

Note: See notes for figure 3.10.

of attainment in environmental indicators. However, none of the green nodes in the countries' network representations is related to the environmental Goals. This could be explained by the peripheral position of environmental indicators. In the absence of synergies represented by dense connections with other indicators, it is relatively more costly to make progress in the environmental indicators. In a similar fashion to the bottlenecks identified in the present section, the absence of progress in the environmental pillar may require special consideration both by national policy makers and by the international community.

5.3 Scenario analysis

The present section compares predicted time series of SDG capacities for the optimal paths and two alternative scenarios.[16] In addition to the optimal scenario, two alternative scenarios are analysed: (a) the pathway that countries follow when they make improvements only on selected Goals associated with the main areas of focus of their respective programmes of action; and (b) a random pathway, which does not give precedence to any particular indicator. The Goals associated with the main areas of focus of a programme of action are those for which the programme of action covers 50% or more of their targets.

As can be seen in table 2.4 of chapter 2, this criterion implies the following areas of focus for each programme of action:

(a) Istanbul Programme of Action: Goal 1 (no poverty), Goal 2 (zero hunger), Goal 4 (quality education), Goal 6 (clean water and sanitation), Goal 7 (affordable and clean energy), Goal 8 (decent work and economic growth), Goal 9 (industry, innovation and infrastructure), Goal 10 (reduced inequalities), Goal 13 (climate action), Goal 16 (peace, justice and strong institutions) and Goal 17 (partnerships for the Goals);

(b) Vienna Programme of Action: Goal 7 (affordable and clean energy) and Goal 9 (industry, innovation and infrastructure);

(c) Samoa Pathway: Goal 2 (zero hunger), Goal 5 (gender equality), Goal 6 (clean water and sanitation), Goal 13 (climate action), Goal 14 (life below water) and Goal 15 (life on land).

The random pathway for progress assumes that countries do not optimize their SDG capacities, randomly choosing indicators for improvement. While this third scenario is rather extreme and unrealistic, it serves as a baseline for comparison purposes. It could also represent a situation in which there is no policy coordination among various government agencies and levels of Government.

Figure 3.13 compares the three scenarios in Bangladesh, Kazakhstan and Fiji. For the three countries, the optimal pathway results in higher levels of SDG capacities compared with the pathway obtained from addressing only the main areas of focus of their respective programmes of action, with the random pathway leading to low or negligible increases in SDG capacities. For comparison purposes, the figure shows the historical trends in the human development index for each country expressed in terms of SDG capacities.[17]

The most interesting differences across countries are those between Bangladesh and the two other countries. In the case of Bangladesh, the optimal pathway and the pathway defined by the Istanbul Programme of Action follow almost identical courses up to 2025, after which the optimal pathway results in a slightly faster growth in SDG capacities. This suggests that the Istanbul Programme of Action is both comprehensive and a good match for the priorities of Bangladesh as regards implementing the 2030 Agenda. The predicted trajectories in SDG capacities associated with both the optimal pathway and the pathway defined by the Istanbul Programme of Action exceed the historical trend of the human development index.

In contrast, in the cases of Kazakhstan and Fiji, the optimal scenarios are predicted to bring about increases in SDG capacities that are substantially higher than the pathway derived from considering only the focus areas of the Vienna Programme of Action and the Samoa Pathway. In the case of the Vienna Programme of Action, this is due to the fact that only Goals 7 and 9 satisfy the criterion for inclusion in the scenario described above. Although Goal 9 is very important to Kazakhstan, as is clear from table 3.2 above, focusing exclusively on infrastructure prevents the country from exploiting synergies between infrastructure and other areas of the 2030 Agenda. This is illustrated by the proximity in the network of Kazakhstan (figure 3.11) of indicators such as the Internet, air transport, ease of doing business, agriculture value added and child mortality.

The figure shows that Fiji also performs poorly when the country focuses exclusively on a relatively small number of Goals. To be sure, the Samoa Pathway covers almost all the Goals of the 2030 Agenda and addresses the social, economic and environmental pillars in a balanced manner. However, when applying the criterion of including in the scenario only Goals for

Figure 3.13 Comparison of scenarios

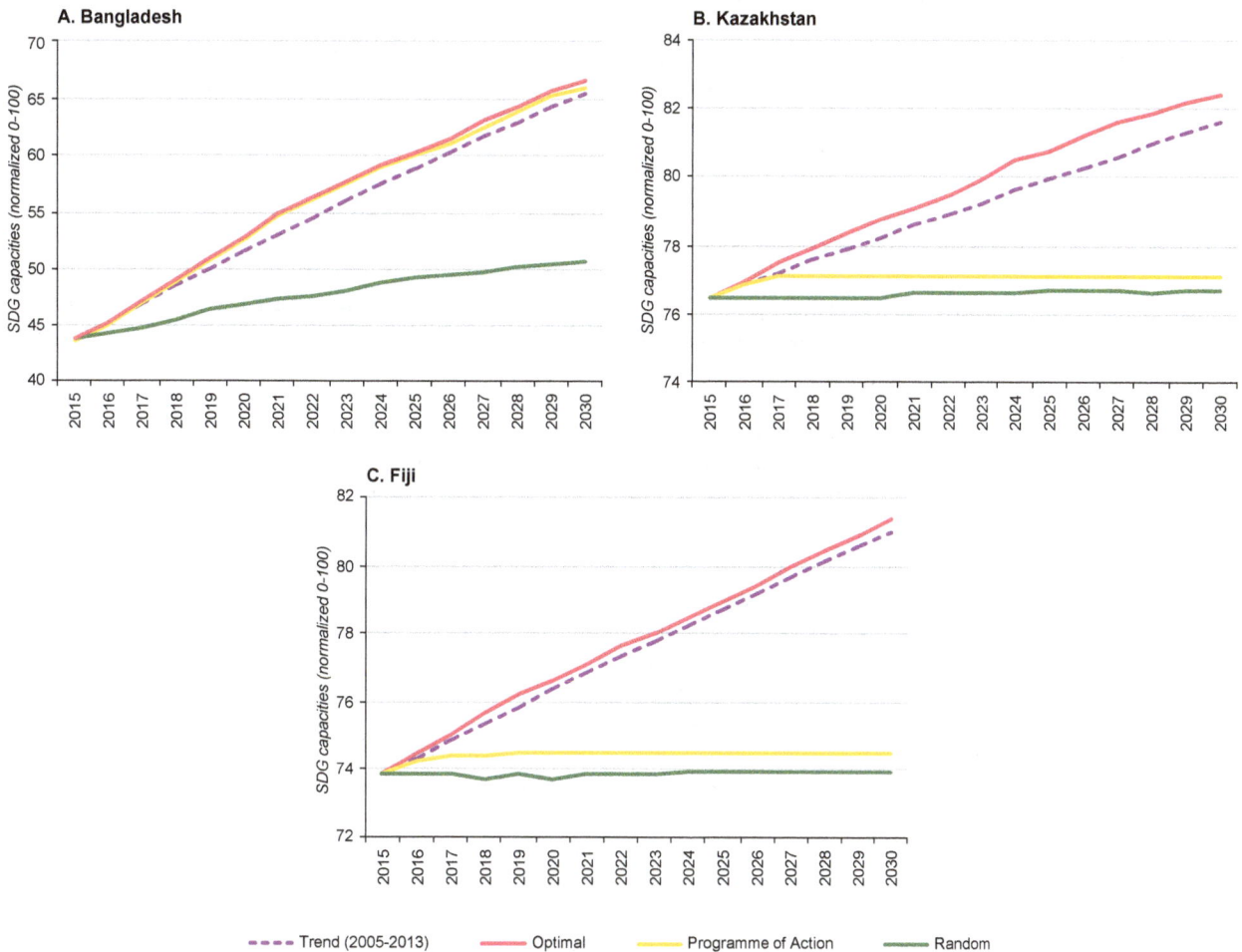

A. Bangladesh

B. Kazakhstan

C. Fiji

- - - Trend (2005-2013) —— Optimal —— Programme of Action —— Random

Source: ESCAP.

Note: See annex III for details about the construction of this figure.

which the Samoa Pathway covers more than 50% of their targets, only Goals 2, 5, 6, 13, 14 and 15 are selected. Of these six Goals, Fiji prioritizes only Goals 2 and 5 in its optimal pathway (table 3.3). As shown in figure 3.9, this leaves out the important priority assigned in the optimal pathway to Goal 8 (decent work and economic growth) and Goal 9 (industry, innovation and infrastructure), as well to other areas with lower but still meaningful priority, such as Goal 4 (quality education) and Goal 10 (reduced inequalities). As in the case of Kazakhstan, restricting the indicators for improvement prevents Fiji from exploiting synergies among indicators, such as those between agriculture value added and the Internet or between the gender index and trade infrastructure (figure 3.12).

In sum, the results show that although the main areas of focus of the Istanbul Programme of Action

provide very good guidance for the implementation of the 2030 Agenda in Bangladesh, those of the Vienna Programme of Action and the Samoa Pathway are too limited to boost sustainable development in, respectively, Kazakhstan and Fiji. To be sure, the criterion of restricting the choice of indicators to Goals for which a programme of action covers 50% or more of their targets may be too strict, and it would be desirable to explore other criteria for the alternative scenarios. The main conclusion of the present section is, however, very clear. It tells us that restricting the indicators may impede the exploitation of synergies across indicators from different areas. Taking full advantage of such synergies, which requires an understanding of the position of a country in the SDG system, can allow the country to make significantly more progress in boosting its SDG capacities and moving faster towards the attainment of the Goals.

CONCLUDING REMARKS

The present chapter has proposed a solution to the very complex problem of how to best prioritize and sequence the attainment of the Goals in the most effective manner, taking into account the unique circumstances, capacities and levels of development of individual countries. The solution is based on viewing a set of 82 indicators that are representative of the 17 Goals and 174 countries for which data are available as comprising a complex system, referred to as the SDG system. The SDG system provides detailed information on the interlinkages, synergies and trade-offs across different indicators from the viewpoint of each individual country. The SDG system also allows the calculation of a summary measure of the attainment of the Goals for individual countries, which we refer to as SDG capacities. This summary measure, along with information in the SDG system, allows us to obtain optimal, country-specific pathways of progress towards the Goals.

The present chapter illustrates the use of the proposed analytical framework to derive optimal pathways towards the Goals in three countries: Bangladesh, Kazakhstan and Fiji. The optimal pathways for the three countries have similarities in that they strongly prioritize attainment in a relatively small number of indicators, and that such priorities are sequenced over time. Another common characteristic is that the countries' priorities tend to include "low hanging fruits" or indicators in which the country underperforms compared with other countries with similar levels of SDG capacities.

In spite of these common, general characteristics, the specific indicators prioritized in each country are unique and distinct. In Bangladesh, for instance, the first phase (2016-2020) of the optimal pathway has a strong focus on education, reduction of inequalities and infrastructure. The first two elements could be related to the importance of human capital for a country to increase the diversification and sophistication of its production and the potential for a more even distribution of income to boost aggregate demand. In Kazakhstan and Fiji, which are more advanced countries than Bangladesh, the focus of the first phase is overwhelmingly on infrastructure. However, the composition of this initial high investment in infrastructure is different for both countries, with Fiji assigning a significantly larger role to telecommunications. This may be due to the greater distance of Fiji from international markets, which may make the cost of international trade in services lower compared with merchandize trade.

The analysis of the optimal pathways also uncovers a number of country-specific bottlenecks, defined as indicators in which the country is not expected to make substantial progress by 2030 that are highly connected with other indicators. The optimal pathways also show a perplexing lack of progress in the environmental indicators, which is explained by their peripheral location in the network representations of the countries analysed. Such a peripheral position indicates a lack of synergies both among the environmental indicators and between them and the socioeconomic indicators, which makes it relatively more costly to address them. The importance of taking into account synergies in planning how to prioritize and sequence the attainment of the Goals is also a strong message from the analyses of alternative scenarios. Finally, the very low performance of SDG capacities in the random pathways justifies the need for policy coordination across government agencies and levels of Government.

Identifying country-specific bottlenecks and under-performing indicators through the derivation of optimal pathways for the implementation of the 2030 Agenda is important because they may call for special measures to address them. This information is useful to both national policymakers and development partners, as they could contribute to maximizing the efficacy of support measures.

Endnotes

1 Multiple imputation utilizes information on the relationships among all 82 indicators, as well as with other indicators, such as nominal GDP, population, population growth and land area, to predict missing values. See Rubin (2004).

2 As in chapter 2, Asia-Pacific CSN that fit into more than one category are grouped so that least developed countries that are also landlocked developing countries or small island developing States are classified as least developed countries.

3 See figure A.1 in annex III. It shows the top-3 Goals, the bottom-3 Goals and the average attainment across all Goals in the 22 CSN for which data for the indicators were available, expressed as percentage deviations from the respective country-group average.

4 See, for example: Arthur (1991; 1999 and 2014); Arthur, Durlauf and Lane (1997); Hidalgo and Hausmann (2009); Hidalgo and others (2007); ICSU and ISSC (2015); and Meadowcroft (2007).

5 See also Le Blanc (2015).

6 The measure of proximity used in this report is based on conditional probabilities, similarly to the one proposed by Hidalgo and others (2007) to make inferences about capacities to export different products. See annex III for details.

7 The figure is constructed so that all indicators are first connected to its closest indicator, forming a skeleton that represents the backbone of the network. Afterwards, links representing probabilities of 0.75 or more are added to this skeleton to differentiate between indicators that are in close proximity to other indicators and indicators that are relatively distant from others. Notice that network diagrams like this are country specific. Figure 3.2 is based on the average values of the indicators for the Asia-Pacific CSN rather than on those for a specific country.

8 Using network theoretic terminology, "importance" is calculated here as the average of an indicator's weighted degree centrality and betweenness centrality. See annex III for more details.

9 Although at the time of writing the official set of indicators has not been finalized, the methodology presented in this chapter can be easily applied to increasingly more complete sets of indicators, eventually including the final list of official indicators.

10 Annex III provides technical details of the optimization problem. See also Cho, Isgut and Tateno (2016a).

11 Beside their representation of the three groups of CSN, the selected countries were chosen on the basis of their data availability: Bangladesh and Kazakhstan had data available for all 82 indicators, while Fiji had data for 75 indicators. See Cho, Isgut and Tateno (2016b) for an application of the proposed analytical framework to Pakistan.

12 Each step represents a small increase in the value of an indicator. The number of steps in each phase is country specific and is derived from historical trends in the human development index, which are used to determine the amount of effort a country is able to exert annually for capacity improvement. See annex III for details.

13 See, for example, Abdallah, Thompson and Marks (2008) and Helliwell and Huang (2008).

14 In 2010, global withdrawals of water for energy production were estimated by the International Energy Agency (2012) to be 583 billion cubic metres or 15% of the world's total water withdrawals. Based on data in current United States dollars from the United Nations National Accounts Main Aggregates Database, the share of mining and utilities in world GDP was 7% that year. Therefore, it is clear that energy is a highly water-intensive sector.

15 A country's peers are defined as a group of 20 countries comprising those that occupy the 10 positions in the ranking of SDG capacities immediately above and immediately below the country. See annex III.

16 To estimate the predicted time series of SDG capacities from the cross-sectional data used in the analysis, a number of steps, described in annex III, were taken. In essence, the calculation involved estimating how many steps countries are likely to undertake each year to increase SDG capacities based on the historical trends of increases in the human development index. This allows each country to be assigned SDG capacity values each year.

17 The regression equation shown in figure 3.6 is used to convert predicted values from historical trends of the human development index into SDG capacities.

CONCLUSION

Although the Asia-Pacific CSN are advancing towards meeting the targets of their programmes of action, they continue to face structural bottlenecks that hamper the development of adequate productive capacities, making sustainable development difficult and expensive. The report finds that 7 of the 12 Asia-Pacific least developed countries have already met the conditions for graduation and three more of them are likely to meet them in the next triennial review of the Committee for Development Policy. However, the report also finds that most least developed countries, particularly small island developing States, have very high levels of economic vulnerability, which casts doubts on their ability to sustain development gains in the long run.

A few landlocked developing countries were highly successful in reducing transit times or improving information and communications technology connectivity, but the majority continues to experience serious challenges in these areas, as well as in diversifying their production. A number of small island developing States have been investing in renewable energy to reduce their exposure to volatile prices of imported fossil fuels. However, investing in renewable energy is characterized by high initial cost of technology, challenges to find solutions that are appropriate for small tropical island conditions, and difficulties in accessing international sources of finance.

The report finds differences in the degree and intensity of coverage of the Sustainable Development Goals by the three programmes of action. The Istanbul Programme of Action covers all three pillars of sustainable development, while placing greater emphasis on the social pillar. The Samoa Pathway also covers the three pillars of sustainable development, but with its focus on the environmental pillar. In sharp contrast, the Vienna Programme of Action is focused just on the economic pillar. All three programmes of action cover governance and means of implementation. Remarkably, the opinion of experts and practitioners on the prioritization and sequencing of the Goals in CSN coincides with the focus areas set forth in the programmes of action of their respective country groups. This suggests that specific actions agreed in such programmes can provide guidance to Governments for the implementation of the 2030 Agenda.

The unique analytical framework proposed in this report allows for the identification of optimal strategies of implementation of the Goals, including specific recommendations for the prioritization and sequencing necessary to achieve each Goal. The report illustrates the functioning of the framework in three CSN: Bangladesh, Kazakhstan and Fiji.

In Bangladesh, for instance, the initial priority is on education, reduction of inequalities and infrastructure.

The first two elements could be related to the importance of human capital for a country to increase the diversification and sophistication of its production and the potential for a more even distribution of income to boost aggregate demand. In Kazakhstan and Fiji, which are more advanced countries than Bangladesh, the initial priority is overwhelmingly on infrastructure. However, the composition of this initial high investment in infrastructure is different for both countries, with Fiji assigning a significantly larger role to telecommunications. This may be due to the greater distance of Fiji from international markets, which may make the cost of international trade in services lower compared with merchandize trade.

The exercise allows not only the identification of optimal strategies but also of indicators that can be considered as bottlenecks for progress and isolated areas of the country networks that represent trade-offs. An important regularity found in the three countries was the absence of progress in the environmental Goals of the 2030 Agenda. As discussed in chapter 3, this result seems to be due to the isolation of the environmental indicators in the countries' networks from the core socioeconomic indicators. This finding suggests that the integration of the three pillars envisioned in the 2030 Agenda is not going to be easy to achieve.

Both the lack of progress of the environmental pillar and the identification of bottlenecks that can potentially impede progress in the attainment of the Goals require careful consideration by national policymakers and development partners. With respect to the latter, they could contribute to focusing the support of the international community on sectors that require the most attention and for which additional financial resources could be most effectively allocated.

A comparison of different scenarios strongly suggests the importance of a thorough understanding of linkages, synergies and trade-offs across Goals, as well as the relative benefits of different implementation plans for each country. Devising an implementation plan based on a narrow selection of sectors could result in a substantially lower attainment of the Goals. The main areas of focus of the Istanbul Programme of Action provide good guidance for the implementation of the 2030 Agenda in least developed countries. However, those of the Vienna Programme of Action and the Samoa Pathway may be limited to boost sustainable development in, respectively landlocked developing countries and small island developing States.

To be sure, the results presented in this report are only preliminary, as the official list of indicators for the 2030 Agenda was not yet available at the time of writing. Future editions of the *Asia-Pacific Countries with Special Needs Development Report* will update the proposed analytical framework on the basis of the most up-to-date data, with the objective of eventually including all the official indicators. In the meantime, we believe that the proposed analytical framework, even if preliminary, can provide useful inputs for discussions on how to adapt the 2030 Agenda at the national level. While analytical results should never be the only basis to support policy decisions, they can nevertheless provide new perspectives and information, which could motivate further explorations and analyses providing a more solid basis for the adoption of policies.

REFERENCES

Abdallah, Saamah, Sam Thompson, and Nic Marks (2008). Estimating worldwide life satisfaction. *Ecological Economics*, vol. 65, pp. 35-47.

Arthur, W. Brian (1991). Designing economic agents that act like human agents: a behavioral approach to bounded rationality. *The American Economic Review*, vol. 81, No. 2, pp. 353-359.

_____ (1999). Complexity and the Economy. *Science*, vol. 284, No. 5411, pp. 107-109.

_____ (2014). *Complexity and the Economy*. New York: Oxford University Press.

Arthur, W. Brain, Steven N. Durlauf, and David A. Lane, eds. (1997). *The Economy as an Evolving Complex System II*, vol. 28. Reading, MA: Addison-Wesley.

Asian Development Bank (2015). *Pacific Energy Report*. Manila.

Azerbaijan (2008). State program on poverty reduction and sustainable development in the Republic of Azerbaijan for 2008-2015, 15 September. Available from www.cled.az/pdf/others/Azerbaijan%20Poverty%20Program%20 for%202008-2015.pdf.

Bhattacharya, Debapriya and Umme Shefa Rezbana (forthcoming). *Challenges of Implementing SDGs at the National Level: Lessons from Nine Country Studies*. Southern Voice Occasional Paper, No. 33. Dhaka: Centre for Policy Dialogue.

Bhattacharya, Debapriya, and others (2013). *Lagging Behind: Lessons from the Least Developed Countries for a Development Agenda Post-2015*. Perspective Series, November. Dhaka: Friedrich-Ebert-Stiftung (FES). Available from http://library.fes.de/pdf-files/iez/10354.pdf.

_____ (2016). *Five Challenges of Implementing SDGs in the Developing Countries: Early Experience from Bangladesh*. Southern Voice Occasional Paper, No. 32. Dhaka: Centre for Policy Dialogue.

Brauer, Michael, and others (2015). Ambient air pollution exposure estimation for the global burden of disease 2013. *Environmental Science & Technology*, 23 November.

Cho, Jaebeum, Alberto Isgut and Yusuke Tateno (2016a). An analytical framework for identifying optimal pathways towards sustainable development. MPFD Working Papers, WP/16/03. Bangkok: ESCAP.

_____ (2016b). Pathways for adapting the Sustainable Development Goals to the national context: the case of Pakistan. MPFD Working Papers, WP/16/04. Bangkok: ESCAP.

Coase, Ronald (1998). The new institutional economics. *The American Economic Review*, vol. 88, No. 2, pp. 72-74.

Dornan, Matthew (2014). Access to electricity in small developing States of the Pacific: issues and challenges. *Renewable and Sustainable Energy Reviews*, vol. 31, pp. 726-735.

Fiji, Ministry of Strategic Planning, National Development and Statistics (2014). *A Green Growth Framework for Fiji: Restoring the Balance in Development that is Sustainable for Our Future*. Suva.

Guillaumont, Patrick (2015). Measuring vulnerability to climate change for allocating funds for adaptation. Working Paper, P136 (October). Clermont-Ferrand, France: Foundation for International Development Study and Research (FERDIi).

Helliwell, John F., and Haifang Huang (2008). How's your government? International evidence linking good government and well-being. *British Journal of Political Science*, vol. 38, No. 04 (October), pp. 595-619.

Hidalgo, César A., and Ricardo Hausmann (2009). The building blocks of economic complexity. *Proceedings of the National Academy of Sciences*, vol. 106, No. 26, pp. 10570-10575.

Hidalgo, César A., and others (2007). The product space conditions the development of nations. *Science*, vol. 317, No. 5837, pp. 482-487.

International Council for Science, and International Social Science Council (2015). *Review of Targets for the Sustainable Development Goals: The Science Perspective*. Paris: International Council for Science (ICSU).

International Energy Agency (2012). *World Energy Outlook 2012*. Paris: OECD/IEA.

_____ (2014). *The Power of Transformation - Wind, Sun, and the Economics of Flexible Systems*. Paris: Organisation for Economic Co-operation and Development/International Energy Agency.

International Renewable Energy Agency (2014). *Renewable Islands: Settings for Success*. Abu Dhabi.

_____ (2015). *Fiji Renewables Readiness Assessment*. Abu Dhabi.

Isgut, Alberto, and others (forthcoming). Complementarities between the global programmes of action and the 2030 Agenda for Sustainable Development. MPFD Working Papers. Bangkok: ESCAP.

Jacomy, M, and others (2014). ForceAtlas2, a continuous graph layout algorithm for handy network visualization designed for the Gepgi software. *PloS One*, vol.9, No.6, e98679.

Johnston, Peter (2012). Pacific perspectives on the challenges to energy security and the sustainable use of energy. Paper prepared for the Asian and Pacific Energy Forum (APEF). Vladivostok, Russian Federation, 27-30 May.

Lao People's Democratic Republic (2014). Country report of the implementation of the Almaty Programme of Action. November. Available from www.lldc2conference.org/custom-content/uploads/2014/06/Lao-PDR-Report-English.pdf.

LDC IV Monitor (2014). *Istanbul Programme of Action for the LDCs (2011–2020): Monitoring Deliverables, Tracking Progress – Synthesis Report*. Dhaka: Centre for Policy Dialogue (CPD). Available from http://ldc4monitor.org/wp-content/uploads/2015/06/istanbul-programme-of-action-for-the-ldcs-2011-2020-monitoring-deliverables-tracking-progress-synthesis-report.pdf.

Le Blanc, David (2015). Towards integration at last? The sustainable development goals as a network of targets. Working Paper, No. 141. New York: DESA.

Meadowcroft, James (2007). Who is in charge here? Governance for sustainable development in a complex world. *Journal of Environmental Policy & Planning*, vol. 9, Nos.3-4, pp. 299-314.

Ocampo, José Antonio (2015). 2015 report of the Committee for Development Policy (CDP). Presentation by the Chairperson of the CDP to ECOSOC. New York, 10 June. Available from www.un.org/en/development/ desa/policy/cdp/cdp_statements/cdp_stmt_ocampo_10jun2015.pdf.

Overseas Development Institute, and others (2015). *European Report on Development 2015: Combining Finance and Policies to Implement a Transformative Post-2015 Development Agenda*. Brussels: European Union. Available from http://ecdpm.org/wp-content/uploads/2015-European-Report-on-Development-English.pdf.

Pacific Islands Forum Secretariat (2015). Forum communique: Forty-sixth Pacific Islands Forum. Port Moresby, 8-10 September. Available from www.forumsec.org/resources/uploads/attachments/documents/2015_Forum_Communique_10Sept2015.pdf.

Papua New Guinea, Department of National Planning and Monitoring (2010a). Papua New Guinea Development Strategic Plan, 2010-2030. Port Moresby. Available from www.treasury.gov.pg/html/publications/files/pub_files/2011/png-development-strategic-plan.2010-2030.pdf.

Papua New Guinea, National Strategic Plan Taskforce (2010b). Papua New Guinea vision 2050. Available from https://sustainabledevelopment.un.org/content/documents/1496png.pdf.

Papua New Guinea, Department of National Planning and Monitoring (2011). *Papua New Guinea the Medium-Term Development Plan, 2011-2015*. Port Moresby. Available from www.pacificdisaster.net/pdnadmin/data/original/PNG_2010_mediumterm_development.pdf.

Rubin, Donald B. (2004). *Multiple Imputation for Nonresponse in Surveys*. Hoboken, New Jersey: John Wiley & Sons.

Samoa (2015). Samoa's intended nationally determined contribution. Available from www4.unfccc.int/submissions/INDC/Published%20Documents/Samoa/1/Samoa%20INDC_Submission%20to%20UNFCCC.pdf.

Samoa, Ministry of Finance (2012a). Samoa energy sector plan 2012-2016. Apia. Available from www.mof.gov.ws/Portals/195/Energy/Samoa%20Energy%20Sector%20Plan-Final%20Version-Master.pdf.

_____ (2012b). Strategy for the development of Samoa 2012-2016. Apia. Available from www.adb.org/sites/default/files/linked-documents/cobp-sam-2016-2018-ld-05.pdf.

Secretariat of the Pacific Regional Environment Programme (2011). Report on the summary of outcomes and proceedings from the Niue Pacific Climate Change Roundtable Meeting. Alofi, Niue, 14-17 March. Available from www.pacificclimatechange.net/components/com_booklibrary/ebooks/Final%20report%20from%20Niue%20PCCR%2027%20April%2011.pdf.

Simon, Herbert A. (1991). The architecture of complexity. In *International Federation for Systems Research International Series on Systems Science and Engineering*, vol. 7, *Facets of Systems Science*, George J. Klir, ed. New York: Springer Science+Business Media.

United Nations (2015). *Global Sustainable Development Report*. Available from https://sustainable development.un.org/content/documents/1758GSDR%202015%20Advance%20Unedited%20Version.pdf

_____ (2016). Summary report: special thematic event "Building Synergy and Coherence in the Implementation of the Istanbul Programme of Action in the Context of the 2030 Sustainable Development Agenda". Available from http://unohrlls.org/custom-content/uploads/2016/02/18-Feb_Thematic-event-on-Building-Synergy-and-Coherence-Summary-18-February-2016.pdf.

United Nations Development Group (2015). Mainstreaming the 2030 Agenda for Sustainable Development: interim reference guide to UN country teams. Available from http://sustainabledevelopment.un.org/content/documents/9478 undgguidancenote.pdf.

United Nations Office of the High Representative for the Least Developed Countries, Landlocked Developing Countries and Small Island Developing States (2012). *Countries with Special Needs: Thematic Think Piece*. New York. Available from http://unohrlls.org/UserFiles/1_countries_with_ special_needs.pdf.

United Nations, Department of Economic and Social Affairs (2010). Five-year review of the Mauritius Strategy for the further implementation of the Barbados Programme of Action for the Sustainable Development of Small Island Developing States: Pacific High-level Dialogue -- Port Vila Outcome Statement. 8-9 February. CSD18/2010/BP10. Available from www.un.org/esa/dsd/resources/res_pdfs/csd-18/csd18_2010_bp10.pdf.

United Nations, Economic and Social Commission for Asia and the Pacific (2012). *Economic and Social Survey of Asia and the Pacific 2012: Pursuing Shared Prosperity*. Sales No. E.12.II.F.9. Available from www.unescap.org/ resources/economic-and-social-survey-asia-and-pacific-2012.

_____ (2015). *Asia-Pacific Countries with Special Needs Development Report 2015: Building Productive Capacities to Overcome Structural Challenges*. Sales No. E.15.II.F.9.

United Nations, and others (2011). Resources for transforming economies, including through climate financing. Paper prepared as part of the Rio+20 Pacific Preparatory Meeting Joint Ministerial Meeting. Apia, Samoa, 21-22 July.

Vanuatu (2013). Vanuatu national energy road map 2013-2020. Available from www.iea.org/media/pams/vanuatu/ Vanuatu_National_Energy_Roadmap20132020.pdf.

World Bank (2014a). Lao PDR trade and transport facilitation assessment. Report, No. 72061-LA (April). Washington, D.C.

_____ (2014b). A sector assessment: accelerating growth of high-speed internet services in Azerbaijan. Working Papers, No. AUS9195 (December). Washington, D.C.

ANNEX I. DEFINITIONS, METHODOLOGY AND DATA SOURCES

Indicators of least developed countries[1]

GNI per capita

The gross national income (GNI) at current prices in local currency Y_t is converted to United States dollars using the World Bank Atlas conversion factor: $Y_t^{Atlas} = Y_t/e_t^{Atlas}$, where e_t^{Atlas} is the average of a country's exchange rate (local currency units per United States dollar) for that year and for the two preceding years adjusted for the difference between domestic and international inflation:

$$e_t^{Atlas} = \frac{1}{3}\left[e_t + e_{t-1}\left(\frac{r_{t-1}}{r_{t-1}^{SDR}}\right) + e_{t-2}\left(\frac{r_{t-2}}{r_{t-2}^{SDR}}\right)\right].$$

The country's inflation rate between year t and year $t\text{-}n$, $r_{t-n} = p_t/p_{t-n}$, is measured as the change in its gross domestic product (GDP) deflator. International inflation between year t and year $t\text{-}n$, $r_{t-n}^{SDR} = p^{SDR}/p_{t-n}^{SDR}$, is measured using the change in the special drawing rights deflator. The GNI per capita uses a three-year moving average of the GNI in United Sates dollars divided by the midyear population: $Y_t^{pc} = (1/3)\ \sum_{s=0}^2 Y_{t+s}^{Atlas}/ N_{t+s}$. The GNI in local prices, GDP deflator and population figures are from the National Account Main Aggregates Database of the United Nations Statistics Division. The special drawing rights deflator is from the World Bank. The graduation threshold is set at 20 per cent above the three-year moving average of the World Bank's GNI per capita threshold between low-income and middle-income countries.

Max-min procedure

For the calculation of the human assets index and the economic vulnerability index, discussed below, the max-min procedure is used in order to reduce the impact of extreme outliers on the distribution of index values. It converts an original indicator value V into a new index score I that ranges between 0 and 100. For indicators that need to increase to attain the graduation criterion, such as the components of human assets index, the formula is the following:

$$I = 100 * \frac{\max\{V, V_{lower}\} - V_{lower}}{V_{upper} - V_{lower}}.$$

For indicators that need to decrease to attain the graduation criterion, such as the components of the economic vulnerability index, the formula is the following:

$$I = 100 * \frac{V_{upper} - min\{V, V_{upper}\}}{V_{upper} - V_{lower}}.$$

Throughout the period covered by this study, the bounds V_{lower} and V_{upper} are kept constant at the levels established for the 2015 triennial review of the Committee for Development Policy of the United Nations Economic and Social Council.

Human assets index

The human assets index is a measure of the level of human capital consisting of the following four indicators using equal weights: (a) percentage of the population undernourished; (b) mortality rate for children aged five years or under; (c) gross secondary school enrolment ratio; and (d) adult literacy rate.[2]

- The percentage of population undernourished represents the probability of a randomly chosen individual to consume less than the minimum amount of calories necessary to maintain a healthy life and carry out light physical activity. The data source is the FAOSTAT database of the Food and Agricultural Organization (FAO) of the United Nations. The lower and upper bounds are, respectively, 5% and 65%.

- The mortality rate for children aged five years or under represents the probability of dying between birth and age five. The data source is the United Nations Inter-agency Group for Child Mortality Estimation. The lower and upper bounds are, respectively, 10 and 175 deaths per 1,000 live births.

---

[1] The calculation of the indicators of least developed countries is based on the methods and sources discussed in United Nations (2015). See also www.un.org/en/development/desa/policy/cdp/ldc/ldc_criteria.shtml.

[2] In future triennial reviews of the Committee for Development Policy of the United Nations Economic and Social Council, mortality will be added as a new component of the human assets index, and undernourishment is likely to be replaced with a measure of stunting as a better indicator of nutrition.

- The gross secondary school enrolment ratio measures the number of pupils enrolled in secondary schools expressed as a percentage of the population in the country-specific official age group for secondary education. The data source is the Institute of Statistics, United Nations Educational, Scientific and Cultural Organization (UNESCO). The lower and upper bounds are, respectively, 10% and 100%.

- The adult literacy rate measures the number of literate persons aged fifteen and above, expressed as a percentage of the total population in that age group. The data source is the Institute of Statistics, UNESCO. The lower and upper bounds are, respectively, 25% and 100%.

Economic vulnerability index

The economic vulnerability index is composed of the following eight indicators (weights in parentheses): population size (1/8), remoteness (1/8), merchandise export concentration (1/16), share of agriculture, forestry and fisheries in the GDP (1/16), share of the population in low-elevation coastal zones (1/8), instability of exports of goods and services (1/4), victims of natural disasters (1/8) and instability of agricultural production (1/8).

- The population size of a country is estimated as of the mid-point of the year. The data source is the World Population Prospects database of the United Nations Population Division. For the max-min procedure, the values are transformed using the natural logarithm in order to address possible distortions caused by highly skewed distributions of indicator values. The lower and upper bounds are set at 150,000 and 100,000,000 people, respectively.

- Remoteness of country A is a trade-weighted average of the distance between country A and all the other countries in the world. The calculation is based on the countries that (i) are geographically closer to country A and (ii) have a cumulative share of the world market of 50 per cent. The trade-weighted average distance is transformed into logarithms and then converted into an index using the max-min procedure, with lower and upper bounds of, respectively, the log of 2,000 km and the log of 10,300 km. The resulting remoteness index r is then adjusted to reflect the higher trade costs of landlocked developing countries using the following formula:

$$r^* = 0.85 \; r + 0.15 \; l,$$

where $l = 100$ if the country is landlocked or 0 otherwise. Finally, the max-min procedure is applied again for r^* with lower and upper bounds of, respectively 10 and 90. The data sources Centre d'Etudes Prospectives et d'Informations Internationales for bilateral physical distances between all countries and the National Account Main Aggregates Database of the United Nations Statistics Division for market shares of each country.

- Merchandise export concentration measures the degree of product concentration of country's exports. It ranges from 0 to 1, with 0 reflecting a country with a series of export products distributed in a homogeneous manner, and higher values indicating that exports are concentrated in few products, i.e., less diversified. The data source is the UNCTADstat database, UNCTAD. The lower and upper bounds for this component of the economic vulnerability index are 0.1 and 0.95, respectively.

- The share of agriculture, forestry and fishing in GDP of a country refers to the GDP share of the agriculture, hunting, forestry and fishing sectors. The data source is the National Account Main Aggregates Database of the United Nations Statistics Division. The lower and upper bounds for this component of the economic vulnerability index are set at 1% and 60%, respectively.

- The share of population in low elevated coastal zones refers to the percentage share of a country's population that lives in areas contiguous to the coast below five meters. The data source is the Center for International Earth Science Information Network, Columbia University. The lower and upper bounds for this component of the economic vulnerability index are 0% and 35%, respectively.

- Instability of exports of goods and services of a country represents the variability of the value of exports around its long-term trend. This indicator is measured by the standard error of the following ordinary least square regression:

$$ln \; x_t = \alpha + \beta \; ln \; x_{t-1} + \gamma t + e_t \, ,$$

where α, β and γ are the regression coefficients; x_t is the value of exports of goods and services at constant United States dollars in year t; t is the time variable; and e_t is the error term in year t. These standard errors are estimated over a 20-year period on a rolling basis, utilizing export data reported at the National Account Main Aggregates Database of the United Nations Statistics Division. The lower and upper bounds of these instability scores are set at 5 and 35, respectively.

- Instability of agricultural production measures the variability of agricultural production around its trend, calculated over a 20-year period. This indicator is measured by the standard error of the same ordinary least square regression as that used to estimate the indicator for instability of exports of goods and services. In this case, x_t refers the index of total agricultural production in volume terms in year t, reported at the FAOSTAT database, FAO. The lower and upper bounds of the instability scores used for the max-min procedure are 1.5 and 20, respectively.

- Victims of natural disasters of a country are measured in terms of the share of the population by dividing the number of persons killed or affected by natural disasters by the total population. This indicator is calculated over a period of 20 years to account for fluctuations of disasters over time and then averaged. The 20-year averages are transformed using the natural logarithm to correct for possibly highly skewed distribution and then converted through the max-min procedure, with the lower and upper bounds of 0.005% and 10% of the total population, respectively. The data sources are the International Emergency Disasters Database of the Centre for Research on the Epidemiology of Disaster for the number of persons killed or affected by the natural disasters and the United Nations Population Division for the population estimates.

Estimating economic vulnerability indices for 2015

ESCAP estimates the economic vulnerability indices for 2015 by updating two of the eight components, population and victims of natural disasters, keeping the other six components unchanged from 2014. The calculations and the setting of lower and upper bounds are the same as those used for the 2015 review of the Committee for Development Policy of the United Nations Economic and Social Council.

At the time of writing, the other six components of the economic vulnerability index are not available for 2015 in the original data sources, and thus the vulnerability scores of these components are carried over from 2014 into 2015. This procedure can be justified in that these six components vary relatively little from year to year compared to the number of victims of natural disaster. The component for victims of natural disaster could change significantly over time, particularly in countries that are prone to natural disasters. In fact, for five out of 12 least developed countries of the region, victims of natural disasters are the most volatile component of the economic vulnerability index, as determined by the standard deviation calculated over the past ten years. Therefore, even though only two out of eight components are updated for 2015, these estimated indices are likely to capture a large variation of actual changes of the economic vulnerability index.

Reference group

In the analysis of indicators for landlocked developing countries and small island developing States, the performance of Asia-Pacific countries with special needs (CSN) is compared to that of a reference group of Asian developing countries that are not CSN. The benchmark is constructed as the value of each indicator for a group of up to 17 non-CSN developing countries: Brunei Darussalam, China, the Democratic People's Republic of Korea, Georgia, India, Indonesia, the Islamic Republic of Iran, Malaysia, Pakistan, the Philippines, the Republic of Korea, the Russian Federation, Singapore, Sri Lanka, Thailand, Turkey and Viet Nam. The group varies from indicator to indicator according to data availability. If the group does not cover all 17 countries, those that are not covered are indicated at the end of the description of each indicator. The reference group is also used for the analysis of the decomposition of the economic vulnerability index. In that case, the reference group included all 17 countries except the Russian Federation.

Indicators of landlocked developing countries

Days to/from ship

The time for the delivery of goods between the main commercial centre of a country and a ship at the nearest seaport, net of land travel, is calculated as follows. First, indicators of the World Bank's Doing Business database on the average time to export and time to import are computed. Second, the number of days it takes to move goods between the main commercial centre of the country and the nearest seaport is estimated by assuming the cargo is shipped by a truck that travels at 40 kilometres per hour with two drivers who each drive 9 hours a day. Third, the estimated travel time is subtracted from the average number of days to export and days to import. Further details of the construction of the indicator are available in ESCAP (2015). The reference group contains all 17 countries but the Democratic People's Republic of Korea.

Access to fixed broadband Internet

Access to fixed broadband Internet is measured by the number of fixed broadband Internet subscribers per 100 people. The source is the International Telecommunication Union. The reference group contains all 17 countries but the Democratic People's Republic of Korea.

Export concentration index

See the economic vulnerability index of the indicators of least developed economies. The reference group covers all 17 countries.

Indicators of small island developing States

Access to improved sanitation facilities

Access to improved sanitation facilities refers to the percentage of the population using improved sanitation facilities. Improved sanitation facilities are defined as facilities that hygienically separate human excreta from human contact, such as flush toilet, piped sewer system, septic tank, flush/pour flush to pit latrine, ventilated improved pit latrine, pit latrine with slab and composting toilet. The source is the Joint Monitoring Programme for Water Supply and Sanitation of the World Health Organization and the United Nations Children's Emergency Fund. The reference group does not include Brunei Darussalam or the Democratic People's Republic of Korea.

Access to mobile phone

Access to mobile phone is measured by the number of mobile cellular subscribers per 100 people in a country. Mobile cellular subscribers refer to users of portable telephones subscribing to an automatic public mobile telephone service, including both post-paid subscriptions and pre-paid accounts. The data source is the International Telecommunication Union. The reference group covers all 17 countries but the Democratic People's Republic of Korea.

Share of renewable in total electricity generation

The share of renewables in total energy generation refers to the ratio of total renewable electricity net generation over total net energy generation. Renewables include hydroelectricity, geothermal, wind, solar, tide and wave and biomass and waste. The data source is the Energy Information Agency of the United States Department of Energy. The reference group includes all 17 countries but the Democratic People's Republic of Korea.

ANNEX II. SURVEY ON THE IMPLEMENTATION OF THE SUSTAINABLE DEVELOPMENT GOALS IN ASIA AND THE PACIFIC

Survey respondents by group and country

Group / Country				
Number of countries:	**38**		**Number of responses:**	**160**
Asia-Pacific CSN:	25		Asia-Pacific CSN:	95
Non-CSN developing Asia:	13		Non-CSN developing Asia:	65
Least developed countries	**71**	**Small island developing States**	**15**
Bangladesh	12	Fiji	4
Lao People's Democratic Republic	11	Micronesia (Federated States of)	3
Nepal	11	Papua New Guinea	3
Cambodia	10	Cook Islands	1
Bhutan	9	Maldives	1
Timor-Leste	6	Nauru	1
Vanuatu	5	New Caledonia	1
Myanmar	3	Samoa	1
Afghanistan	2	**Non-CSN developing Asia**	**65**
Kiribati	1	India	10
Tuvalu	1	Malaysia	9
Landlocked developing countries	**9**	Sri Lanka	9
Mongolia	3	Philippines	8
Kyrgyzstan	2	Thailand	8
Azerbaijan	1	Viet Nam	8
Kazakhstan	1	China	4
Tajikistan	1	Indonesia	2
Uzbekistan	1	Iran (Islamic Republic of)	2
		Pakistan	2
		Georgia	1
		Republic of Korea	1
		Russian Federation	1

Source: ESCAP.

The survey

Survey on the Implementation of the Sustainable Development Goals in Asia and the Pacific

Question 1. How familiar are you with the 2030 Agenda for Sustainable Development and the Sustainable Development Goals?

Question 2. In your view, what is the degree of priority for your country of each of the Goals? Please rate each Goal using the following scale: 1 - very low priority; 2 - low priority; 3 - high priority; and 4 - very high priority.

Question 3. Which of the Goals should be emphasized initially, between 2016 and 2020, in the implementation process in your country? Please select up to five Goals.

Question 4. Are there, in your view, any "unfinished businesses" from the Millennium Development Goals that your country should address as a priority in the next five years (2016-2020)? If yes, please indicate which ones.

Question 5. What, in your view, are the main challenges for the implementation of the Sustainable Development Goals in your country? Please rate each challenge using the following scale: 1 - not challenging; 2 - somewhat challenging; 3 - moderately challenging; and 4 - very challenging.
  (a) Integrating the Goals into national development plans (such as five-year plans)
  (b) Integrating the Goals into annual budgets
  (c) Institutional mechanism to coordinate different government agencies and ministries levels of government for the implementation of the Goals
  (d) Institutional mechanism to coordinate the implementation of the Goals among the national government and different tiers of local governments
  (e) Technical and administrative capacities of government officials and policymakers
  (f) Availability of data and statistics
  (g) Others, please provide details

Question 6a. Regarding financing the Goals, with which priority should the following domestic sources of finance be (further) developed for the implementation of the Goals in your country? Please rate each source of finance using the following scale: 1 - very low priority; 2 - low priority; 3 - high priority; and 4 - very high priority.

(a) Domestic public resources – national government revenue
(b) Domestic public resources – local government revenue
(c) Improved management of domestic public expenditures
(d) Commercial banks (public and private, including subsidiaries of foreign banks)
(e) National development banks
(f) Affordable financial services for disadvantaged and low-income segments of society (financial inclusion)
(g) Domestic capital markets
(h) Public-private partnerships

Question 6b. With which priority should access to the following international sources of finance be enhanced for the implementation of the Goals in your country? Please rate each source of finance using the following scale: 1 - very low priority; 2 - low priority; 3 - high priority; and 4 - very high priority.

(i) Official development assistance (ODA)
(j) Multilateral development banks, including regional development banks (such as the World Bank and the Asian Development Bank)
(k) Foreign direct investment (FDI)
(l) International capital markets
(m) Blended finance (complementary use of ODA and non-grant foreign financing from private or public sources to provide financing on terms that would make projects financially viable)

Question 6c. Which of the above mentioned sources of finance should be emphasized initially, between 2016 and 2020, in the implementation process of the Goals in your country? Please select up to three sources.

Question 7. To what extent are global systemic issues important for the implementation of the Goals in your country? Please rate each systemic issue using the following scale: 1 - not important; 2 - somewhat important; 3 - moderately important; and 4 - very important.

(a) Global economic growth
(b) Multilateral trade negotiations
(c) Global financial stability
(d) Transfer of technology and intellectual property rights
(e) Climate negotiations
(f) Stability of global commodity prices (of food, fuel, minerals, etc.)
(g) Others, please list

Question 8. With which priority should the following actors be engaged by your country's government for the implementation of the Goals? Please rate each actor using the following scale: 1 - very low priority; 2 - low priority; 3 - high priority; and 4 - very high priority.

(a) Foreign private sector
(b) Domestic private sector – SMEs
(c) Domestic private sector – others
(d) Non-governmental organizations (NGOs)
(e) Civil society organizations (CSOs)
(f) Public representatives (such as parliamentarians and local government members)
(g) Media
(h) Others, please list

Question 9a. In your view, what role should the United Nations and its agencies play to support your country in implementing the Goals?

Question 9b. In your view, what role should other agencies, including multilateral development banks, bilateral donors, regional organizations, etc., play to support your country in implementing the Goals?

ANNEX III. INDICATORS AND TECHNICAL NOTES

List of indicators used for analysis in chapter 3

Goal	Indicator	Source	Notes
1	Population below $1.25 per day (purchasing power parity, percentage)	World Bank	High income countries with missing values are assumed to have a value of 0.
	Poverty gap ratio at $1.25 a day (purchasing power parity, percentage)	World Bank	
2	Population undernourished (percentage)	FAO	Percentage of the population whose food intake is insufficient to meet dietary energy requirements.
	Arable land (hectares per person)	FAO	Includes land defined by the FAO as land under temporary crops, temporary meadows for mowing or for pasture, land under market or kitchen gardens, and land temporarily fallow.
	Crop production index (2004-2006 = 100)	FAO	Crop production index shows agricultural production for each year relative to the base period 2004-2006.
	Food production index (2004-2006 = 100)	FAO	Food production index covers food crops that are considered edible and that contain nutrients.
	Livestock production index (2004-2006 = 100)	FAO	Livestock production index includes meat and milk from all sources, dairy products such as cheese and eggs, honey, raw silk, wool, and hides and skins.
	Food supply (kcal/capita/day)	FAO	
	Agriculture value added per worker (constant 2005 US$)	FAO/World Bank	A measure of agricultural productivity. Value added in agriculture measures the output of the agricultural sector (ISIC divisions 1-5) less the value of intermediate inputs.
3	Health index	United Nations Development Programme (UNDP)	Life expectancy at birth expressed as an index using a minimum value of 35 years and a maximum value of 85 years.
	Tuberculosis detection rate under DOTS (percentage)	World Health Organization (WHO)	Percentage of estimated new infectious tuberculosis cases detected under the internationally recommended tuberculosis control strategy directly observed treatment shortcourse (DOTS).
	Tuberculosis incidence rate	WHO	Estimated number of new tuberculosis cases arising in one year per 100,000 people.
	Tuberculosis prevalence rate	WHO	Estimated number of tuberculosis cases in a given point per 100,000 people.
	Tuberculosis death rate	WHO	Estimated number of tuberculosis deaths per 100,000 people.
	Children immunized against measles (percentage)	United Nations Children's Emergency Fund (UNICEF)	Children refer to those that are 1 year old.
	Health expenditure, total (% of GDP)	WHO	Recurrent and capital spending from government budgets, external borrowings and grants, and social health insurance funds.
	Maternal mortality ratio	UNICEF	per 100,000 live births.
	Children under five mortality rate	UNICEF	per 1,000 live births.
	Infant mortality rate	UNICEF	per 1,000 live births.
4	Education index	UNDP	Calculated using Mean Years of Schooling and Expected Years of Schooling. For technical notes, see http://hdr.undp.org/sites/default/files/hdr14_technical_notes.pdf.
	Government expenditure on education, total (% of GDP)	UNESCO	
	Population with at least some secondary education (percentage)	UNDP	Percentage of the population ages 25 and older that reached at least a secondary level of education.
5	Seats held by women in national parliament (percentage)	Inter-Parliamentary Union	Inter-Parliamentary Union data used by the United Nations Statistics Division.
	Gender Parity Index in primary level enrolment	United Nations Statistics Division (UNSD)	Ratio of the number of female students enrolled at primary, secondary and tertiary levels of education to the number of male students in each level.
	Labour force participation rate, female (percentage)	International Labour Organization (ILO)	Modelled ILO estimate (% of female population ages 15-64).

Goal	Indicator	Source	Notes
5	Gender inequality index	UNDP	A composite measure reflecting inequality in achievement between women and men in three dimensions: reproductive health, empowerment and the labour market.
	Female to male ratio of Human Development Index	UNDP	Ratio of female to male Human Development Index (HDI) value.
	Account at a financial institution, female (percentage age 15+)	World Bank	Denotes the percentage of respondents who report having an account at a bank or another type of financial institution.
6	Proportion of the population using improved drinking water sources	UNICEF/WHO	Percentage of the population who use any of the following types of water supply for drinking: piped water into dwelling, plot or yard; public tap/standpipe; borehole/tube well; protected dug well; protected spring; rainwater collection and bottled water.
	Proportion of the population using improved sanitation facilities	UNICEF/WHO	Percentage of the population with access to facilities that hygienically separate human excreta from human contact.
	Water productivity	FAO/World Bank	Constant 2005 (United States dollar) GDP per cubic meter of total freshwater withdrawal.
7	Renewable electricity output	International Energy Agency (IEA)	Renewable electricity is the share of electricity generated by renewable power plants in total electricity generated by all types of plants.
	Renewable energy consumption	IEA	Percent of total final energy consumption.
	Energy intensity level of primary energy (MJ/$2011 purchasing power parity, GDP)	IEA	Ratio between energy supply and gross domestic product measured at purchasing power parity. Energy intensity is an indication of how much energy is used to produce one unit of economic output.
	Access to electricity (percentage of population)	World Bank	
8	Labour force participation rate	ILO	Modeled ILO estimate (% of total population ages 15-64).
	Unemployment rate	ILO	Modeled ILO estimate (% of total labour force).
	Ease of doing business index	World Bank	Ease of doing business ranks economies with first place being the best. A high ranking (a low numerical rank) means that the regulatory environment is conducive to business operation.
	GDP per capita, logarithm (current United States dollar)	World Bank	
	GDP per capita, purchasing power parity, logarithm (constant 2011 international dollar)	World Bank	
	Number of commercial bank branches per 100,000 adults	International Monetary Fund	Calculated as: (number of commercial banks + number of commercial bank branches) X 100,000 / adult population.
	GDP growth (annual %)	World Bank	
	Export diversification index	International Monetary Fund (IMF)	Higher values indicate lower diversification.
9	Fixed-telephone subscriptions per 100 inhabitants	UNSD	
	Mobile-cellular subscriptions per 100 inhabitants	UNSD	
	Internet users per 100 inhabitants	UNSD	
	Air transport, registered carrier departures worldwide per capita	International Civil Aviation Organization (ICAO)	Civil Aviation Statistics of the World and ICAO staff estimates.
	Air transport, passengers carried per capita	ICAO	Civil Aviation Statistics of the World and ICAO staff estimates.
	Logistics performance index: Quality of trade and transport-related infrastructure	World Bank	1=low to 5=high. Evaluates the quality of trade and transport related infrastructure (e.g. ports, railroads, roads, information technology).
	Average area covered by a permanent post office (km²)	Universal Postal Union (UPU)	
	High-technology exports (percentage of manufactured exports)	United Nations Commodity Trade Statistics Database (Comtrade) Database	High-technology exports are products with high research and development intensity, such as in aerospace, computers, pharmaceuticals, scientific instruments, and electrical machinery.
	Scientific and technical journal articles	National Science Foundation of the United States	Number of scientific and engineering articles published in the following fields: physics, biology, chemistry, mathematics, clinical medicine, biomedical research, engineering and technology, and earth and space sciences.
	Manufacturing, value added (percentage of GDP)	World Bank/ Organisation for Economic Co-operation and Development	Manufacturing refers to industries belonging to International Standard Industrial Classification divisions 15-37. Value added is the net output of a sector after adding up all outputs and subtracting intermediate inputs.

Goal	Indicator	Source	Notes
10	GINI index	World Bank/ United Nations University - World Institute for Development Economics Research (UNU-WIDER)	World Bank PovcalNet data is supplemented by UNU-WIDER and the Standardized World Income Inequality Database (SWIID). Documentation for UNU-WIDER data can be found at www.wider.unu.edu/project/wiid-world-income-inequality-database. Documentation for SWIID can be found at http://myweb.uiowa.edu/fsolt/swiid/swiid.html.
	Coefficient of human inequality	UNDP	Average inequality in three basic dimensions of human development. See Technical note 2 at http://hdr.undp.org/en.
11	Proportion of the population using improved drinking water sources, urban	WHO/UNICEF	
	Proportion of the population using improved sanitation facilities, urban	WHO/UNICEF	
	Access to electricity, urban (percentage of urban population)	World Bank	World Bank Sustainable Energy for All (SE4ALL) data.
12	PM2.5 air pollution, mean annual exposure (micrograms per cubic meter)	Brauer and others (2015)	Data taken from World Bank database.
	PM2.5 air pollution, population exposed to levels exceeding WHO guideline value (percentage)	Brauer and others (2015)	
	Natural resource depletion	UNDP	Monetary expression of energy, mineral and forest depletion, expressed as a percentage of total gross national income (GNI).
13	Carbon dioxide (CO_2) emissions (metric tons of CO_2 per capita)	UNSD	Uses Carbon Dioxide Information Analysis Center and United Nations Framework Convention on Climate Change data.
	Carbon dioxide (CO_2) emissions (kg CO_2 per $1 GDP, purchasing power parity)	UNSD	
	Population affected by natural disasters (per million)	Emergency Events Database, Centre for Research on the Epidemiology of Disasters	People requiring immediate assistance during a period of emergency as a result of a natural disaster, including displaced, evacuated, homeless and injured people, expressed per million people.
	Emissions of methane and nitrous oxide produced from agricultural activities	FAO	Contains all the emissions produced in the different agricultural emissions sub-domains, providing a picture of the contribution to the total amount of greenhouse gas emissions from agriculture.
14	Renewable internal freshwater resources per capita	FAO	Renewable internal freshwater resources flows refer to internal renewable resources (internal river flows and groundwater from rainfall) in the country.
	Fertilizer consumption (kilograms per hectare of arable land)	FAO	Fertilizer consumption measures the quantity of plant nutrients used per unit of arable land. Fertilizer products cover nitrogenous, potash, and phosphate fertilizers.
	Fish species, threatened	Fish Base database	Fish species are based on Froese, R. and Pauly, D. (eds). 2008. Threatened species are the number of species classified by the International Union for Conservation of Nature (IUCN) as endangered, vulnerable, rare, indeterminate, out of danger, or insufficiently known.
15	Terrestrial and marine areas protected to total territorial area (percentage)	United Nations Environment Programme (UNEP)	Terrestrial protected areas are protected areas of at least 1,000 hectares designated by national authorities as scientific reserves with limited public access, national parks, natural monuments, nature reserves or wildlife sanctuaries, protected landscapes, and areas managed mainly for sustainable use. Marine protected areas are areas of intertidal or subtidal terrain that have been reserved by law or other effective means to protect part or all of the enclosed environment.
	Mammal species, threatened	UNEP	Mammal species are mammals excluding whales and porpoises. Threatened species are the number of species classified by the IUCN as endangered, vulnerable, rare, indeterminate, out of danger, or insufficiently known.
	Plant species (higher), threatened	UNEP	Higher plants are native vascular plant species. Threatened species are the number of species classified by the IUCN as endangered, vulnerable, rare, indeterminate, out of danger, or insufficiently known.
	Percent change in forest area (1990-2011)	FAO	
	Percentage of the population living on severely or very severely degraded land	FAO	Land degradation estimates consider biomass, soil health, water quantity and biodiversity.

Goal	Indicator	Source	Notes
16	Refugee population by country or territory of origin per capita	UNHCR	Refugees are people who are recognized as refugees under the 1951 Convention Relating to the Status of Refugees. Country of origin generally refers to the nationality or country of citizenship of a claimant.
	Homicide rate	UNODC	Number of unlawful deaths purposefully inflicted on a person by another person, expressed per 100,000 people.
	Overall life satisfaction index	UNDP	Average response to the Gallup World Poll question relating to the indicator.
	Satisfaction with local labour market	UNDP	Average responses to related Gallup World Poll questions. These three indicators are averaged into a single indicator relating to communities and society.
	Trust in other people		
	Satisfaction with community		
	Satisfaction with efforts to deal with the poor	UNDP	Average responses to related Gallup World Poll questions. These three indicators are averaged into a single indicator relating to government.
	Satisfaction with actions to preserve the environment		
	Trust in national government		
17	Foreign direct investment, net inflows (Balance of payment, logarithm, current United States dollar)	IMF	Foreign direct investment refers to direct investment equity flows in the reporting economy. It is the sum of equity capital, reinvestment of earnings, and other capital.
	Tax revenue (percentage of GDP)	IMF	Tax revenue refers to compulsory transfers to the central government for public purposes.
	Time to prepare and pay taxes (hours)	World Bank	
	Statistical capability	ESCAP calculations	The total number of indicators out of the 81 used for analysis that are available for each country.

Attainment across Goals for selected Asia-Pacific countries with special needs

Figure A1. Top and bottom three Goals according to deviations from the group averages (percentage)

A. Least developed countries

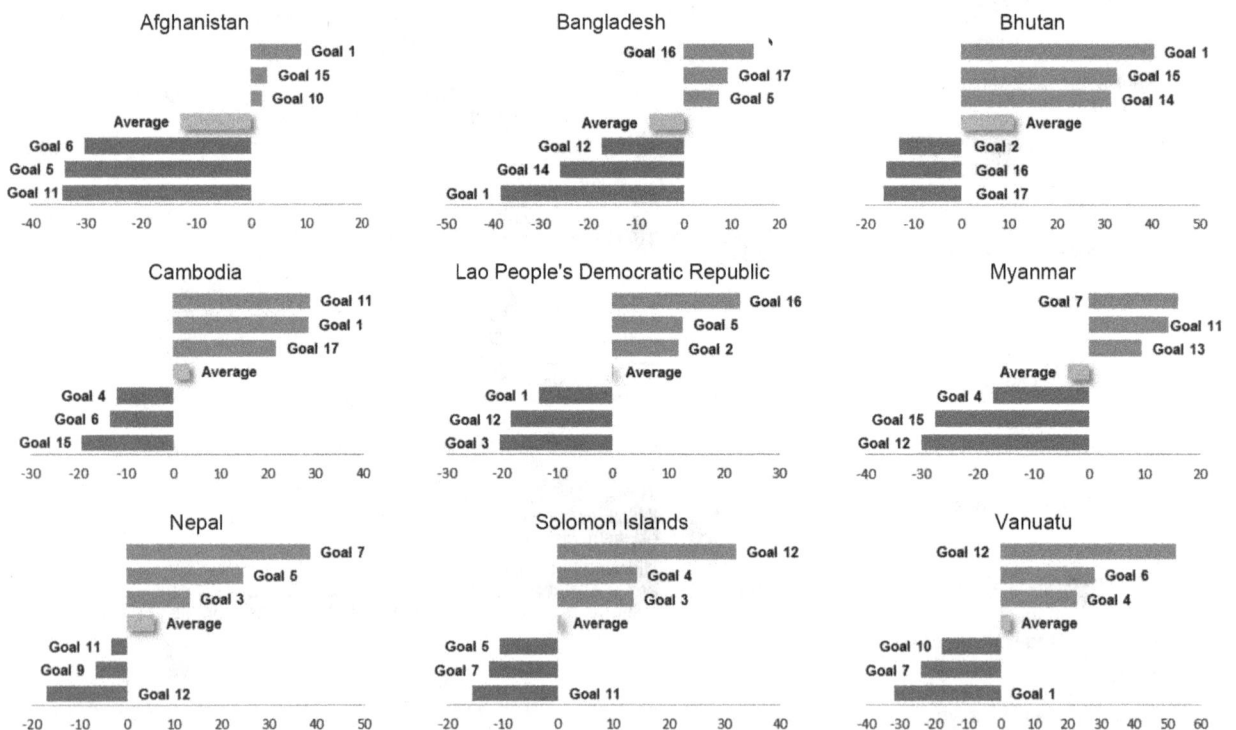

Figure A1. *(continued)*

B. Landlocked developing countries

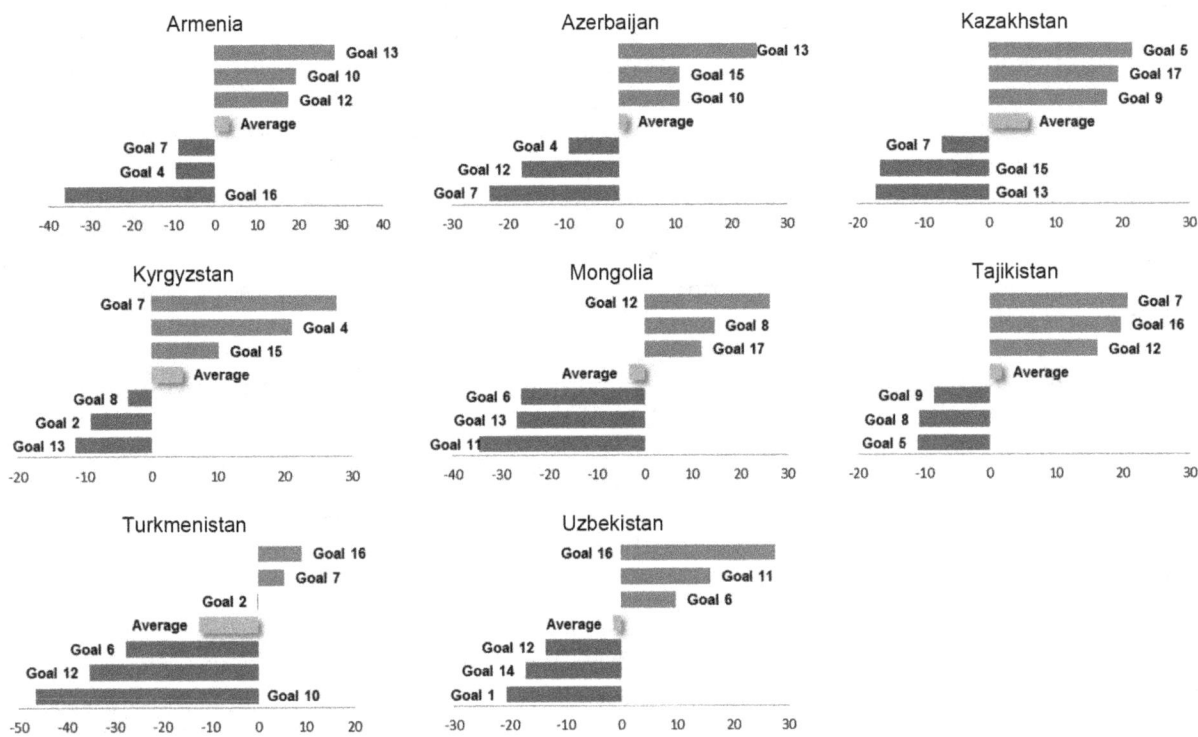

C. Small island developing States

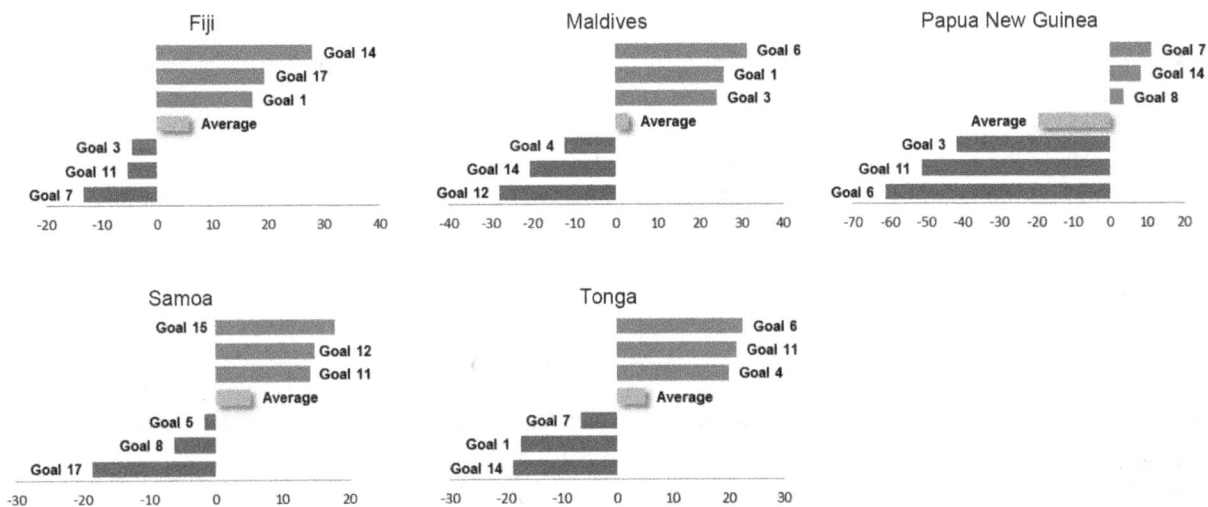

Source: ESCAP.

Measuring and optimizing SDG capacities

Normalization of indicator attainment levels

For the indicators used in this analysis, there are no clear thresholds (i.e. maximum and minimum values that an indicator can take) that can be used as reference in normalization. Thus as one possible alternative, the maximum value for an indicator can be set to be the highest observed value for the indicator given the countries in the sample, and vice-versa for the minimum value. However, setting the threshold in this manner is vulnerable to the existence of outliers, for the scale (the difference between the maximum and minimum) can be greatly increased by a data point with an extreme value. For example, if Greenland were included in the sample, the scale of normalization for the indicator related to internal freshwater resources per capita would be extremely large, with Greenland having maximum attainment while other countries uniformly having attainment levels close to zero. Thus in order to control for such extremities, the 90th and 10th percentiles are used instead of the absolute maximum and minimum. For a country that is above the 90th percentile, the 90th percentile value is replaced with the original value, and a country that is below the 10th percentile is given the corresponding 10th percentile value. Then, the normalized attainment levels are calculated such that

$$Normalized\ attainment = \frac{actual\ value - 10th\ percentile}{90th\ percentile - 10th\ percentile} \times 100$$

for indicators where a larger value is better, and

$$Normalized\ attainment = \frac{90th\ percentile - actual\ value}{90th\ percentile - 10th\ percentile} \times 100$$

for indicators where a smaller value is better. The normalized attainment for any indicator thus takes a value between 0 and 100, with a higher value corresponding to higher levels of attainment.

Calculating the SDG capacity measure using the Method of Reflections

To measure the Sustainable Development Goal (SDG) capacities of countries, the Method of Reflections proposed by Hidalgo and Hausmann (2009) is used, with some modifications. The Method of Reflections uses the information of the constructed bipartite network of 1) countries and 2) indicators to calculate measures of SDG capacity and indicator complexity. Here, the links connect only countries with indicators, and no links exist between countries or between indicators. Any link between a country and indicator is defined by the country's normalized attainment for the particular indicator in question, where the link weights take a value between 0 and 100.

Taking countries as a starting point, the simple sum of normalized attainment across the indicators for a particular country is calculated to produce a first order measure of "SDG capacity." Countries with relatively high levels of attainment across the 82 indicators used will have high first order SDG capacities. The same can be done for the indicators, where the normalized attainment across countries is summed up for a particular indicator. Indicators with high first order "ubiquity" will be ones where many countries having comparatively high attainment levels. Thus such indicators are considered to be less complex, or in other words easier to improve upon. Consider a bipartite network $\mathbf{M}$ described by the adjacency matrix $\mathbf{M}_{ci}$, where each element in the matrix m_{ci} is defined as the normalized attainment values of country c in indicator i. Then,

$$S_{c,0} = \sum_i \mathbf{M}_{ci}$$
$$K_{i,0} = \sum_c \mathbf{M}_{ci}$$

where $S_{c,0}$ is the first order SDG capacity for country c, and $K_{i,0}$ is the first order ubiquity for indicator i.

However, this measure in itself is not very enlightening in that the first order measures are the simple sum of attainment levels. The Method of Reflections iterates by using the information collected at the first order to calculate a second order measure, using information provided by second order (the link weights between a link neighbour and the link neighbour's neighbour) linkages. Subsequent iterations of higher order utilize more and more information regarding indirect linkages between distant neighbours. For example, the second order SDG capacity measure for countries would not simply sum the link weights of first order linkages, but would weight these links based on the ubiquity levels calculated for the indicators in the first order. Higher reflections for countries represent generalized measures of SDG capacities in that the difficulty in achieving a certain level in a particular indicator is taken into consideration, rather than simply summing up the raw attainment levels. The same applies for indicators, where the higher order reflections generate generalized measures of ubiquity in that the SDG capacities of countries are taken into consideration.

Higher order reflections are the recursive set of calculated values defined as

$$S_{c,N} = \frac{1}{S_{c,0}} \sum_i \mathbf{M}_{ci} K_{i,N-1}$$

$$K_{i,N} = \frac{1}{K_{i,0}} \sum_c \mathbf{M}_{ci} S_{c,N-1}$$

for $N \geq 1$. For countries, the even reflections ($S_{c,0}$, $S_{c,2}$, $S_{c,4}$, . . .) are generalized measures of attainment, and thus reflective of SDG capacities, while the even reflections for indicators ($K_{i,0}$, $K_{i,2}$, $K_{i,4}$, . . .) are generalized measures of ubiquity (inverse of complexity). In network terms, $S_{c,1}$ and $K_{i,1}$ are the average nearest neighbour degree. Higher order reflections can be interpreted as linear combinations of the properties of all of the nodes in the network. In the analysis for this chapter, $S_{c,8}$ is used as the generalized measure of SDG capacity for a country, and $K_{i,8}$ is used as the measure of indicator ubiquity. The 8th reflection for countries and indicators is used, for higher order reflections did not result in any substantial change in rank among countries or indicators given the data.

Node importance: degree and betweenness centrality

(Weighted) degree centrality is one of a family of measures that can quantify how important a node is within a network. Quantifying the importance of a node – or in network terms its "centrality" – is helpful in distinguishing nodes that exert more influence within the greater network, where influence can be defined in many ways. Degree centrality is a simple measure of influence that is defined as the number of connections a node possesses. It is intuitive in the sense that a better connected node (thus having higher "degree") will have more power in the network, compared to a node that has fewer links and is thus relatively isolated. Weighted degree centrality is identical to degree centrality, with the difference that it weights each link by its strength. Thus it can be seen that $S_{c,0}$ and $K_{i,0}$ from the previous section are essentially the weighted degree centrality of the countries and indicators within the network.

However, there are other ways a node can be influential within the network. Consider a node that is connected to only two neighbours, where the neighbours are part of distinct clusters. Consider further that without the particular node, the two clusters would be disconnected. This particular node has relatively low degree centrality compared to other nodes that are part of a cluster, since a node within a cluster will have many connections to other nodes within the same cluster. However, this node is influential in the sense that it serves as the sole connection between clusters, and thus will always be crossed when something is exchanged between the two groups (such as information, cars, electricity etc.). The intuition for measuring this type of influence is quantifying how many pairs of individuals (i.e. nodes) would have to go through you in order to reach one another. Formally, this type of influence is measured using betweenness centrality, where its name derives from the fact that it measures how "between" a certain node is relative to others in a network. It is measured as

$$Betweenness\ centrality\ (i) = \sum_{j \neq k} \frac{g_{jk}(i)}{g_{jk}},$$

where $g_{jk}(i)$ is the number of shortest paths connecting j and k that pass through i, and g_{jk} is the total number of shortest paths.

The concept of proximity within the network of indicators

It is assumed that the SDG system is comprised of a set of indicators i and a set of countries c, including the reference country c^*. The *proximity* $\varphi_{i,j}^{c^*}$ between indicators i and j for country c^* is the minimum of the pairwise conditional probabilities that a country c has a higher level of attainment l in one indicator compared to country c^*, given that those countries have a higher level of attainment in the other indicator. Formally,

$$\varphi_{i,j}^{c^*} = \begin{cases} \min \{ P(l_i^c > l_i^{c^*} \mid l_j^c > l_j^{c^*}), P(l_j^c > l_j^{c^*} \mid l_i^c > l_i^{c^*}) \} & \forall\ i \neq j \\ \\ 0 & otherwise \end{cases}.$$

This proximity measure captures the idea that, if two indicators are related due to the similarity of the underlying capacities needed to achieve a certain level of attainment for an indicator, they will move in tandem. Unrelated indicators utilize different sets of underlying capacities and, thus, would have a lower chance to move together. The networks represented in figures 3.10-3.12 are constructed using this measure of proximity as the link weights. Figure 3.2 also uses this proximity measure, yet the conditional probabilities in this case are specific to *average* levels of attainment for the Asia-Pacific CSN. Formally, the proximity measure used in figure 3.2 is identical to the one specified above, after replacing l_i^{c*} with $l_i^{\bar{c}}$, where $l_i^{\bar{c}}$ is the average level of attainment across the Asia-Pacific CSN for indicator i. The proximity measure used to calculate the network of countries in figure 3.3 is conceptually identical, replacing countries with indicators and indicators with countries in the setup above.

The proximity measure $\varphi_{i,j}^{c*}$ between any two indicators is interpreted as the link weights that connect the two indicators in a one-mode network of all indicators. Under this interpretation, the network structure can be represented by the $N{\times}N$ adjacency matrix Φ^{c*}, where each element $\varphi_{i,j}^{c*}$ in the matrix is the proximity measure defined above and N is the number of indicators used in the analysis. By construction, this matrix is symmetric about the diagonal, with zeros on all diagonal elements.

Network visualization based on proximities

The network visualizations found in figures 3.2, 3.3, and 3.10–3.12 are based on the method used in Hidalgo and others (2007), where the links in the network are defined to be the proximity values derived from the equation above. In the first step, a "skeleton" of the network represented by Φ^{c*} is constructed using the Maximum Spanning Tree (MST) algorithm. In essence, the MST algorithm produces a set of N-1 links (N being the number of indicators or countries) that connect all nodes in the network with its most proximal partner. It is implemented by first considering the strongest link within the network, and connecting the two nodes that are at the opposite ends of this strongest link. Subsequent links are added by considering the set of nodes that are not already connected, and choosing the maximal link that connects the otherwise unconnected node to the set of nodes that are already connected. The algorithm stops when all nodes are connected to each other.

While the skeleton of the network constructed by the MST algorithm is enlightening on its own, nonetheless there exists some strong links that are not necessarily in the MST. Thus in the second step, all the links above a certain threshold are added to the MST, to differentiate between nodes that are strongly connected to many other nodes and those that are relatively isolated. The threshold chosen is 0.75, which gives a good representation of the network that is not too overwhelmed by links, while still being able to differentiate between better and less connected nodes. After construction of the underlying network, the Force Atlas 2 algorithm (Jacomy and others, 2014) was implemented in Gephi (an open source network analysis software package) for final visualization.

Optimal pathways for progress

The optimal pathway for progress regards maximizing a country's gain in SDG capacities with respect to increases in attainment in particular indicators. This optimization is based on the premise that the goal for countries under the 2030 Agenda for Sustainable Development is to improve upon all areas of sustainable development, including economic, social and environmental aspects. Since the measure of SDG capacities by construction encompasses all aspects covered by the indicators included in the analysis, it is a superior measure to other indicators such as GDP or GDP per capita growth.

However, a particular country's position within the SDG network of indicators most likely dictates which indicators a country is more easily able to improve upon. This is analogous to the example of trade diversification given by Hidalgo and others (2007) where it is shown that countries diversify their export baskets incrementally, first diversifying into new products that are similar to the products they export currently.

Before we formalize the optimization exercise, we must identify how a country is constrained by its current circumstances, including SDG capacity and current attainment levels. To do this, first, the set K of country $c*$'s peers is defined as countries that have similar levels of SDG capacities (denoted as v) calculated from the Method of Reflections. Formally,

$$K = \{c \in C: v_{c*} - \bar{v} \le v_c \le v_{c*} + \bar{v}\},$$

where $\bar{v}$ is the threshold value that is used to select the group of a particular country's peers. Country $c*$ is said to be *populating* indicator i if country $c*$ has a higher level of attainment in indicator i compared to the average level of attainment for that indicator among a group of the country's peers K. The group of indicators that country $c*$ is populating determines the position of that country within the network of indicators. For example, if a particular country is populating indicators related to Goals 4 (quality education), 5 (gender equality), and 16 (peace, justice and strong institutions), it can be said that the country is positioned within the social area of the SDG network. For the analysis, the threshold value $\bar{v}$ was chosen such that the number of peers for each country was 20.

After identifying which indicators a country populates, a *density* measure is constructed which in essence measures the average proximity of a particular indicator to other indicators that a country is populating in the SDG network. Formally,

$$\omega_j^{c^*} = \frac{\sum_i \left(x_i^{c^*} \varphi_{i,j}^{c^*} \right)}{N-1}, \quad i \neq j$$

where $\omega_j^{c^*}$ is the density around indicator j given the position of country c^* within the SDG network, N is the number of indicators, and $x_i^{c^*}$ is 1 if country c^* is populating indicator i and 0 otherwise. A high density value means that a country has many indicators with high proximity relative to indicator j that are populated. If $\mathbf{X}^{c^*}$ is defined to be a column vector where each element is $x_i^{c^*}$, the above can be rewritten in matrix notation as

$$\mathbf{\Omega}^{c^*} = \frac{1}{N-1} \left(\mathbf{\Phi}^{c^*} \mathbf{X}^{c^*} \right),$$

where each element of the $N \times 1$ column vector $\mathbf{\Omega}^{c^*}$ is the corresponding density value $\omega_j^{c^*}$ for each indicator.

In addition, it is assumed that not all indicators are equal in their *complexity*. For example, indicators such as scientific and technical journal articles encompass a wide range of different capacities including education, infrastructure and technology, and thus would be harder to improve upon compared to other more basic indicators such as crop production. The "ubiquity" measure u_i, which is $K_{i,8}$ for indicator i calculated from the Method of Reflections, is used as a proxy for complexity, with lower values indicating higher complexity. u_i is normalized to be between 0 and 1, with 1 being the highest and 0 being the lowest ubiquity levels observed given the set of indicators used for the analysis. Here, $\mathbf{U}$ is defined to be a $N \times 1$ column vector such that the row values correspond to the ubiquity measure u_i $K_{i,8}$ for each indicator. Notably, $\mathbf{U}$ is not country specific for it refers to the ubiquity calculated using the information of all countries, and thus has no country superscript.

Finally, it is assumed that the attainment level for any indicator also determines the relative cost of improvement. This is because, given any indicator (such as CO_2 emissions per capita), it is relatively easier to improve upon the indicator early on, when attainment levels are relatively low. However, it is more costly to improve upon the indicator as attainment levels increase, for more involved measures need to be taken in order to improve upon an indicator that already has a relatively high level of attainment. The cost of improvement can be defined using an inverted distance measure $d_i^{c^*}$ such that it is more costly to improve upon an indicator for which a country is further away from the mean attainment of its peers. Formally,

$$d_i^{c^*} = \begin{cases} 1 - \left(\dfrac{l_i^{c^*}}{100} - \dfrac{\bar{l}_{c \in K}}{100} \right)^2 & \forall \ l_i^{c^*} > \bar{l}_{c \in K}, \\ 1 & otherwise \end{cases}$$

where $l_i^{c^*}$ is the attainment level for indicator i in country c^*, and $\bar{l}_{c \in K}$ is the average attainment level in indicator i for country c^*'s peers K. Higher levels of $d_i^{c^*}$ close to 1 indicate that the indicator is less costly to improve upon.

Then, the overall ease $e_i^{c^*}$ in improving upon indicator i, given its density value, ubiquity, and effort needed is defined as

$$\mathbf{E}^{c^*} = \mathbf{\Omega}^{c^*} + \mathbf{U} + \mathbf{D}^{c^*},$$

where $\mathbf{E}^{c^*}$ and $\mathbf{D}^{c^*}$ are $N \times 1$ column vectors where the elements correspond to $e_i^{c^*}$ and $d_i^{c^*}$ respectively. $\mathbf{E}^{c^*}$ takes a value between 0 and 3, for each element $\mathbf{\Omega}^{c^*}$, $\mathbf{U}$, and $\mathbf{D}^{c^*}$ takes values between 0 and 1.

Defining a certain threshold $\bar{e}$ for the measure of ease $e_i^{c^*}$, the indicators for which country c^* can improve upon is limited such that only indicators that are above the threshold are eligible for improvement. Here,

$$\bar{I}^{c^*} = \left\{ i \in I : e_i^{c^*} \geq \bar{e} \right\},$$

where $\bar{I}^{c^*}$ is the set of indicators that are above threshold $\bar{e}$. For the analysis, the threshold of 1.5 is chosen, which does not constrain too heavily the set of indicators eligible for improvement while also being able to differentiate between indicators of varying ease. The optimization problem is such that country c^* chooses to improve on an indicator by an amount a out of the set of indicators that are above the threshold $\bar{e}$ which maximizes the unobserved capacity v_{c^*}. Formally,

$$\max_a \ v_{c^*}\left(a_1^{c^*}, \dots, a_N^{c^*} \right) = v_{c^*}\left(a_1^c + l_1^{c^*}, \dots, a_N^c + l_N^{c^*} \right) \quad s.t.$$

$$\sum_{i=1}^{N} a_i^{c^*} = 1$$

$$a_i^{c^*} \in \{0, 1\} \quad \text{for all} \ i = 1, 2, \dots, N$$

$$a_i^{c^*} + l_i^{c^*} \leq 100$$

The optimization problem is simplified by assuming that for one step, country $c*$ can only increase attainment in one indicator by an amount of 1, which is captured in the first two constraints. Subsequent rounds of the optimization using updated levels of attainment from the previous round provide for a detailed, optimal pathway that a country should follow in order to maximize its capacities.

Algorithm for optimization

A computational algorithm was implemented to derive the optimal pathway for progress of a country. The algorithm was implemented in 11 steps, defined below.

1. Calculate the SDG capacities of country $c*$ as well as the ubiquity matrix U for indicators using the Method of Reflections.
2. Calculate the adjacency matrix Ω^{c*} defined by the proximity values.
3. Calculate the column vector X^{c*} indicating which indicators country $c*$ populates, based on country $c*$'s peers determined by the Method of Reflections.
4. Calculate density Ω^{c*} based on Φ^{c*} and X^{c*}.
5. Calculate distance D^{c*} based on country $c*$'s peers determined by the Method of Reflections.
6. Calculate the "ease" index E^{c*} based on Ω^{c*}, U, and D^{c*}.
7. Choose indicators that are above threshold $\bar{e}$ (1.5 in this case) as being eligible for improvement.
8. Calculate the new potential SDG capacities through the Method of Reflections for each eligible indicator, where each calculation assumes that only one indicator will be improved upon by an increment of 1. Here, the number of times the Method of Reflections needs to be run will be equal to the number of indicators that cross the threshold in a particular step.
9. Choose the indicator that results in the highest level of increased SDG capacities.
10. Update raw attainment levels I_i^{c*} for country $c*$.
11. Iterate from steps 1 to 10 for as many rounds as needed.

Defining phases within the optimal pathway

Each step of the optimization exercise highlighted above encompasses a certain amount of "effort" needed by a country in order to improve attainment on an indicator. Thus, a measure of how many steps a country can take in one year needs to be calculated. To do this, first the cross-sectional relationship between aggregate raw attainment $S_{c,0}$ and the human development index for countries was examined, where

$$HDI_c = \beta_{0,step} + \beta_{1,step} * S_{c,0} + \epsilon .$$

The R-squared value for this regression was 0.86, sufficiently high enough (and higher than when using GDP per capita instead of the human development index) to predict the human development index levels based on raw attainment. Since the unit increase in $S_{c,0}$ is the piecewise input used to calculate the increase in SDG capacity in each step, examining this relationship allows for the calculation of the increase in the human development index brought about by one step of optimization. $\beta_{1,step}$ was estimated to be 0.0001227, suggesting that one unit increase in $S_{c,0}$ results in an increase in the human development index of 0.0001227.

Afterwards, historical trends in the human development index for Bangladesh, Kazakhstan, and Fiji were used to predict yearly increases in the human development index for each country. It was estimated that given historical trends (from 1980 to 2014), Bangladesh, Kazakhstan, and Fiji would experience yearly increases in the human development index of roughly 0.0071, 0.0041, and 0.0038 respectively (the R-squares for all country regressions were greater than 0.95). This information, coupled with the increase in the human development index brought by one step of optimization, allows for the calculation of the number of steps the countries can take in one year. Thus the number of steps that can be taken for Bangladesh, Kazakhstan, and Fiji yearly were calculated to be 58, 33, and 31 respectively. The phases are defined as the number of steps that each country can take in one year, multiplied by the number of years in each phase.

www.ingramcontent.com/pod-product-compliance
Lightning Source LLC
Chambersburg PA
CBHW080426270326
41929CB00018B/3182